Essays from t
on Industrial History 1983

D1149129

The Popular Perception of Industrial History

Edited by
Robert Weible
and
Francis R. Walsh

Published by the AASLH LIBRARY and
the Museum of American Textile History

University Publishing Associates, Inc.
4720 Boston Way
Lanham, Maryland 20706

3 Henrietta Street
London WC2E 8LU England

Printed in the United States of America

British Cataloging–in–Publication Information Available

Co–published by arrangement with
The Museum of American Textile History

Library of Congress Cataloging–in–Publication Data
Lowell Conference on Industrial History (1985)
The popular perception of industrial history.
1. United States—Industries—History—Congresses. 2. United
States—Industries—Public opinion—Congresses. 3. Public
opinion—United States—Congresses. I. Weible, Robert.
II. Walsh, Francis R. III. Title.
HC103.L69   1985   338.0973   88–349 CIP
ISBN 0–8026–0029–8 (alk. paper)
ISBN 0–8026–0030–1 (pbk. : alk. paper)

Dedicated to

the memory of

Herbert G. Gutman

Contents

The Popular Perception of Industrial History

Introduction

This book is the fourth publication in a series drawn from proceedings of the annual Lowell Conference on Industrial History. The year 1985 was a particularly eventful one for the Lowell Conference, because it marked the expansion of the conference from a two-day to a three-day event. The 1985 meeting was also the first Lowell Conference to be held in the National Park district of downtown Lowell. Since National Park programs are mandated to interpret the American Industrial Revolution to the public, it seemed logical that the Lowell Conference recognize its new location by addressing the ways in which the American public's understanding of its industrial heritage has been shaped. Consequently, the 1985 conference was organized around the theme "The Popular Perception of Industrial History."

The choice of "The Popular Perception of Industrial History" as the conference theme also reflected the growing nationwide interest in public history. It seemed then--and it seems now--that universities everywhere are adding public history offerings to their curricula; professional historical organizations are showing increased sensitivity to public history concerns; and more and more academically trained historians are finding employment with museums and historic sites, libraries and archives, publishing houses, private industries, government agencies, and numerous other off-campus employers. No doubt most of these employers are benefitting from the skills and insights of their historian-employees, and no doubt history departments are grateful that their graduates are finding work.

Still, the definition of public history as simply "historians working outside the academy" is one which the 1985 Lowell Conference sought to avoid. After all, as Michael Scardaville recently argued before the National Council on Public History, the tendency for historians to define their professional roles in terms related almost exclusively to their university-based responsibilities is a relatively new--and unfortunate--development in the history field. Scardaville emphasizes the fact that, earlier in the century, historians considered their primary audience to be the public, broadly defined, and not simply themselves.[1]

The organizers of the 1985 Lowell Conference were, likewise, less interested in the professional practitioners of history than in the relationship of historical scholarship to history's public audiences. To be sure, the public's historical consciousness has been formed to some degree by professionally trained historians (those working in museums, for example), but it has also been molded, somewhat more cynically and self-servingly, by non-historians (commercial filmmakers, for example, or corporate advertisers). The lay public also interprets its own history through community history projects. The Lowell Conference consequently sought to foster a better understanding of the public's historical awareness and the forces which have affected it, so that historians might ultimately work to free popular audiences from many of the myths which serve the public's cultural and political interests so poorly. In other words, Lowell Conference organizers and attendees understood the term "public history" to mean, essentially, "the public's history," and they were as concerned with the future of public history as they were with its past.

The conference program began with a discussion of museum interpretations of industrial history, featuring the papers by Mary Blewett, Jacqueline Hinsley, and Nicholas Westbrook and commentary by Thomas Leary which are all reprinted here. This was followed by a session describing the planning of the large and significant exhibits being developed in the Boott Mill area of Lowell. The discussion here was led by Lawrence Gall of the National Park Service and Shomer Zwelling of the Center for History Now, the exhibit design contractor working on the Lowell project. Conference attendees were then treated to a performance of labor songs by Alex Demas and Bobbie McGee before hearing Minnesota Congressman Bruce Vento's dinner presentation on historic preservation and National Park Service issues.

The second day of the conference featured a survey of community history programs which have addressed various industrial and labor issues. Papers included the articles in this volume by Brent Glass, Marsha Mullin, and Loretta Ryan, along with a talk by

John Herbst on the American Labor Museum in Paterson, New Jersey and a commentary by Mike Wallace. Robert Asher of the University of Connecticut offered additional comments. Afternoon sessions began with papers exploring the roles of individual industrialists and inventors in driving American industrial history. Papers by Michael Folsom and co-authors Frances Robb and Michael Workman provided the basis for Gary Kulik's commentary here. The day concluded with a look at the ways in which private industry has influenced the public's understanding of its industrial past. This discussion included papers by Patrick Furlong, Pamela Lurito, and Helena Wright and comments by Richard Tedlow.

The entire morning of the third day was devoted to issues related to labor history and film. Stephen Nissenbaum (University of Massachusetts) chaired a panel discussion on the role historians play in making such films. Discussants included James Dougherty (Indiana University of Pennsylvania), Elsa Rassbach (Made in USA Productions), and Daniel Walkowitz (New York University). This was followed by a presentation of the two papers on Hollywood films reprinted here, one by Francis Couvares and Daniel Czitrom and the other by Francis Walsh. Richard Gid Powers offered his thoughts on the subject at the conference. The meeting concluded with a discussion of industrial history exhibits that had recently opened in northern New England. William Kemsley (Vermont Labor History Society), Paul Rivard (Maine State Museum), and William Taylor (Plymouth State College) all offered insightful presentations on the subject.

The 1985 Lowell Conference owes a considerable debt of gratitude to its four sponsors: President William T. Hogan of the University of Lowell, Executive Director Peter Aucella of the Lowell Historic Preservation Commission, Superintendent Sandy Walter of Lowell National Historical Park, and Director Thomas W. Leavitt of the Museum of American Textile History. The conference was planned by a committee consisting of Frank Walsh and David Lewis of the University of Lowell, Paul Marion and Rosemary Noon of the Preservation Commission, Thomas Leavitt of the Textile Museum, Richard Candee of Boston University, and Maude Salinger and Robert Weible (Chairman) of the National Park. Other contributors to the conference's success included Raymond Laporte, who was then Acting Director of the Preservation Commission; National Park Service Curator Andrew Chamberlain,

who organized conference exhibits; Edward Miller and
Theresa Daigle of the University of Lowell Research
Foundation, which handled administrative
responsibilities; and Brian Foye of the Preservation
Commission staff and Peter Richards of the Lowell
Historical Society, who together assisted with
registration at the conference. Finally, this publication
benefitted from the considerable support and assistance
of Jonathan Sisk of the AASLH Library, Edward Jay
Pershey, the Director of the Tsongas Industrial History
Center, and his staff at the Tsongas Center. Created in
1987 by the University of Lowell, in cooperation with
Lowell National Historical Park, the Tsongas Center has
become a leading sponsor of the Lowell Conference on
Industrial History.

Robert Weible
Francis R. Walsh

Notes

1   Michael C. Scardaville, "Looking Backward Toward the
Future: An Assessment of the Public History Movement," *The
Public Historian* 9 (Fall 1987), 34-43.

REVISIONS WAITING IN THE WINGS: THE NEW SOCIAL HISTORY AT NEW ENGLAND TEXTILE MUSEUMS

Mary H. Blewett

This paper is a preliminary report on initial exhibit observations, archival research, and interviews with directors and staff at the major public and privately-funded museums of textile history in New England. It is part of a larger project to assess the impact of the new social history on interpretation at various historic sites and museums throughout the United States, especially museums concerned with the history of native Americans, women, blacks, workers, and ethnics. My responsibility is workers and industrialization. The end result will be a book of analytical essays designed for use in museum and public history programs and by museum professionals.[1]

I have chosen to concentrate my efforts on the interpretation of workers and industrialization in the New England textile industry because of the institutional richness of the region, the opportunities for comparisons, and the high level of physical expansion and interpretive activity during the past two decades. The expansion of existing historic sites and museums, such as Slater Mill Historic Site and the Merrimack Valley Textile Museum(the Museum of American Textile History since 1984 [MATH]), and the creation of new sites, Lowell National Historical Park, the State Heritage Park system, the Charles River Museum of Industry, the Maine State Museum, the proposed Massachusetts Labor History Center, the abandoned Mill Village at Old Sturbridge Village, and the defunct exhibit of the Lowell Museum, has involved social historians as consultants, as museum personnel, and on teams of exhibit designers. Here is an unusual opportunity to evaluate how social history can offer a new vision of the story of early industrial capitalism.

The new social history is an effort to demonstrate the powerful ways in which social experience shapes work, politics, and ideology.[2] Its methodologies range from quantitative analysis of demographic data to the impressionistic reminiscences of oral history. Its fundamental focus is mass experience as an active force in the process of history. Its subjects are family, ethnicity, race, urban and rural life, gender and sex roles, mobility, and work places. Its vision is to link the past with the present through a systematic study of the changing experience of ordinary people. Its politics are activist and democratic, often radical.

One way to capture the dynamic of the new social history is through the words of ordinary people such as Mabel Delehanty Mangan, a textile worker interviewed as part of the Working People of Lowell Oral History Project in 1984. She remembered what it was like to be fifteen years old in 1916:

> "Every morning at...quarter of six,...every door on the Acre would open, and we'd all troop out, down to the Merrimack, the Prescott, the Boott or the Tremont and Suffolk. We'd all be going. Merrimack Street, in those days, in the early morning was crowded with the mill workers, going to work.... And we'd be laughing and singing, going along.... Some of us. And some of us were...very upset at getting up, you know and figuring, uh, there wasn't much to look forward to. But...so what, some of us looked at it this way, it's got to be. What else are you going to do? You can't stay home, your mother won't let you....You've got to go to work..."[3]

This image of a work force, some willing, some resentful, many fatalistic, leaving their neighborhoods, entering the mills, and bringing the machines to life is an apt illustration of the interconnections between work and life which the new social history seeks to explore and interpret to a wide public audience.

The past two decades of rising interest in the new forms of social history paralleled a number of economic and political changes for New England museums. The professional growth of museum staffs in the 1960s and 1970s benefitted in part from the collapse of the academic market for historians, the development of public history programs, and increased grant funding for new exhibits, notably by the National Endowment of the Humanities which prolonged the bicentennial impulse into the late 1970s and early 1980s. New investment of public monies by the National Park Service and the Commonwealth of Massachusetts transformed urban policy from renewal by wrecker to revitalization through adaptive reuse--not in time, however, to save the splendid Dutton Street boardinghouses in Lowell from destruction. Although high costs for energy and high interest rates in the late 1970s created serious challenges for some New England museums and led Sturbridge to abandon its plans for a mill village,[4] financial pressures on private museums were balanced by steady growth and seemingly endless funding for public developments at Lowell and throughout the State Heritage park system.

The interest of the museum-going public in industrial history is harder to account for. New England museums and historic sites depend on grants and community support for their programs, and public attitudes seem to encourage a reconstruction of the American industrial experience even as major industries close their plants in the Northeast and high tech moves its assembly lines to Asia and Latin America. Is it nostalgia or a subtle form of politics? When exhibits interpret and extol the vitality of nineteenth century industrial development as the creator of American wealth, it is hard to avoid questioning contemporary national economic policy. Interpretations which explore the importance of worker skills and contributions to the workplace raise questions about the disappearance of industrial work and the future of a work force trained to serve as hamburger chefs and copy clerks.

How accurate a paradigm of early industrialization is the textile industry of New England? As an integrated and centralized system of mass production, early textile manufacturing in Waltham, Lowell, and Lawrence stands in sharp contrast to what historians know about the decentralized and discontinuous development of other forms of pre-Civil War production such as the New England boot and shoe industry and the nineteenth century experience of many Eastern seaboard industrial cities such as New York, Newark, Baltimore, and Philadelphia.[5] Not then a very accurate model, but most museum interpretation avoids this discrepancy by arguing that the textile industry became a precursor to and predictor of future industrial organization, mass production, and a high material standard of living in American society. Despite a reluctance in the current exhibits to mention the other historic sites by name (aside from British precedents which are always mentioned as examples avoided by canny American entrepreneurs) or to provide the visitor with a clear regional sense of industrial development, (specifically who borrowed and enhanced what organizational forms and technology from whom), one of the strengths of the New England sites is the variety of forms they take and the exploration of small-scale textile manufacturing in addition to large-scale factory production. Development can be traced from pre-industrial methods at Sturbridge, Slater, and MATH to mechanization at Slater to the integrated factory at Charles River to large-scale production and its subsequent demise in the twentieth century at Lowell and Lawrence (MATH). As a convenient social overview for this, Edward Thompson's model of the shift from pre-industrial seasonal rhythms to industrial time discipline is alive and well at all New England museums whether or not local experience actually confirms it.[6] For example, the presence of mill villages and small-scale production along the Blackstone, Merrimack, Concord, and Charles Rivers suggests a less dramatic shift.

The major tradition of interpreting industrialization in New England textile museums is the interpretation of technology as process and as a part of a large culture, a critical reaction by technology and culture advocates to exhibits which used machines as artifacts. Paul Rivard's exhibit of 1974 at Slater Mill and the first wool technology exhibit of Bruce Sinclair at MATH embody this approach.[7] Both used working machinery in spaces which suggest or actually reconstruct the mill or the shop, but which also demonstrate technical change and the process of industrialization. Both emphasize the impact of machines on production and the evolution of technology and its influence on American economic development. The emergence of the new social history in these exhibits in the 1970s and the early 1980s has largely taken the form of temporary exhibits or of overlays of comment by tour guides on the reactions of the community and workers to economic change. For example, Slater Mill borrows heavily from the work of Gary Kulik on the reaction and resistance of the community of Pawtucket and its workers to early water power development and mechanization. But, the tour guide's comments are delivered of necessity before the commencement of the tour because the exhibit as yet does not embody the findings of social historians.[8] The understandable reluctance of one Slater guide to grasp and stop the whirling flyer on a throstle spinning frame, despite the fact that children of ten years and younger were required to do so in order to piece broken threads, became a lost opportunity for social interpretation. The guide also explained the dangers of the "kiss of death" shuttle, but not the pressures on the weaver who devised this lethal way of changing the bobbins as quickly as possible.

Intensive efforts to plan and develop new exhibits in the late 1970s and early 1980s provide clearer evidence of the revisioning of museum interpretation by social history at Slater and other New England textile museums new and old, but all of these plans are yet to be realized. One of the best is the master plan at the Charles River Museum of Industry. Developed primarily by Michael Folsom, this stunning and ambitious interpretation of industrial life at Waltham insists in a unique way on seeing the slave economy of the Cotton South as integral to the textile factory system of New England.[9] Other strengths of this master plan include articulated links with other sites and a regional focus on industrial development with textiles as one major component.[10]

In addition to the new attention paid to the social implications of industrial development--reactions of workers, traditions of protest, the social environment of the community with its class and status hierarchies-- one element seems common to most of the planning in New England textile museums. All attempt to interpret the entire story of the pre-industrial setting, early industrialization, and the mature factory system. Gone is the limited focus on the early nineteenth century or on one aspect of textile production or on fibre, a context in which social experience might assume some interpretive weight. The ambitious overview has replaced the specific emphasis on one stage of industrial development, raising questions about the space that might remain for the rich detail of social life. The technology and culture approach continues to shape this fundamental drive to see textile production as the model for the national experience of industrial capitalism.

MATH is currently planning for what is purported to be the "exhibit of record on the development of factory labor in the United States" at its new site in the former Pacific Mill weave shed in Lawrence.[11] The exhibit design features four work places: a weaver's shop, a water-powered carding mill, a small mid-nineteenth century integrated factory, and a mature factory of the twentieth century. Rejecting technological determinism, the focus of the exhibit developed primarily by Laurence Gross and Paul Hudon is the changing nature of work as the result of human choice and decision.   One fascinating element is the emphasis on contingency in industrial development by suggesting alternative paths to industrialization other than the factory system: the carding mill.   This water-powered mill mechanized one step in production, but left the rest of the work process decentralized and the materials owned (and when finished marketed) by the worker. The interpretation suggests that centralized and integrated   production   financed   by   large   capital represents only one option for early industrialization.

The overall interpretation in the proposed MATH exhibit centers on workers, machines, and supervisors in the work place, and the major theme is the deskilling of workers   by   decisions   which   produced   the   factory system.   There is, however, a curiously abstract quality to   the   exhibit.   All   workplaces   are   generic   without specificity of time and place.   Social   history   in   the interpretation is limited to labor history and of that only the shop floor variety.   All values are assumed to be created by the relations of production.   Missing here are   the   social   contexts   of   gender,   religion,   politics, ethnicity, sentiment, and family.   Despite the historic importance of the textile factory as the first employer of women,   the   work   force   remains   ungendered   and culturally neutral.   There is no discussion of a specific and changing tradition of labor protest.   In spite of the focus   in   the   interpretive   text   on   human   choice   and decision-making, these decisions remain off-stage in the exhibit which focuses instead on the results of these choices in the form of altered work relationships and spaces.   Although the theme of increasing productivity and profits by deskilling the work force is compelling and unique in museum exhibits, the danger in the final analysis is to create a victimization model.

*   *   *

How might the vision of the new social history revise exhibit planning on the New England textile industry?   At Slater, for example, the Sylvanus Brown House, now interpreted primarily as a domestic location of textile production, might be interpreted more as a pre-industrial household composed of family and kin who ate, drank, slept, prayed, gave birth, and made cloth.   The Wilkinson Machine Shop might explore the development of a working class culture which produced David Montgomery's functionally autonomous craftsmen who refused to work when the boss was watching them. The Slater Mill itself might be interpreted as a space where five men, fifteen women, and fifty-two children worked together to spin yarn by water-powered machinery. How all of that was accomplished is the story of the social experience of early industrialization. Or Slater Mill might focus its interpretation just on the spinning process and related operations as they developed in the eighteenth, nineteenth, and twentieth centuries and explore the social consequences of the shifts from spinning wheel to jenny to throstle to mules and rings, an emphasis in which the changing nature of the work force would be central.

Lowell National Historical Park is currently in the throes of the planning process for its major exhibit in the Boott Mill. The initial plan for a weave room might be reconstructed not simply as a noisy and unpleasant place to work, but as a work place where the piece rate and the consequent need to avoid spoiled work brought weavers, loomfixers, smash piecers, bobbin boys, and other workers into a complex relationship with their machines and their supervisors, a relationship shaped by special languages, behaviors, and tensions--what Tom Leary has called an "industrial ecology."[12]   The Lowell Park planners might also look beyond the walls of the Boott Mill into the adjoining neighborhood of tenements, boardinghouses, schools, and streets and use the memories of early twentieth century mill workers to develop the story of community life outside of but immediately adjacent to the mill.

*   *   *

Whatever the reaction of planners, museum professionals, and exhibit designers to this vision, the new social history, as most of its practitioners would readily acknowledge, has not provided the interpretive link to the national experience that is the strength of exhibits based on the technology and culture approach. The long awaited synthesis of social history as a central theme in American development or even the amalgamation of the old and the new labor history have yet to appear.[13]   Furthermore, social historians and museum professionals who stress harmonious inclusiveness and organic community in their interpretations of social life and who ignore conflict and political struggle cannot offer an explanation to replace technology as the source of change and process in history.[14]

Whatever the shortcomings of social history, it is an exciting time to observe the ways in which the history of technology and industrialization has become enriched by new interest in social experience--at least in the planning process. We all look forward to the time when these plans are realized and take their place on center stage.

Notes

My thanks to Patrick Malone, Theodore Penn, Michael Folsom, Thomas Leavitt, Robert Weible, Laurence Gross, and Paul Hudon for their generosity with their time and with the files of their institutions.

1   This book project,*Toward An Accessible Past: History Museums and Historic Sites in the United States*, has been organized by Warren Leon of Old Sturbridge Village and Roy Rosenzweig of George Mason University.

2   For recent definitions of the new social history designed for use by museum specialists, James B. Gardner and George Rollie Adams, eds., *Ordinary People and Everyday Life: Perspectives on the New Social History* (Nashville, 1983).

3   The exclusion of the Acre, the oldest and most vibrant site of the city's working class and ethnic culture, from the original design of the Lowell Park seems a major disaster for meaningful social interpretation, see *Lowell, Massachusetts, Report of the Lowell Historic Canal District Commission to the Ninety-Fifth Congress of the United States of America*(Washington, D.C., 1977). On Lowell's development, Robert Weible, "Lowell: Building a New Appreciation for Historical Place," *Public Historian* 6 (Summer, 1984), 27-38.

4   Interview with Theodore Z. Penn, July 24, 1985.

5   Paul G. Faler, *Mechanics and Manufacturers in the Early Industrial Revolution: Lynn, Massachusetts, 1780-1860* (Albany, 1981); Alan Dawley, *Class and Community: The Industrial Revolution in Lynn* (Cambridge, 1976); Sean Wilentz, *Chants Democratic: New York City and the Rise of the American Working Class* (New York, 1984); Susan E. Hirsch, *Roots of the American Working Class: The Industrialization for Crafts in Newark, 1800-1860* (Philadelphia, 1978); Bruce Laurie, *Working People of Philadelphia, 1800-1850* (Philadelphia, 1980); Philip Scranton, "Varieties of Paternalism: Industrial Structures and the Social Relations of Production in American Textiles," *American Quarterly* 36 (1984), 235-258; Charles G. Steffen, *Mechanics of Baltimore: Workers and Politics in the Age of Revolution* (Urbana, IL, 1984); Mary Blewett, *Men, Women, and Work: A Study of Class, Gender, and Protest in the New England Shoe Industry, 1780-1910* (Urbana, IL,1988)

6   E.P. Thompson, "Time, Work-Discipline and Industrial Capitalism," *Past and Present* (December, 1967) 56-97. In contrast, see the sense of a gradually shifting concept of time and work discipline which distinguishes the weaver's shop in the proposed exhibit at MATH, Draft of an NEH grant proposal for an exhibit, "A Necessity of Life: The Path of Textile Factory Production," c. October 1985, Files of MATH.

7   For a 1969 critique of the use of machinery as artifact at Slater Mill, James C. Hippen, "Industrial Textile Machinery: Five North American Museums," *Technology and Culture* 10 (October, 1979), 570-586. Paul E. Rivard, *The Home Manufacture of Cloth,1790-1840* (Pawtucket, 1974) and *Wool Technology and the Industrial Revolution* 1965. Also see J. Bruce Sinclair, "The Merrimack Valley Textile Museum: A New Institution for an Important Aspect of American History," *Transactions, 1956-1963, Colonial Society of Massachusetts* 43 (Boston, 1966), 406-416.

8   Visit to Slater Mill, June 1985, and Training Manual for Tour Guides, Slater Mill Historic Site, June 1985, Slater Mill Files. A rich knowledge of industrial history will enhance a visitor's appreciation of exhibits, but ordinary visitors must take the exhibit at face value. For an appreciation of Slater Mill from the first viewpoint, Theodore Z. Penn, "Exhibit Review: The Slater Mill Historic Site and the Wilkinson Mill Machine Shop," *Technology and Culture* 21 (January, 1980), 56-66. MATH also depends heavily on its tour guides for flexibility in interpretation.

20   Mary H. Blewett

9   Also see the traveling exhibit, "Negro Cloth: Northern Industry and Southern Slavery."

10   Despite a primary focus on industrial production, the Master Plan includes other unique ideas handled in exciting and imaginative ways: a focus on multiple industries, textiles, watches, autos, and electronics and developmental relationships, attention to the sources of mercantile capital for industrialization, situating all industrial production within a market context, a humanistic interpretation of technology with emphasis on human choice, will, and decision making, the use of museum education techniques in exhibits, the consideration of issues of public policy within the exhibits, a unique working model of the integrated system of textile production at the Boston Manufacturing Company, and a consideration of the impact of industrialization on both rural and urban society.   Charles River Museum of Industry, *Master Plan for Exhibits and Programs* (Waltham, 1983).   For recent planning at Slater Mill, Patrick M. Malone, "Industrial Power in Nineteenth-Century America," Final Report, NEH Grant #PM-26871-77-58, October 26, 1977; "Machines and Workers in the Textile Industry," NEH Planning Grant Application, November 11, 1979;   Herbert Gutman to Steve Victor, August 20, 1980, Ted Penn to Steve Victor, n.d., especially the injunction to "Simplify! Simplify!"; Laurence F. Gross to Stephen Victor, August 12, 1980, Correspondence re NEH Conference, Summer 1980; Gary Gerstle, "Looking Ahead: A Plan for Rearranging the Machinery and Revising the Tour in the Slater Mill," September 23, 1981, Files of the Slater Mill Historic Site.

11   My thanks to Tom Leavitt, Larry Gross, and Paul Hudon for generously sharing with me a copy of their grant proposal in draft.

12   T.E. Leary, "Industrial Archeology and Industrial Ecology," *Radical History Review* 21 (Fall, 1979), 171-182.

13   For a recent sense that the new synthesis may be emerging, Thomas Bender, "Making History Whole Again," *New York Times Book Review*, October 6, 1985.

14   Compare, for example, the emphasis on organic community and social harmony in Cary Carson, "Living Museums of Everyman's History," *Harvard Magazine* (July, 1981), 22-32 with the emphasis on conflict and struggle strongly insisted upon by consultant Thomas Dublin and reflected in Lowell National Historic Park's media show "Lowell: The Industrial Revelation."   Also see the emphasis in the proposed MATH exhibit on alternative paths of industrial development and on human choice and decision making.

THREE DECADES
OF GROWTH AND CHANGE
AT THE HAGLEY MUSEUM

Jacqueline A. Hinsley

The Hagley Museum opened on May 24, 1957, on the site of the Du Pont Company's early powder mills along the Brandywine River, near Wilmington, Delaware. This paper takes a retrospective look at the forces that shaped Hagley and traces its development from an industrial museum rooted in the traditional scholarship of technology and culture to a museum that only recently has embraced the new social history.

It was a corporate celebration of the company's 150th anniversary in 1952 that drew attention to the decaying mills built by Eleuthere Irenee du Pont in 1802, and expanded in 1814, for the manufacture of black powder. Since the closing of the yards and dismantling of machinery in 1921, little notice had been taken of the historical significance of the abandoned site. In 1933, J. Victor Dallin, a former World War I pilot, made a series of aerial photographs of the more than two hundred acre stretch of mills ranged along the river banks. And in 1935 a survey team from the Historical American Buildings Survey recorded two of the surviving early nineteenth-century stone structures, a small dwelling in the Eleutherian Mills yard, undated, and the Birkenhead Mills, 1822-24, a pair of rolling mills in the Hagley yard.

In 1952, as plans were underway for the anniversary festivities to take place on the exact location of du Pont's first manufactory, another plan began to take shape: to preserve the historic industrial site. For that purpose, company and family leaders organized the Eleutherian Mills-Hagley Foundation[1], which takes its name from the two adjacent powder yards. It was originally intended that the Foundation would administer the property as a public park, but by 1954 its creators had decided to establish a museum of industrial

21

history. The location of the site was, indeed, fortuitous, for the Brandywine had had an unusually long and varied industrial history.   The museum's approach, however, was not to be parochial but was intended to place the local story of water-powered industry within the broader context of the development of industry and technology in America's Industrial Revolution.   That was the immediate task to be undertaken as soon as a professional staff could be brought together.

In April 1954 Walter J. Heacock was appointed Director of Research and Interpretation. While Du Pont engineers gutted the 1814 textile mill that would become the museum, Heacock and a small staff developed a story line. By the end of the year, Walter Dorwin Teague had been selected to design the exhibits. Teague had been in the vanguard of industrial designers of the 1920s whose work suggested "progress through industry" and had helped to popularize the "streamlined" style of the 1930s and 40s.[2] He had designed trade shows for Eastman Kodak, Consolidated Edison, National Cash Register, Ford, U.S. Steel, and Du Pont, including Du Pont's exhibit at the 1939 World's Fair.   After a preliminary visit to the Brandywine site in January, 1955, Teague wrote his impressions to Heacock:

> There is an unusual combination of values here: an extremely picturesque site, a dramatic story to tell, and really beautiful remains to start with. If carried out your project should be one of the show spots of the country, and have profound educational value as well.[3]

Because of earlier work he had done, the most compelling reason for Teague's interest in the project was in the basic premise of the story line sent to him a few weeks after his visit:

> The Hagley Museum is devoted to the industrial history of the United States. Concentrating upon the Brandywine area, it endeavors to show how the diversified industries which drew their power from this small stream in the colonial and early Federal periods epitomized the beginnings of industry in other areas of the country. The museum exhibits establish the essential relationship between the growth of these infant industries and the growth of the nation.[4]

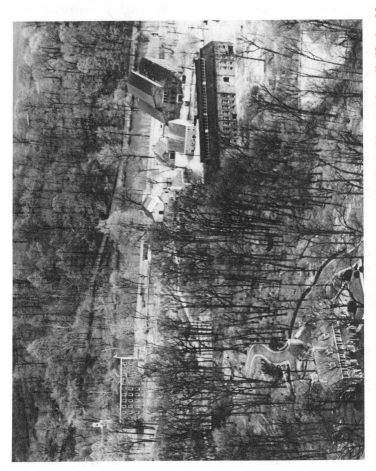

Figure 1. Section of photo by Dallin Aerial Surveys Co., April 25, 1933 showing Henry Clay textile mill (Hagley Museum) far left. Building with clerestory roof, right rear, is a 1904 machine shop acquired by Hagley in 1984 from the estate of S. Hallock Du Pont (home in foreground). (All photographs courtesy the Hagley Museum and Library.)

The most important of those infant industries on the Brandywine was the manufacture and marketing of flour.   In the 1940s Walter Dorwin Teague had been commissioned to design a museum of flour-milling for General Mills in Minneapolis.   After extensive research and design, the project was never carried out.   Here, in a sense, was a second chance--and anyone who has visited Hagley will remember the superb models that trace flour milling from the first Swedish grist mill in Delaware to the automated flour mill designed by Oliver Evans.   As work progressed on the Hagley Museum, the designer and the historian did not always see eye to eye, but on one point they agreed: the museum would be neither *quaint* nor *trade show*.

In the context of the 1950s and early 60s, Hagley may be viewed as a case study of industrial sites saved from oblivion through the efforts of historically-minded businessmen working with designers and historians to preserve America's industrial past.   A replica of Saugus Iron Works funded by the American Iron and Steel Institute opened to the public in 1954; Slater Mill Textile Museum in 1956; Hagley in 1957; Merrimack Valley in 1964.   What gave Hagley an advantage not immediately enjoyed by the others was that its exhibits were developed with a basis of sound scholarly research of remarkable quality.   Putting together a research team was the director's first concern.   In cooperation with Professor John Munroe at the University of Delaware, he initiated a graduate program that provided two fellowships a year for students seeking training in historical agency work and M.A. degrees in American history or American studies.   Under the direction of Peter Welsh, who was both the first Hagley Fellow and its first program coordinator, students devoted about one-half of their time to the development of the museum.   Working from the story line, staff historians and Hagley Fellows began a study in depth of every subject for which information was needed to interpret the site and for which an exhibit was planned.   Unlike most museums created to house existing collections, Hagley would consist largely of constructed exhibits arranged sequentially to tell a story.   The research team, truly a community of scholars, labored intensively for three years, producing volumes of research reports, many of them published in journals of history or technology.   Historical research was supplemented by extensive archaeology and a sustained oral history program of interviews with some fifty or sixty men, or

Figure 2. Walter Dorwin Teague (far right), Walter J. Heacock (second from right), and Du Pont Company executives study plans for adapting 1814 textile mill to use as Hagley Museum.

descendants of men, who had worked in the du Pont mills.[5]   The questions asked were oriented primarily toward understanding the process and sequence of making black powder and identifying surviving structures.

With the first floor exhibits completed, the museum was dedicated on May 24, 1957. That month's issue of *Fortune* magazine carried a pictorial portfolio by Walker Evans of the gunpowder mills and the new Hagley Museum. In a brief, but perceptive essay, Evans noted that "the powder mills at Wilmington are not quaint. For the time being, at least, the Du Ponts are leaving them standing just as they are--mysterious, remotely druidic, and unmistakably haunted."[6]

Locally, the opening of the museum inspired proud, if less poetic, rhetoric: "Scenes from America's childhood: a new museum depicts some of the little-known beginnings of U.S. manufacturing"; "The Hagley Museum, site of first Du Pont mills, depicts birth of U.S. industry"; "Cradle of firm along Brandywine banks slated to be industrial Williamsburg." One editor predicted that in the years to come visitors from all parts of the country would thank the Eleutherian Mills-Hagley Foundation for an "imaginatively conceived and meticulously developed contribution to the social history of the United States."[7]

With the opening of the museum, and the gradual enlargement of its professional staff, the work of graduate students became somewhat less critical to its building and operation. Today's students in the Hagley Program in the History of Industrial America continue to experience museum work first-hand but with greater flexibility in the pursuit of primary research. The program's alumni number more than 120 historians, archivists, museum professionals, and others. Hagley alumni have won many distinguished awards for their published works, including the Dexter Prize for the best book in the history of technology. The graduate program was only the beginning of a consciously conceived mechanism for scholarship that has informed and shaped the museum since its beginning. In 1962 the trustees approved the appointment of an Advisory Committee of distinguished academicians, museum and library professionals. They have been a sounding board and a voice of reason of inestimable value in charting the museum's direction. Early on they recommended appointments of senior resident scholars, encouraged an active publications program, and suggested a regular schedule of temporary exhibits.

The decade of the sixties was a period of

Left to right, Daniel Hadley, James Ackerman, and restoration archaeologist Roland W. Robbins take measurements of 1880s turbine Birkenhead mills.

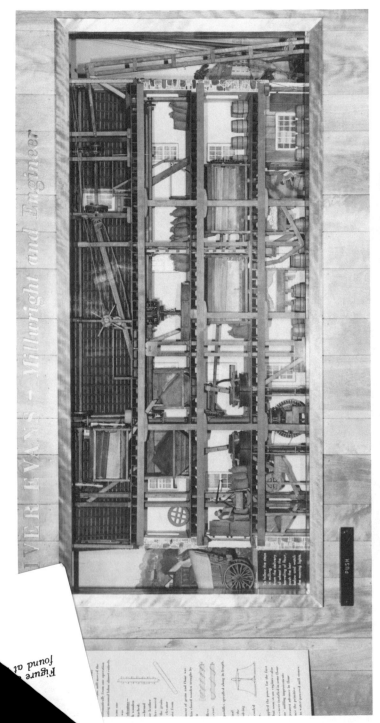

Figure 4.   Model of Oliver Evans automatic flour mill, one of the first floor museum exhibits opened in 1957.

5. *Hagley Fellows at drive pulley for textile mill, Lowell, 1984. Left to right, Brian Greenberg, program coordinator, Beth Hager, Strong, Betsy Bahr, Sarah Heald, Kathy McKay, David Driscoll, Preston Thayer, and Duncan Hay.*

phenomenal growth and expansion of programs, collections, and restorations, summarized below:

1961 Opening of a modern research library devoted to American business and industrial history with a regional focus on the Mid-Atlantic.

1962 Opening of a second exhibition building, an 1850s millwright and machine shop, with working models of the powder making process (many of which were based on the Diderot plates of powder making in France).

Acquisition of a collection of some 800 U.S. patent models.

1964 Restoration of the Birkenhead mills with reconstruction and installation of an operating wooden water wheel.

1965 Arrival of George Rogers Taylor, first senior resident scholar.

1966 Designation of museum property as a National Historic Landmark.

1967 Opening of second floor exhibits on industrial development of United States, an extension of the first floor theme of industry on the Brandywine.

Appointment of a Director of Publications.

1968 Archaeological dig of E. I. Du Pont's 1803 garden in anticipation of restoration.

1969 Restoration of first Du Pont company office.

As interpretive areas increased, school programs devel~ \d, and collections grew slowly but steadily, iverse professional expertise was needed. rs, educators, and curators joined historians on It was a fully functioning museum that official accreditation by the American of Museums in 1972. Citing the diversity of , ranging from mechanical arts to decorative

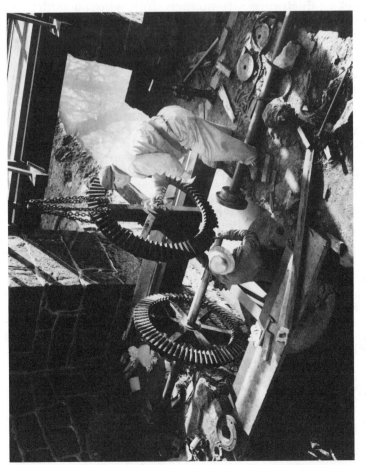

Figure 6. Installing gear wheels at Eagle Roll Mill, 1974.

arts, the visiting inspection team's report expressed the hope that the museum "will continue to reconstruct the nineteenth-century ambience of the site as well as to restore the technological aspects of industry."

The Museum's coming of age brought international attention. After a visit from John Cornforth, editor of the English journal *Country Life*, the Hagley Museum was the subject of a two-part article in the magazine's issues of November 2 and 9, 1972. Cornforth pointed out to his countrymen the lessons that Hagley had to offer to those who were trying to create industrial museums in Britain, in particular Hagley's dual use as a museum and a research center. He observed that "the two parts complement each other and give the whole place an intellectual vitality that is stimulating, as well as solving the purely practical problem of coping with the bulk of industrial archives."[8]

Having gained professional recognition at home and abroad, the museum coped with the practical problems of the energy crisis, spiraling costs, staff cutbacks, declining attendance following a shift from free to paid admission, natural disasters, and, not least, changing ideologies.

In 1976 Hagley joined the rest of the country in observing the bicentennial with a major exhibit that celebrated Wilmington, Delaware as a diversified industrial city at its zenith in 1976. More important to the museum's on-going interpretation of industrial power were the installation that same year of an 1870s box-bed steam engine (fully operating and regularly demonstrated by interpreters) and the reconstruction of a turn-of-the-century hydroelectric plant. Together they completed the museum's full-scale examples of industrial power sources in the Hagley yard. The water wheel at the Birkenhead mills and a water turbine that powers the cast-iron wheels of the Eagle Roll Mills are the others. The turbine installation was under way in 1972 when Brooke Hindle cited it as one of very few examples of operating machinery in industrial museums. "The Hagley Museum," he wrote, "is still developing its fine presentation of a few significant stories in industrialization, such as the restored powder mill." Hindle recognized the effectiveness of working scale models as a technique of museum presentation *if done well*, again citing Hagley's successful example, but his concluding message was that "In today's world, presentation of industrialization is an essential museum mission. The need is critical. The eager audience is there. The first step is to get the machines running.

Figure 7. Students reenact 1844 political campaign rally, Henry Clay Day at Hagley, 1972.

Beyond that lies an endless frontier in interpreting man's relationship to his machines."[9] The message did not fall on deaf ears at Hagley. Close associations with scholars in the history of technology--like Brooke Hindle, Eugene Ferguson, George Basalla, and Merritt Roe Smith--are but another facet of the mechanism for scholarship at Hagley that both challenges and confirms the instincts of the museum's curators.

By the end of its second decade, in the mid-seventies--with full-scale restorations, operating machinery, and some two dozen buildings connected by hillside and riverside paths, or by bus--Hagley had clearly become an indoor/outdoor museum with a major focus on education.

In 1970 Hagley developed a special program called Henry Clay Day for one local school district as a climax to a fifth grade study of "America in Transition: an Agrarian to an Industrial Society." The annual event, described by a local journalist as "a gigantic role play in craft and chore activities" culminated in a political rally for Henry Clay's 1844 presidential campaign among textile and powder mill workers in the villages surrounding Hagley. It was so well publicized that other schools requested the same kind of experience. In response, museum educators developed a nineteenth-century lifestyle program with pre-visit materials available in a kit developed by two NEH interns. To accommodate the popular program, the only surviving nineteenth-century workers' house at Hagley was renovated and furnished as a see-and-touch exhibit of appropriate domestic artifacts. The overwhelming success of the John Gibbons house sparked a growing interest in re-creating the physical setting of a workers' community.

In 1975, a Regional Economic History Research Center, under the direction of Dr. Glenn Porter, was created at Hagley to support research in economic history, broadly interpreted to include the study of the industrial revolution, its social context and consequences. Through his involvement with the research center and Hagley graduate students, Porter perceived the need for a synthesis of academic research and museum programs. After consulting with museum staff, he applied for, and received, a National Endowment for the Humanities grant to fund a major joint Research Center/Hagley Museum exhibition on "The Workers' World: the Industrial Village and the Company Town," which would encompass both a temporary indoor exhibit and permanent outdoor exhibits and restorations.

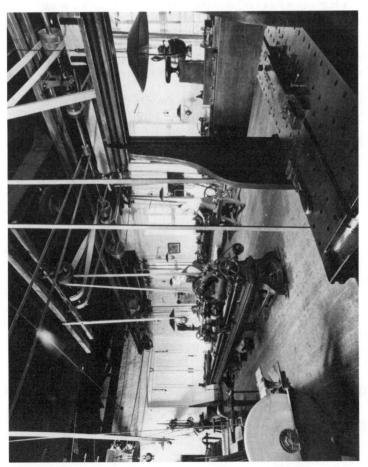

Figure 8.   Nineteenth-century machine shop installed at Hagley as a permanent part of the Workers' World exhibit, 1981.

The "Workers' World" opened in September of 1981 and closed in May 1982. It was the permanent outdoor part of the exhibit that moved Hagley's interpretive focus in new directions, building on the existing school program in nineteenth-century lifestyle. The foreman's home and the restored Brandywine Manufacturers' Sunday School in the workers' community called Blacksmith Hill are now open to all visitors. The "jewel in the crown" of these new exhibits is the machine shop where a corps of dedicated volunteers demonstrate fully operating machinery.

Before the formal exhibit closed, *History News* published an article by assistant editor Tracey Linton Craig. In "Delicate Balance," subtitled "Hagley Museum traces the impact of technology and its products on society and the individual," Craig reviewed the steps leading to the Workers' World exhibit and its impact on Hagley's interpretation:

> Seeing the work in progress here, the visitor begins to sense interrelationships. The shop worker who stood at this machine some 70 years ago made parts to fit the big mill upstream. He went home to the house up the hill. He sent his children to the Sunday School over that way.
>
> In the Eleutherian Mills mansion overlooking the factory site, the visitor makes similar linkages concerning the mill owner. The visitor begins to put the pieces together in a new and important way.
>
> And that's the project's aim--to present the visitor with a complete sense of the human experience in an industrial setting.[10]

What about scholarship for this new interpretation? In the 1950s Harold Hancock's pioneering research at Hagley on "The Industrial Worker on the Brandywine," resulted in a series of excellent reports. But the impetus for the Workers' World exhibit came largely from current scholarship *outside* the museum, primarily from work supported by the Regional Economic History Research Center from 1975 to 1980, for example, Donald R. Adams, Jr.'s studies of wages, incomes, cost of living, and savings of Du Pont Company workers in the nineteenth century.[11] Since 1981, however, new research is being generated at a steady pace *within* the museum on such topics as the role of women, boarders, servants, storekeepers, bookkeepers, and children; ethnicity; the work force at Hagley; work hierarchy reflected in housing; recreation; foodways.   Of these recent research efforts, one of the most productive was a quantitative study of pupils in the Brandywine Manufacturers' Sunday School, 1816-1850, a research project carried out by a team of volunteers under the direction of a Hagley Fellow under a summer internship.   The oral history program has been reactivated under the direction of Curator Frank McKelvey and archaeology is being conducted in the area of the workers' community.   In the spring of 1985, with funding from the National Endowment for the Humanities, the University of Delaware offered a course at Hagley in Historical Archaeology and Museum Interpretation.   The Workers' World exhibit was more than a catalyst for bringing social history to the workplace.   It was also a catalyst for renewed intellectual vigor at Hagley.

With a demonstrated capacity for change, and an inherent ability to respond to scholarship, there is every reason to believe that the Hagley Museum will be able to maintain a delicate balance between man and his machines, industrial history and social history, through many more decades of growth and change.

Notes

1 Eleutherian Mills-Hagley Foundation continues as the legal corporate name of the organization but, since 1983, Hagley Museum and Library is the official name of the institution.

2 Rosemarie Haag Bletter, "The World of Tomorrow: the future with a past," essay in catalog of exhibit "High Styles: Twentieth Century American Design," Whitney Museum of American Art.

3 Correspondence of Walter Dorwin Teague and Walter J. Heacock, Hagley Museum Archives.

4 Storyline, February 11, 1955, Research Department files, Hagley Museum.

5 Transcripts of oral interviews conducted by Hagley Museum 1954-74 in Research Department files, original tapes in Pictorial/Audio-visual Department archives, the Hagley Museum and Library.

6 Walker Evans, "The Stones of Du Pont," Fortune (May, 1957) 167-169.

7 Quaesita C. Drake, The Del-Chem Bulletin, November 1955.

8 John Cornforth, "The Hagley Museum, USA" part 1, "Powder for Pioneers" and part 2, "Interpreting Industrial History," Country Life, November 2 and 9, 1972.

9 Brooke Hindle, "Museum Treatment of Industrialization: History, Problems, Opportunities," Curator, XV, 3 (1972).

10 Tracey Linton Craig, "Delicate Balance--Hagley Museum traces the impact of technology and its products on society and the individual," History News, 37:5 (May, 1982).

11 Glenn Porter, The Workers' World at Hagley, 1981.

INTERPRETING "THE WORKSHOP OF THE WORLD": MUSEUMS AND BRITISH INDUSTRIAL HISTORY

Nicholas Westbrook

Our engineers may be regarded in some measure as the makers of modern civilization.

Samuel Smiles, Lives of the Engineers, 1861

Prologue

In the century between 1750 and 1850 Britain led the world into a new form of civilization. British entrepreneurs, engineers, and mechanics launched an industrial revolution--both a revolution in forms of power, transportation, and technique, and a revolution in living conditions, relationships, perceptions and metaphors. Many of the innovations in mechanisms and materials crucial to our modern world occurred first to British minds during that century. The Industrial Revolution generated forces which continue--even in their decline in the Anglo-American world--to disrupt, ease, and transform lives far beyond the factory gates.

Today easily half the world is still struggling to bring to itself the benefits of mechanization won by the British more than a century ago. At the same time the long-industrialized nations are caught in the throes of what portends to be another profound transformation of civilization, a revolution in information access and processing. We live simultaneously, then, in *two* worlds of kaleidoscopic change, one aborning and the other shifting in locus to formerly colonial and still dependent lands. And out of these two concurrent revolutions arise anxieties concerning personal and national identity.

Nowhere are those anxieties so close to the surface of daily lives as in the land which cradled the Industrial Revolution. Nowhere are the burdens of the past and the challenges of the future so confounded and compounded as in Britain today: empireless, yet fervent in defense of its Falklands outpost, a democratic socialist society still misty-eyed at the marriage of its crown prince, an aged industrial plant scarcely resuscitated by its off-shore oil boom, its symbols of technological achievement such as "Concorde" silhouetted against played-out mines, uneconomical smelters, and strike-bound assembly lines, a land where inequities of education continue to reinforce a still strong ideology of class difference, a nation where the remains of brilliant engineering achievements taunt a present that too often seems not to work.[1]

How may we begin to comprehend the forces and effects of historical change which began transforming Britain and then the rest of the world more than two centuries ago? As we ourselves begin to witness and direct a new revolution in the forms of our own civilization, we may be usefully mindful of the origins and evidences of the Industrial Revolution. Perhaps in so doing we will be better able to understand and defuse the economic and psychological tensions arising between North and South as each hemisphere begins a revolutionary overturn of the customary relationships between its technics and its civilization, to adapt Lewis Mumford's memorable phrase.[2]

Today, of course, the evidences of the Industrial Revolution are omnipresent in the objects, the sounds and smells, the comforts and constraints which entwine our lives. In Britain we can also see physical evidence of the birthing and adolescent years of the Industrial Revolution, evidence that has survived by grace of Providence, national choice, and the preservative inertia of habit and custom. In the nineteenth century, the British boasted that their island kingdom was "the workshop of the world." In that island today it is readily possible to see in museums and in the landscape the workshops wherein British engineers constructed the framework for modern civilization.[3]

Direct ties link museums to industrialization. Museums are themselves artifacts of the cultural changes set in motion by the Industrial Revolution. Rapid change created a new reverence for things past. Forces of democratization brought collections of treasures out of aristocratic palaces and into a new form of public institution, the museum. The profits from industrialization endowed these new *pro publico*

collectors.   Antiquarians and local history societies
organized to preserve the supplanted "by-gones" of
village and farm.   As the pace of mechanization and
urbanization accelerated, folk museums were established
to attempt boldly the encapsulation of a by-gone way of
life--traditional, landbound, and energized by little more
than muscle power.   In our own time, we have seen the
rise--especially since the Second World War--of the
industrial museum, direct testimony to the tremendous
economic dislocations and mechanical improvements
which sprang forth from the war years.   Whole
factories, whole industries became obsolete and were
shortly museumized.[4]

Risen from a civilization created by the Industrial
Revolution, what is the destiny for museums as their
society is transformed by the Information Revolution?
We say professionally as curators that we preserve
because we wish to teach.   We hold an abiding faith in
our particular form of texts.   We believe that artifacts,
though too often intransigently silent, may often enough
be made to speak of the lives which created and
consumed them.   Can the powers inherent in objects
hold their own against the hypnotic sway of video
display terminals and computerized data banks?   In a
world instantaneously informed by bytes and bits, will
it any longer be necessary or economical to decode the
information tenaciously embodied in objects?

These questions are being tested today in Britain
as its economy deindustrializes.   This is a profoundly
nostalgic society, after all, where the imagined as well
as the remembered past hold extraordinary sway.
"Merrie olde England," say people fondly; "there will
always be an England," they reassure themselves.   But
deindustrialization is changing class relationships and
prospects.   How will British society adjust as the
referent past increasingly becomes a world of "dark,
satanic mills" rather than an agricultural "green and
pleasant land?"   British industrial museums illustrate the
role of history and nostalgia in this ongoing process of
social change.

Formal Museums
Industrial museums sprang from the first world's fair,
the 1851 Crystal Palace Exhibition in London.   Prince
Albert's "Great Exhibition" celebrated the plenitude and
possibility of mechanical production.   It represented to
its contemporaries the apogee of moral and economic
progress and the triumph of empire and machine.   Out
of its fantastic popular success came the Science

Museum and the Victoria and Albert Museum in the same Kensington Gardens, perpetuating the fair's notion that the products of our Industrial Revolution ought to be exhibited for public marvel and inspiration.[5]

Today the Science Museum preserves and exhibits pieces of the "True Cross" in more than two dozen technologies. Formal exhibits in vast galleries display and sometimes explain the artifacts which began and expanded the Industrial Revolution: James Watt's steam engines, the Parsons turbine, *Puffing Billy*, the world's oldest surviving locomotive, Maudsley's lathe, the crucial inventions in textile machinery by Kay, Hargreaves, and others, Brunel's pulley-making equipment which helped introduce mass production, Babbage's proto computer, . . . the list goes on and on. But this enormously important collection is presented and interpreted erratically. The level and quantity of information and the sophistication of design by which it is communicated vary greatly. Obviously untouched since the 1920s and almost wholly uninterpreted are the machines which formed the basis of the great technologies of the nineteenth century. There they rest in public view, waiting for anyone to make what sense of them one can. Such major topics as *Power* (steam engines), *Materials Processing* (machine tools), *Textiles* (wool and cotton), and *Transportation* (railroads) rest unexplored, largely bereft of an historian's help in understanding.

The modern technologies of our era clearly receive the bulk of curatorial attention and budgetary allotment. Envigorated by quite recent reinstallations are major exhibits treating the twentieth-century manifestations of the topics enumerated above. We find fresh, lively, engaging exhibits on petrochemicals and electricity, computers, synthetics, space travel, and medicine. Gradually, within straitened resources, the permanent exhibits are being transformed from typological displays to intentionally interpretive exhibitions. And so the museum struggles to keep intellectually attune, adjusting from a nineteenth-century sensibility that naming meant understanding to the contemporary museum's insistence on finding contexts and connections.

But the question remains: can the Science Museum survive the slow pace of that adjustment in a civilization where video and computers offer instantaneous access to whenever, wherever worlds? Can the preservation and interpretation of the "Real Thing" retain significance for a new generation? A hopeful note is struck by the recent appointment as

Director of Neil Cossons, the innovative former director of the Ironbridge Gorge Museum Trust and the National Maritime Museum.

The major national collections, the Science Museum and its kin, the Victoria and Albert Museum, London, and the National Railroad Museum, York, are role models in organization and technique for smaller museums across the land. Frequently the national model has not been re-examined in living memory, as is obvious in the systematic presentations of steam engines at the Birmingham Museum of Industry or in the display of Saxon projectile points and medieval coins at Moyses' Hall, Bury St. Edmunds.

Elsewhere, in such freshly refurbished museums of science and industry as those in Swansea and Newcastle on Tyne, the dual purposes of being both systematic and interpretive have been accomplished. In most instances, however, these museums of formal exhibits have been unwilling to acknowledge that action is a necessary context for understanding machinery.[6] An exemplary exception is the Bradford Industrial Museum, where virtually every machine displayed in the four-story woolen mill operates, with explanation. Even here, however, the emphasis is upon machines as artifacts, upon process, rather than the relationship of the technology to the world beyond the shop floor.

Examining the relationship between technology and culture from the other end of the telescope are several urban history museums. Demonstrating the enthusiastic response toward such an interpretive trend are the audiences crowding the City Museums of London and Birmingham, both recent, comprehensive, and sprightly urban history presentations, the latter with a particularly strong attention to the city's industrial past. Effective use of industrial artifacts and a broad perspective on social history reinforce our understanding of how this industrializing nation had become the world's first urban society by the mid-nineteenth century.[7]

Open-Air Museums
Surely the most important development in British museum practice since World War II has been the rise of the open-air museum, modelled on the century-old Scandinavian folk museums and the American outdoor history museums established in the 1920s and 1930s such as Colonial Williamsburg and Old Sturbridge Village.

In Britain, the movement began at war's close with the Welsh Folk Museum near Cardiff. The museum preserves a sprawling collection of traditional farm homes and outbuildings, completely furnished. Additions in recent years have tended to center on the industries necessary to an agricultural economy: a gristmill, woolen mill, tannery, and so on.

But the open-air concept has been applied with particular energy and imagination to the interpretation of industrial history. The educational advantages are considerable. In this way complete industrial complexes can be preserved, retaining large machines in their original settings. With their surrounding houses and shops, such open-air museums have the potential to powerfully illuminate the social context of industrial work. Beamish, the museum of coal-centered life in the North of England, County Durham, pioneered this development. In the last fifteen years, many more open-air industrial museums have been established, with phenomenal success by both public and professional standards. Gladstone Pottery in Stoke-on-Trent shows with rich nuance how the city's products came to grace the Victorian world. Ironbridge Gorge Museum Trust is an almost insanely ambitious complex of half-a-dozen museums concentrating on the origins of iron as a structural material, but also including major museums on Severn river transportation, nineteenth-century engineering, and pottery and tile production.

The vigor of the older group of open-air industrial museums (Beamish, Ironbridge, and Gladstone) may well prove telling in the rising competition for leisure-time pounds. Those older institutions have been blessed with strong, clear-visioned leadership, combined with an entrepreneurial sensibility uncommon in British life. Despite recent changes in leadership, all three seem not to have faltered in their forward momentum.

The success of such really quite young institutions has spread an enthusiasm for imitation and competition. So we find the Museum of Black Country Life, in the Midlands near Dudley, being built purposely where no such buildings stood before. We find the staid National Trust, customarily the guardian of castles and cathedrals, museumizing both Samuel Greg's cotton-spinning mill of the 1780s and his thoroughly paternalistic village of Styal (near Manchester). Both had languished in the Trust's care for half a century, and now resound with the thump of looms, whir of spindles, and chatter of schoolchildren.

Today the wisdom of finding public usefulness for historic structures seems apparent to almost everyone from regional tourism boards to typically insensitive agencies like the National Coal Board. After production at Chatterly-Whitfield Colliery near Tunstall was shut down in 1977, it shortly reopened as a museum of coal mining. Today visitors are frisked for inflammables, kitted out with miner's helmet, lamp, and safety gear, and whisked by "man-engine" down 700 feet to workings where, in best museum period room fashion, the activity seems to have stopped only moments before. There is no disputing the authenticity. The guides are now-retired colliers who had worked those shafts from school-leaving at age fourteen until the mine shut down in the Coal Board's grand national scheme of rationalizing production.

Financial Foundations

The museum enthusiasms and the economic resources of a community are often unevenly matched. The cutlery museums of Abbeydale and Shepherd's Wheel in Sheffield enjoy considerable City Council and business support. Thriving wholly on volunteer labor, organized in the best English village tradition by the vicar's wife, is the Framework Knitters' Museum in Ruddington, preserving an industry mechanized early enough for Daniel Defoe to despair in 1725 about the cultural transformation being wrought by a new technology.[8] On the other hand are some more desperate mis-matches of will and ability. Higher Mill in Lancashire houses a highly significant collection of Arkwright cotton-spinning machinery. It aspires to become the National Textile Museum, but so far has trouble enough generating support in the local community. In Wales, the remains of Blaenavon Furnace, site of important refinements in what we know as the Bessemer steel process, have been in public trust since 1969. But can-- or should--the frail Welsh economy, struggling to survive the on-going demise of its modern steel industry, afford the wholesale reconstruction of the furnaces at Blaenavon?

Few young organizations manage to be as shrewd about their own futures as the Arkwright Society which preserves its namesake's great cotton mill at Cromford. The Society has wisely resisted the temptation to plunge, with scant resources, into a comprehensive museum development. Instead members have concentrated energies upon public education, especially on an excellent set of two-dozen regional guides. As a constituency is firmed up, so too will be its museum's realization.

Entrepreneurial Spirit

Concern over such practicalities as long-term finance aside, open-air industrial museums are the brightest facet of British museums today. As institutions they are quite young, and therefore tend to have attracted younger staff, professionally trained and willing to plan boldly and defy tradition. In general these museums are independent trusts (or non-profit organizations), not supported from public revenues. They have had to become quite entrepreneurial, earning income, for example, through museum-shop sales. They make thorough use of government employment schemes. They depend in good measure on admissions; charges of £3 a head contrast sharply with the 10p admission to County museums. And from that contrast the open-air museums derive much of their vigor. To stay alive, to continue their inordinately expensive development, they need to keep alive in the public eye. So they advertise. They promise kaleidoscopic activity. They present craft demonstrations. They raise historical livestock. They operate machinery, and trains, and trolleys. They offer education programs for school children and adults. The very activity in these open-air industrial museums stands out in sharp contrast to many Council-supported local history museums housing crowded dusty cases of Roman relics.

The public response to that open-air industrial liveliness is so substantial that the last ten years or so have seen the rise of the corporate industrial museum.[9] In some instances, such as Colman's Mustard in Norwich and Clark Shoe in Street, historically sensitive management sees an opportunity to promote its product while preserving important artifacts. Bass Brewery, in Burton-on-Trent, for example, has a long heritage of innovative marketing. In the early heyday of automobiles in the 1920s, Bass made its product visible through a humorous beer-bottle auto. Today, in the heyday of the industrial museum, and the Campaign for Real Ale, the brewery asserts the authenticity of its product through a richly endowed and well-visited museum.

Occasionally the result is less satisfactory, as at the Poldark Mining Museum (renamed after the BBC/PBS TV series on life in a Cornish mining community) in Cornwall. A private collection gone "for-profit," the Poldark Museum fails to honor its public trust in its care of a just-inherited collection assembled by Holman's, a major Cornish heavy engineering firm. And then there is the gloriously eclectic Wookey Hole Museum, recently purchased for profitable operation by Madame Tussaud's Wax Museum. This mad-cap conglomeration includes a spectacular cavern, a seventeenth-century paper mill still hand-casting paper (including that used for the invitations to the recent Royal Weddings), an American collection of carousel figures, and--in the curatorially-proper constant environment of the caverns, the spare limbs and deposed heads of Madame Tussaud's London effigies!

Wholly voluntary, where the only profit is enormous satisfaction, are the numerous interpretive efforts undertaken by buffs. Britain has a lively popular tradition of amateur interest in history and technology. Children are raised to consider the landscape a rich text; many spend some intense period of their adolescence as "spotters"--of birds, of trains, of traces of Roman roads.[10] In adult life, those enthusiasms often coalesce into purposeful and meticulous preservation of steam engines, canal boats, and railroads. Lovingly kept in steam by volunteers are the magnificent municipal pumping engines at Kew Bridge, London, and Ryhope, Sunderland. Volunteers resurrected Britain's nineteenth-century canals from virtual abandonment by the Inland Waterways Board after World War II.[11] Preserved locks, boats, and considerable sections of canals now enjoy intensive leisure-time use. Canalling history is told today in many places, perhaps most vividly at the Waterways Museum, Stoke Bruerne.[12] Similarly *volunteers* have largely powered the phenomenal restoration of steam railways beginning in the late 1940s and really accelerating after the demise of steam on BritRail in the late 1960s. More than 900 steam locomotives are now preserved. Today those volunteers provide both an important constituency and source of colorful public programming for the several railroad and transport museums around the country.[13] And there are many, many volunteer efforts which verge on the professional as in the re-creation of Trevithick's *Penydarren* locomotive, undertaken as a high school project in Cardiff.

The Impact of Industrial Archeology
Very much a related development has been the popular involvement in and growing academic respectability of industrial archeology. In the thirty years since the term came into general use, most industrial regions of the country have been systematically inventoried by

amateurs, curators, and scholars often working in
tandem to identify surviving industrial and engineering
evidence in the landscape. National handbooks, regional
guides, and studies of individual technologies find an
apparently insatiable market.[14] Those resources--in the
landscape, in people, and in their books--constantly
propel one out into the hinterlands in search of
industrial ruins: tin ore-crushing stamps mouldering in a
Cornish vale at Nancledra, arsenic-refining flues
zigzagging up the sterile hills above the Leadworker's
Reading Club in Nenthead, and so on. A surprising
feature of this popularly-based fascination for industrial
remains is the consistent quality of the simultaneous
efforts to identify, preserve, and interpret. Academic
historians clearly have no monopoly on good work![15]

Interpretation and Collections
The best British industrial museums are adopting the
latest interpretive techniques, such as participatory
exhibits. Many British open-air industrial museums
have adopted the familiar American practice of live
interpreters who assist visitors in making sense of a
recreated historical environment. But often in Britain
the results are quite uneven. Costumed interpreters are
simply not very gregarious. It may in part be a matter
of cultural difference, as staff at Ironbridge Gorge
suggested. Neither British interpreters nor visitors
respond with a ready "hail-fellow-well-met" attitude as
Americans do. Yet much of the problem has clearly to
do with morale. In the best instances, at Bewdley brass
foundry, at Ironbridge Gorge, at Morewellham, staff feel
good about themselves and proud of their institutions,
and that is reflected in their eagerness to talk with
visitors. Sad to encounter, but happily few, are
instances such as Beamish where staff were simply
peckish and made visitors quickly feel unwelcome.
Regional and national museum organizations in Britain
urgently need to develop administrative skills in
training and motivating interpreters.
     British industrial museums seem to concentrate
their energies on doing one thing well: Beamish, for
example, has a thoughtful and amusing orientation
exhibit. Others manage a publications program or
invest in intensive collections research. Some provide
museum education for regional schoolchildren. But few,
indeed, including the national museums, are those
institutions which develop simultaneous strengths in
several areas. Ironbridge Gorge Museum Trust, the City
Museums of Birmingham and London, and the National
Railroad Museum are in that handful of exceptions.

British industrial museums make considerably greater use than we do of television as an interpretive tool--even, sometimes, to the detriment of visitors momentarily on site. They reason that more people will be exposed to the educational resources of the museum though the medium of television than will be inconvenienced by a camera crew during a day's taping. And when the results are such distinguished series as "The Past at Work" and "The Rise and Fall of King Cotton", perhaps they are right![16]

Conservation protections for artifacts on display (and in industrial museums, frequently in use) are practically non-existent. In many cases the cavalier attitude seems to be the result of a pragmatic sense of the plentifulness of replacements rather than any well-cooked philosophy of museum teaching or curatorial responsibility.

What, finally, can be said about the *content* of the museum interpretation of industrial history? It is antiquarian, focusing on artifacts in isolation. It is heavily process-oriented. It generally portrays innovation as springing *de novo* from the minds of individual Great Men. It is heartily progressivist. The technological mechanisms of improvement are more clearly understood, and more pridefully presented, than are the social mechanisms--much less the dark-side causes of decline.[17]

The social ramifications of technology are too often implicit, suggested only contextually by a period room or two. C. P. Snow observed that "nine English traditions out of ten spring from the latter half of the nineteenth century."[18] For nine English industrial museums out of ten, the social meanings of industrialization seem to spring only from the Victorian parlour!

The impact of recent historiography is not apparent. One learns nothing about demography, politics, working-class *mentalite* at the museum. Even the simple questions go unanswered. How many people were required to keep such a mill running? How many others depended for their very lives on it? What were the patterns of training and paces of work? How did innovation and empire feed one another? An Englishman once observed that "history is chaps." But that is not true, *yet*, in museums of British industrial history.

Museums and Public Policy
For Britain to endure its present deindustrialization, the

society and its museums must come to terms with "the chaps" in the nation's industrial history. Industry has liberated, divided, and undermined British society. Today one must worry about where in Britain's industrial life the nation will find the energies necessary to sustain the culture. (For example, during my visit, a lengthy strike over the distribution of tea breaks nearly broke the surviving remnant of Britain's auto industry.) Britain's industrial museums do well at asking the technical "hows" and "whys," but too rarely do they address the loaded social question of "so what".[19]

History empowers a society and its citizens, as the leftish History Workshop demonstrates in a succession of worker-written craft histories.[20] If British industrial museums can become the popular medium for the historical voice and perspective of the "working chaps," then these museums of the world's first industrial civilization can contribute mightily to shaping a vigorous new society for the post-industrial age.

Notes

1.   A burgeoning literature struggles to understand the deindustrialization of the British and American economies. For an analysis of the British situation, see, for example, Correlli Barnett, *The Pride and the Fall: The Dream and Illusion of Britain as a Great Nation* (New York, 1987). A literary perspective may be found in Martin J. Wiener, *English Culture and the Decline of the Industrial Spirit, 1850-1980* (New York City, 1981).

2.   Lewis Mumford, *Technics and Civilization* (New York City, 1963).

3.   This essay is based upon a study-tour of British industrial museums under the Winston Churchill Travelling Fellowship of the English-Speaking Union of the United States (E-SU) in the winter of 1981-82. Opinions expressed are those of the author alone, and represent neither E-SU, the National Park Service, nor the Lowell Conference.

4.   On the evolution of museums from aristocratic to publicly accessible collections, see Alma Wittlin, *Museums: In Search of a Usable Future* (Cambridge, Massachusetts, 1970). Charles R. Richards, *Industrial Art and the Museum* (New York City, 1927), discusses the rise of industrial and technical museums which could serve as the inspiration for improved design of mass-produced objects. Michael J. Ettema, "History Museums and the Culture of Materialism," in *Past Meets Present: Essays about Historic Interpretation and Public Audiences*, Jo Blatti, ed. (Washington, D.C., 1987), carries the discussion further. Darwin Kelsey, "Outdoor Museums and Historical Agriculture," *Agricultural History*, xlvi, no. 1 (1972), 105-127, discusses the rise of outdoor museums created to preserve a memory of agricultural heritage in the face of industrialization.

5.   A useful introduction to the first world's fair is Yvonne French, *The Great Exhibition: 1851* (London, n.d.). For a contemporaneous report on the Exhibition, see *The Crystal Palace Exhibition Illustrated Catalogue* [from *The Art-Journal*] (New York City, 1970). C.H. Gibbs-Smith, *The Great Exhibition of 1851* (London, 1950), is a catalogue of a centennial exhibit at the Victoria and Albert Museum. Eugene S. Ferguson, "Technical Museums and International Exhibitions," *Technology and Culture*, 6, 1 (1965), 30-46, discusses the reciprocal relationships in presentation and pedagogy.

6.   Brooke Hindle argues the point eloquently in "Museum Treatment of Industrialization: History, Problems, Opportunities," *Curator*, xv, 3 (1972), 206-219.

7.   The Census of 1851 showed that 51% of the population lived in urban places.

8.   Daniel Defoe, *A Tour Through the Whole Island of Great Britain*, 1724-26 (New York, 1979).

9.   Victor J. Danilov, "The New Thrust of Corporate Museums," *Museum News* (June, 1986), 37-47.

10.   W.G. Hoskins has been a principal catalyst for understanding the landscape as text: see his *Fieldwork in Local History* (London, 1967); and *The Making of the English Landscape* (London, 1955). The latter was produced as a BBC-TV series in 1972-77, and subsequently as a book, *One Man's England* (London, 1978).

52   Nicholas Westbrook

11.   L.T.C.Rolt launched this preservation effort with his autobiographical account of a journey through 400 miles of Midland canals on the eve of WW II in *Narrow Boat* (London, 1944).

12.   Countless guidebooks exist to Britain's restored canals.   A good place to begin study is Charles Hadfield's *British Canals: An Illustrated History* (Newton Abbot, 1950).   (Mr. Hadfield is the eponymous Charles of David and Charles, Ltd., major publishers of industrial archeology guides and histories.) David and Charles has published more than a dozen regional volumes on British canals.

13.   Similarly David and Charles, Ltd., has published an extensive series on steam railroading, thanks to the interest of the firm's co-founder, David St. John Thomas, in railroad history.   A good place to begin is the regional "Forgotten Railways" series, also in some dozen volumes.

14.   Kenneth Hudson, *Industrial Archaeology: An Introduction* (London, 1963).   Arthur Raistrick, *Industrial Archaeology: An Historical Survey* (London, 1972).   R.A. Buchanan, *Industrial Archaeology in Britain* (Harmondsworth, 1977).   Neil Cossons, *The BP Book of Industrial Archaeology* (Newton Abbot, David & Charles, Second Revised edition, 1987).   County-by-county handbooks have been systematically published since the late 1960s by David and Charles.

15.   Typically, Ironbridge Gorge Museum Trust has undertaken to bridge that gap.   With the University of Birmingham, it has collaborated in the establishment at Ironbridge of an Institute for Industrial Archaeology offering graduate and diploma courses.

16.   Anthony Burton has produced three series, each of which has resulted in a book of the same title: *The Past at Work* (London, 1980), *The Past Afloat* (London, 1982), and *The Rise and Fall of King Cotton* (London, 1984).

17.   For an extended discussion of the problem, see George Basalla, "Museums and Technological Utopianism," *Curator*, 17, 2 (1974), 105-118.

18.   C.P. Snow, *The Masters* (New York, 1951), 349.

19.   See Michael Wallace, "Industrial Museums and the History of Deindustrialization," in this volume.

20.   See, for example, *Miners, Quarreymen, and Saltworkers*, Raphael Samuel, ed. (London, 1977), and Paul Thompson with Tony Wailey and Trevor Lummis, *Living the Fishing* (London, 1983).

COMMENT
THE VULTURE
AND THE OWL:
MUSEUMS AND INDUSTRIAL
HISTORY

T.E. Leary

On the connections between scholarship and society, the eminent historian, David Brody, has remarked, "If research is not absorbed into the way in which society understands its history, then those labors ultimately become futile." Brody has also noted that "the dissemination of social history scholarship may well move out of the traditional literary channels by which history has found its public in the past."[1] The papers presented here demonstrate that dialogue between the scholarly community and public audiences is indeed transpiring through the medium of industrial history museums--a fact of considerable significance given the potentially popular appeal of both recent research and of museum programs as conduits for diffusing that knowledge.

It is now not uncommon for practitioners to straddle--however uncomfortably--the fields of academic and public history. Those who try to keep a foot in both camps would, I suspect, agree with Mary Blewett's contention that asserting the value of social history has proven easier than translating its diverse dialects into museum exhibits. Nevertheless, the prospect for reinterpreting the popular perception of industrialization on the basis of concepts drawn from social history continues to be attractive. Programming in progressive museums has probably passed the point of subjecting visitors to displays conflating industrialization with mechanization or confounding capitalism with the personalities of entrepreneurs.

However, we have also reached a point where blanket exhortations to inspire stale exhibits with the fresh breath of social history are no longer sufficient. It is necessary to recognize that the nature of learning opportunities at industrial museums may not be equally compatible with all areas of recent social history scholarship. Although museum programming can cover a wide range of activities, the primary characteristic distinguishing museums remains the collection and display of physical objects. In a crudely materialist sense a museum of ideas must be founded on tangible things and visual images; much to their dismay, historians-turned-museum interpreters have realized that more is involved in preparing exhibit text than simply ripping the pages out of a monograph and pasting them up on the walls.

Since museum exhibits cannot rely exclusively on verbal communication, they may be most effective in interpreting for visitors those areas of industrial history where the artifactual record is visually compelling. The richest of these opportunities lies in depicting the realm of work and the process of capitalist production on the shop floor. In the best of such projects artifacts and exposition can be melded into a realistic or evocative environment. Opportunities for reconstituting with equal immediacy and drama the more ephemeral cultural dimensions of industrialization may prove less plentiful, short of freezing in place the entire panoply of community institutions now collapsing in industrial villages and neighborhoods throughout North America. Museums concentrating on the legacy of work are admirably situated to preserve artifacts and educate the public concerning such topics as changes in the meaning of "skill" within particular occupations.

Decades hence, the gigantic machinery of twentieth-century factories may possess the aura now reserved for the handicrafts of Williamsburg or Sturbridge. To stifle romanticism those artifacts must be augmented by a meaningful interpretive framework that avoids reducing the history of an industry to a synopsis of its extant production technology. Even on such an optimal stage for recreating yesterday's work as an authentic industrial building with operating vintage equipment, realization of the full potential inherent in such a setting remains contingent on the quality of the script.

Recent literature on industrial capitalism and the labor process contains three themes of mutually-reinforcing value for reinterpreting existing industrial history exhibits and devising new ones. These three themes are: uneven development; the value of local case studies; the interrelationships between technology and the organization of work in specific industrial settings.[2]

The general theme of uneven development offers a refined context for interpreting artifacts associated with a variety of workplaces. For example, Raphael Samuel's portrait of industrialization in mid-Victorian Britain demonstrates graphically how mechanized and handicraft modes of production continued to co-exist within industries or even within the same factories.[3] On a more abstract and synthetic level, the troika of David Gordon, Richard Edwards, and Michael Reich has formulated a complex schema linking changes in the labor process to periodic restructuring of the institutions sustaining or inhibiting capital accumulation.[4] This controversial refinement of earlier linear periodizations such as Lewis Mumford's serves as a useful caution against telescoping the rate of change in production processes or homogenizing the work experiences of distinct generations.[5] If local industrial history is to find its way to the public on a level transcending antiquarianism, then museums should adopt some standard interpretive framework such as the uneven development theme.

The second point industrial museums can extract from current scholarship is the importance of case studies and disaggregated data. As Nicholas Westbrook emphasized, the pursuit of industrial history in Britain relies on a heterogeneous mixture of institutions and individuals. A comparable situation now exists in many areas of the United States. Local and regional historical societies, specialized public and private industrial history museums, and professional or amateur researchers all have in their custody artifacts and archival records requisite to reconstituting the industrial ecology and occupational cultures of particular work processes. Intensive investigation of specific industries can provide a useful antidote against overgeneralizations based on extrapolations from known conditions in leading sectors such as textiles or small arms during the early nineteenth century. Certainly David Hounshell's careful study of armory metalworking practice and its episodic adoption in sewing machine and agricultural implements factories offers a case in point.[6] Moreover, interpretive exhibits on labor processes in local industries provide an appealing avenue for recovering the human dimension of industrial work, right down to the details of identifiable individuals' careers when possible.

The third bequest from contemporary scholarship to industrial history exhibits highlights the effects of changes in the social organization of production on established shop floor routines. For example, the research of Daniel Nelson, David Montgomery, Dan

Clawson, and Katherine Stone demonstrates that important developments in factory supervision occurred during the late nineteenth and early twentieth centuries.[7] Management consolidated authority over production previously decentralized among clusters of skilled workers and laid upon their successors the visible hand of a new ideology. Museum interpretation of work environments during that period should focus visitors' attention upon the impact of such organizational changes on prevailing customs, wages, and work loads. Effective recreation of labor processes should involve rendering the envelope of social relations surrounding production as transparent as the hardware of manufacturing technology would be if the factories' skin were to be peeled away.

Exhibits interpreting industrial capitalism and the labor process can thus draw on a growing body of literature for guiding concepts. It is no longer justifiable to remain content with typological displays whose logic derives solely from object classification categories. Moreover, as Jacqueline Hinsley has indicated, museums such as the Hagley are not limited to passive consumption of academic scholarship. In-house research capability is integral to the success of exhibits, particularly with respect to specialized collections or local subject matter.

In practice, many museums that present past worlds of work to the public must incorporate the results of continuing research into existing physical plants and collections strategies. For museums dealing with earlier phases of the industrial labor process, such as the New England textile industry, new interpretive strategies are applied primarily to collections that will remain relatively static in terms of the range of artifacts represented. Where the universe of possible acquisitions has become finite, the primary problem becomes one of selecting the most appropriate interpretive techniques for acquainting visitors with the ecology of shop floor production that represents the sum of technology, organization, and workforce composition at any given moment. Within an overall exhibit design there are four possible ways of conveying information: labels; tour guides; audio-visual presentation; and publications such as exhibit catalogues or guide books. Each has its strong points and drawbacks. More important than choosing the ideal combination of interpretive techniques is insuring that the conceptual framework contains certain basic information about the particular work process under consideration. If a particular machine is on display, for example, visitors need to be given an opportunity of discovering which features still require human intervention; what effects the exhibited equipment had on prior handicraft or mechanical methods; the extent of operatives' autonomy within the workplace; some details about the age, sex, and ethnicity of the people who most likely would have run the machine during different years of capitalist development, and some sense of how the exhibited apparatus affected old or new traditions of labor protest.

Museums treating the initial stages of industrialization thus implement new exhibit strategies primarily by reinterpreting existing collections. Institutions confronting the current legacy of deindustrialization, including the contraction of the steel and auto industries around the Great Lakes, may find that planning exhibits also involves basic questions about collections policy and preservation capability. What should be collected in order to give present and future generations a chance to understand daily work routines in the plants that so vividly represent a particular phase of American industrial capitalism? Can significant portions of giant complexes be preserved intact as monuments to the role of industry in particular communities and as settings which simply cannot be duplicated in any conventional museum environment? If the scale of twentieth-century industry mocks the limited resources available for annual maintenance, can industrial museums compensate by collecting business records, photographs, job descriptions, union grievance records, small tools, safety equipment, training manuals and films, T.V. news footage, oral histories, and video documentation of operations prior to shutdown? Should such prosaic items find their way onto contemporary collections agendas, it will be due in no small measure to the explicit influence of social and labor history in shaping the overall direction of the museums that will eventually contain the most recent residue of deindustrialization. Ideally, concepts relevant to interpreting the labor process through material culture will also guide other areas of museum activity such as collection and preservation. In this sense, the core of a museum's identity and purpose might be defined as much by the themes which it wishes to bring to public attention as by the physical artifacts in its possession. One example of museum development along these lines is presently being undertaken by the Ohio Historical Society in Youngstown.[8]

For unionized, mass-production industries, grievance records are a particularly endangered species; international union archives may not systematically retain all documents when locals fold.[9] Grievance records also represent an indispensable element in reconstructing daily life on the shop floor over the past half-century of collective bargaining. Viewed in this light, grievance records represent common ground for reintegrating the institutional focus of the old labor history with the rank-and-file perspective of newer scholarship. Collecting grievance records is also important because they will be useful in discussing the causes of the capital redeployment that has relegated so much of American industry to the scrap heap and the museum.

In dealing with expiring industries museums mix ecology with eschatology. For in communities where plants have recently shut down, the sense of having passed a watershed is pervasive; denial of death coexists with desire for remembrance. It is precisely at this moment when a phase of capitalism has run its course that industrial history museums must seize their transitory chance to fashion for future visitors both exhibits and judgments out of the wreckage left behind. Minerva's owl wheels among the vultures over Lackawanna.

Notes

1   David Brody, "Workers and Work in America: The New Labor History," in *Ordinary People and Everyday Life: Perspectives on the New Social History*, ed. James B. Gardner and G. Rollie Adams (Nashville, 1983), 152, 153.

2   Historians of higher management or the capitalist state may discern in this interpretive agenda a certain syndicalist bias.   These comments focus on a specific theme--industrialization and labor--where the interplay between the academy and the museum seems potentially rich.   Other types of public programming may be more effective in engaging issues that lie outside the workplace.

3   Raphael Samuel, "The Workshop of the World: Steam Power and Hand Technology in Mid-Victorian Britain," *History Workshop*, 3 (Spring, 1977), 6-72.

4   David M. Gordon, Richard Edwards, and Michael Reich, *Segmented Work, Divided Workers: The Historical Transformation of Labor in the United States* (Cambridge, 1982).

5   Lewis Mumford, *Technics and Civilization* (New York, 1963), especially chapters III-V.   This pioneering history of technology was first published in 1934.

6   David A. Hounshell, *From the American System to Mass Production, 1800-1932: The Development of Manufacturing Technology in the United States* (Baltimore, 1984).

7   Daniel Nelson, *Managers and Workers: Origins of the New Factory System in the United States, 1880-1920* (Madison, WI, 1975); David Montgomery, *Workers' Control in America: Studies in the History of Work, Technology, and Labor Struggles* (Cambridge, 1979); Dan Clawson, *Bureaucracy and the Labor Process: The Transformation of U.S. Industry, 1860-1920* (New York, 1980); Katherine Stone, "The Origins of Job Structures in the Steel Industry," *Review of Radical Political Economics*, 6/2 (Summer, 1974), 61-97.

8   For further information on the Youngstown project contact Youngstown Museum Planning Office, Ohio Historical Society, 47 Federal Plaza, Suite 903, Youngstown, OH 44503.

9   Some industrial unions have established archival programs in conjunction with universities.   For example, the official repository for United Steel Workers of America records is Pennsylvania Labor Archives, West 342 Pattee Library, University Park, PA 16802.   See also Roger A. Meade and Marjorie J. Myers, comps., *Guide to Primary Sources in Ohio Labor History* (Columbus, 1980).

MAKING SENSE OF TEXTILE HISTORY: PUBLIC HUMANITIES PROGRAMS IN NORTH CAROLINA

Brent D. Glass

The first generations of textile mill workers in North Carolina referred to industrial work as "public work" meaning non-agricultural wage-earning work. It is appropriate, therefore, that we take this opportunity to talk about public humanities programs and the history of textiles in North Carolina since these programs represent the efforts of scholars to reach general audiences and to bring the insights, discoveries, and explanations of historical research into public view. I am going to provide a survey of public humanities programs sponsored by the North Carolina Humanities Committee that have sought to interpret the history of the textile industry in North Carolina. What is striking about these programs is that they represent the efforts of scholars to reach a new audience and to tell the story of the textile industry from the point of view of the workers themselves. Reaching new audiences has required working within more popular formats--plays, television broadcasts, musical performances, tours, and exhibit building. Emphasizing the worker's perspective has opened up new thematic categories for historical analysis--industrial work, collective action, family and mill village life, race relations, and religion. The result has been to stimulate a greater interest and understanding of the meaning and significance of North Carolina's largest industry and--more important--has encouraged a confrontation with difficult and disturbing questions about the impact and legacy of that industry upon the lives of those who have worked in textiles.

A brief background comment is in order before I proceed. There is a strong tradition in North Carolina that supports the kind of scholarship and public

61

programming I am describing in this paper. Back in the 1920s, Howard Odum led a team of notable sociologists based in Chapel Hill who examined in detail the life and culture of working-class people in the South. Their pioneering studies and monographs about tenant farmers and mill workers created an awareness of Southern working-class culture that had never been acknowledged or considered a proper subject for serious inquiry. Odum's journal, *Social Forces*, provided an intellectual framework for historians, novelists, and sociologists who raised important critical questions about the quality and meaning of life in the South.

Chapel Hill also served as the center for other educational and scholarly activities that focused attention upon the lives of ordinary citizens. One of the earliest "life history" projects in the country began under the direction of W.T. Couch, director of the University of North Carolina Press and regional director of the Federal Writers Project. Couch proposed to provide a complete picture of Southern life and culture through interviews which allowed individual Southerners to "speak for themselves." In 1938 and 1939, he and his staff collected 900 biographical interviews with Southerners from all walks of life. Thirty-five of these stories were published in the critically acclaimed *These Are Our Lives*. During this same period, the university also demonstrated a concern for reaching non-academic audiences. Its drama department, through what was known as the Playmakers Theatre, regularly traveled throughout the state bringing classical and contemporary drama to small towns and rural communities. One of the Playmakers' leading writers and performers was Paul Green who created the outdoor or symphonic drama in the early 1930s to depict historical themes and characters.

These traditions of Southern regionalism, historical drama and documentary realism are important because they inform and shape so much of the public humanities programs sponsored in North Carolina today. Much of this activity continues to be based in the Research Triangle--Chapel Hill and at Duke University in nearby Durham--with ambitious and innovative educational leadership also coming from the colleges and universities around Charlotte, especially the University of North Carolina at Charlotte.

I am going to discuss four projects that have been sponsored by the North Carolina Humanities Committee. The first is a play written in 1981 by Roland Reed, a professor at UNC-Charlotte. The play was called "Vera" and it tells the story of a woman facing her final day of work after 39 years working in textiles for a family-owned mill in Salisbury. Through a series of flashbacks, Vera confronts various events and dilemmas that have occurred in her life, each reflecting her personal development as well as containing symbolic meaning for the lives of textile workers in general.

The heart of the play is Vera's complex relationship with Randolph Laws, the mill owner whose family established the company and whose paternalistic managerial style dominates the life and work of all the workers in the mill. Vera's loyalty to Laws and the company is a powerful force in her life. Nevertheless, she clings to her independence, her ability to distinguish between right and wrong actions and decisions, and her dedication to the truth. Although Vera never joins a union during her career at the mill, she emerges as a natural leader among the workers because of her sense of fairness and her candor, and this position inevitably leads her into several conflicts with Laws. Laws himself faces a dramatic dilemma at the conclusion of the play when absentee owners purchase his company and force him to relinquish control of the day-to-day management of the mill.

The play creates an atmosphere of tension and ambiguity. The ambivalence the audience feels toward the characters and events in the play suggests a larger uncertainty in public opinion concerning mill workers, textile mill owners, and unions in North Carolina's Piedmont region throughout most of this century. The closeness of the mill community, for example, is played off against the all-consuming nature of the mill village and the control the company exercises over individual lives. The normally independent worker is forced to confront a series of demands to conform, first to the machine itself, and then to the rules of the company or the discipline of the union. In these circumstances, "Vera" develops the themes of autonomy and loyalty, class and corporate culture, paternalism and authority, work and family. The play offers no answers and deliberately seeks to establish a feeling of empathy for both the major protagonists, Vera and Laws, and by extension, for the workers and managers confronting dramatic changes in the textile industry.

The critical response to "Vera" was positive and enthusiastic chiefly because the playwright succeeded in creating characters and dialogue that were believable and that allowed working-class audiences to respond directly and to identify personally as the drama unfolded. Another important reason for the success of the play was the setting and format for each performance. The play was performed in 1983 in working class neighborhoods of north Charlotte, and in mill villages in and around Charlotte. Community centers such as churches, agricultural extension buildings, and retirement homes served as hosts for "Vera" and these locations invited greater attendance by non-academic audiences who might have been intimidated by a downtown theatre or a college campus auditorium. A potluck supper with audience and actors--the staple of most cultural events in the South--preceded each performance and served to reinforce the idea that this was an event that would be within the common experience of most ordinary citizens. As a result of this approach, nearly 90% of the 1,200 people attending these performances were present or former textile workers or managers.

Each performance was followed by a discussion led by Paul Escott, a historian from UNC-Charlotte and a leading scholar of the history of the South. Escott's role was perhaps the most sensitive and important in the entire project. He had served, along with other scholars, as an advisor and critic to the playwright and had written short articles on the history of textiles that appeared in local newspapers prior to each performance. In the post-performance discussions, Escott sought to make connections between specific events and characters in the play and some of the broader issues that have historically affected the textile industry. He also tried to build a bridge through dialogue between the academic perspective based upon research and observation and the point of view of the workers in the audience who responded to the play and to Escott's questions in light of their direct experience.

Paul Escott also figured prominently in the second project considered in this paper. As researcher for a television documentary called "From Uncle Tom to Jim Crow," Escott supplied a rich collection of primary source materials that were used to form the text of the production. The catchy title of this program suggests an examination of black history in the second-half of the nineteenth century, however, this presentation actually dealt with issues that also concerned the industrial development of North Carolina and the rest of the South. The program was produced by WTVI, an independent public television station in Charlotte, and appeared in February, 1984. The central idea conveyed in the program was that racial segregation developed in North Carolina as a response to the political success of populism, and that populism gave expression to the grievances and anxieties of the new industrial class of the South as surely as it addressed the plight of black and white farmers in the region.

"Uncle Tom to Jim Crow" called special attention to the writings of Daniel A. Tompkins, a textile mill engineer and industrial promoter, who spent his career turning Charlotte from a backcountry trading-post to the hub of the growing textile industry in the South during the late nineteenth and early twentieth centuries. Tompkins' brand of Social Darwinism is set apart in the documentary from the autobiographical writings of the late Pauli Murray, a North Carolina native, and selections from oral histories of former slaves, farmers, and mill workers. Excerpts from these texts were performed by professional actors who were filmed at various historic sites associated with the period. A live studio panel discussion followed the program when it was broadcast in February, 1984. The discussion of this panel helped to clarify the major points of the program and helped make connections with the challenge of industrial development still facing the South a full century after D.A. Tompkins and his colleagues pioneered in the first New South period. The most divisive issue that arose during this panel discussion was arriving at a definition of progress. One member asserted that Tompkins and his generation had opted for technological values over human values and that civic leaders in Charlotte and other Sun Belt cities seemed determined to replicate the spirit of those times, especially with regard to their attitudes toward the environment and the working class.

A third project took place in 1985 and attempted to examine the textile history of a single county. Gaston County, located about twenty miles west of Charlotte, was known as the combed yarn capital of the United States and as the home of more textile mills per square mile than any county in the country. Its county seat, Gastonia, achieved notoriety in 1929 as the site of the Loray Mill strike which resulted in the murder of the city's police chief and of Ella May Wiggins, a textile worker who wrote songs that chronicled the conditions faced by workers in the 1920s. The project was sponsored by Belmont Abbey College, a small Catholic school in Gaston County, and about ten co-sponsors representing education, business, and local history museums.

The project was called "Crafted with Pride: Historical perspectives on the Textile Industry in Gaston County." The purpose of the project was to provide a learning experience that allowed area residents to participate on several levels. A series of lectures examined various issues in the textile history of the South and of Gaston County specifically. These lectures concentrated on material culture, religion, and union activity and also offered a comparative view between the South and New England. A reading group met on alternate weeks to discuss the lectures and to review excerpts from several historical and sociological studies concerning the textile industry. Another group met to study oral history techniques and then collected about 25 interviews with people who are working or who have worked in the textile industry in Gaston County.

The most ambitious part of the project called for the construction of a model of a typical North Carolina mill village as it would have looked in 1900. The southern mill village is very different from company towns in the northeast or mid-west and these communities have recently begun to receive serious scholarly consideration. The purpose of constructing the model was to invite residents to reconstruct the physical environment of mill workers, to cause them to reflect upon the meaning of mill village life, and to consider the implications of "paternalism" as a system of labor management. The project sponsors posed these questions in their proposal: "Were the mill villages simply a necessary part of mill building that required the creation of whole towns by the owners, or were they constructed primarily to serve as a controlling force over labor? Was the paternalism which evolved reflective of "humanistic values" embedded deep in religious traditions, or was it simply used to thwart union organizing?" Participants in this phase of the project conducted research in census records, insurance maps, oral histories, and company records. They conducted reconnaissance surveys in the many villages that still exist in Gaston County especially in one town-- McAdenville--that became the chief model for the exhibit builders.

The last project I want to discuss is still in the process of becoming a full-fledged public program. In 1984, the Southern Oral History Program at the University of North Carolina-Chapel Hill sought our support to produce a script for a play that would be based upon its extensive collection of interviews on industrialization in the Piedmont region of North and South Carolina. Under the direction of Jacquelyn Hall, the Oral History Program had begun conducting interviews on this subject in 1975 with the intention of publishing a book on the subject. (The book was published by the University of North Carolina Press under the title *Like a Family: the Making of a Southern Cotton Mill World* in 1987. It was awarded the Merle Curti Award by the Organization of American Historians as the best American social history book published in 1987-8. Ed.) In developing their statement of purpose for the public program, Dr. Hall and her colleagues voiced the hope that their research and interpretations could go beyond the constraints of a monograph that would be read chiefly by an academic audience. They were also influenced by the positive critical response to the play "Echoes from the Valley" based upon interviews with textile workers from Yorkshire, England, which was performed in North Carolina as well as in South Carolina, Rhode Island, and Connecticut during 1984. They were so impressed with this production that they engaged the playwright, Garry Lyons, to review the transcripts and tapes in the oral history collection in Chapel Hill and to prepare a script based upon this collection. I have recently read the first draft of Lyons' effort which he is calling "Plant Me A Garden" and I found it to be a remarkably sensitive portrait of black and white workers undergoing a period of significant change in the twentieth century.

The play is intended to provide a text for what the sponsors hope to be a series of history workshops held in the industrial communities in which many of the interviews took place. The model for these workshops comes from England where Ruskin College, Oxford sponsored meetings between workers and historians in the 1960s. A similar format has been transplanted to Massachusetts in the 1980s. The purpose is "to make history a more democratic activity and a more urgent concern by bringing industrial workers and social historians together in an informal workshop setting. The workshop will include a pot-luck lunch, a slide-illustrated talk, and a performance of Lyons' play. Small group discussions will be led and tape-recorded by a humanities resource person. Quotations from these tapes, along with photographs, other commentary, and an evaluation form will be compiled in a follow-up newsletter and sent to each participant."

"The need for such a project," writes Jacquelyn Hall, "is twofold. First, . . . rapid social change since World War II has tended to separate the generations and make it difficult for people to use history to understand the present and chart the future. Our study has shed new light on such issues as the values of self-sufficiency and reciprocity fostered by rural life; the capacity of working people for cultural creativity as they adjusted those values to the exigencies of factory labor; and the forces that promoted or undermined group identity and affected workers' ability collectively to shape their community and work experiences." Professor Hall's hope is that through the history workshop format, she can make the research of the oral history program "common property, conveying to a lay audience a sense of connectedness . . . and a perception of themselves as makers of their own history."   In addition, she hopes to demonstrate not only a respect for "the eloquence and analytic ability of the people . . . interviewed", but also to create a dialogue among scholars and workers that is truly reciprocal.

Many of the programs I describe are ambitious and I would be the first to admit that these programs often fall short of their original intentions.   The play "Vera", for example, stirred vigorous criticism from some social historians who felt that the playwright Roland Reed had stereotyped mill workers while going easy on the actions and decisions of the mill owner. "From Uncle Tom to Jim Crow" struck many observers as lacking any dramatic quality.   One critic found it flawed in its conceptualization and called it "one-sided, pedantic, and moralistic."   Even the creators of "Crafted with Pride" recognized the limitations of their effort when they pointed out in their final evaluation that the project failed to attract significant numbers of Gaston County   textile   workers.   This   last   point--the participation of workers in these programs--is crucial. In the final analysis, a central measure of success or effectiveness of public programming in this area is the degree of ownership that working people in North Carolina are able to claim over the public interpretation of their history.   Industrial workers, black and white and young and old, need to come forward and offer themselves and be included as project sponsors, as panel members, as evaluators, and as critics.   At this point, this has not happened in North Carolina.   The scholars in our state have made significant strides in opening up the interpretive process and in sharing the fruits of their research.   Nevertheless, they are still the singular custodians of the historical record.   How can we use public programs in the humanities to further develop the capacity of working citizens to critically examine and explain the historical record?

These are not academic issues in North Carolina. The state is alive with issues and public concern over the fate of the textile industry.   The history of the textile industry has occurred for the most part within the living memory of many of our citizens. Many more are no more than one generation removed from the earliest years of industrial development and the dramatic transformation of much of the state from a rural to an industrial society, from farming to "public work." Furthermore, that experience continues to shape the lives of thousands of residents along with the popular perceptions of anyone who lives in the state. Remember, the film "Norma Rae" did not depict some remote society in a far off land but called attention to the struggle to organize a major American textile company in North Carolina in the 1970s.   In October, 1985, another attempt to organize workers at Cannon Mills failed miserably chiefly because of the tenacity of basic assumptions that support individual autonomy and respect for authority. Moreover, the violence associated with an earlier period of textile history can erupt again as we saw in the streets of Greenboro in 1979 when Ku Klux Klansmen, many of whom were mill workers, fired upon members of the Community Workers Party who were trying to organize the mills, leaving five dead and many others wounded.

I am convinced that the proper role of the North Carolina Humanities Committee is to continue to support efforts to critically assess the impact of textiles and other industries upon our lives, to examine the choices and tradeoffs we have made, to discover the connections between industrialization in our state and in other societies, and to do these things in public among everyday citizens.

The overall strength of these public programs, indeed the strength of the humanities, is that they wrestle with difficult issues, raise disturbing questions about the meaning of our public and private lives, and call attention to those values and beliefs that direct us and make us human. The study of industrial history focuses upon many of the most enduring questions about what it means to be human and I view the willingness of academic historians to "go public" with their research and interpretation to be a positive and necessary step in the continuing process of reaching an understanding about who we are as a people.

DISCOVERY HALL MUSEUM: INTERPRETING SOUTH BEND'S INDUSTRIAL PAST

Marsha A. Mullin

South Bend, a city of 110,000 people located in northern Indiana, has long had a self image as a busy industrial city. However, in the past twenty years much of that image has changed, as industries have closed down, moved elsewhere, or contracted their activities. At the same time, Discovery Hall, a city-sponsored museum of the industrial history of the South Bend community, has been collecting and interpreting artifacts and archives from the city's industrial past. During 1984 the museum served about 35,000 visitors from a diverse public: local residents, general tourists, Studebaker fans, school children, and scholars. Interpreting a past which so strongly bears on the present presents many problems. The museum itself, as well as the city's industrial history it seeks to preserve, has been a subject for much public discussion and this has affected the ways in which the museum interprets South Bend's industrial history.

Since the establishment of South Bend in the 1830s manufacturing industries have played an important role in the development of the area. Indeed one portion of South Bend was originally called Lowell after Lowell, Massachusetts, in hopes that industrial development in South Bend would mirror activity there. The coming of the railroad in the 1850s and the impetus given to manufacturing by the Civil War gave the city its first growth spurt.

In the late nineteenth and early twentieth centuries the name of South Bend was carried throughout the country, and the world, by dozens of products made by companies named after the city--South Bend Chilled Plow, South Bend Woolen, South Bend Toy, South Bend Watch, South Bend Lathe, among many others. Many of the products made in the city were a result of its midwestern location, near sources of lumber and markets for farm equipment. The three largest companies to spread the city's fame were the Studebaker Brothers Manufacturing Company, the country's largest wagon maker; the Oliver Chilled Plow Works, one of the largest agricultural implement manufacturers; and the Singer Sewing Machine Cabinet factory. Studebaker and Oliver, along with the Bendix Corporation which moved to South Bend in 1923, became South Bend's industrial leaders in the twentieth century as Studebaker turned to the manufacture of cars and trucks, Oliver diversified into a wider range of farm equipment, and Bendix became a major supplier for the auto and aviation industries.

Immigrants, primarily from Germany, Poland, and Hungary, came to South Bend to work in the factories. By 1920 the community had the second largest percentage of foreign born residents in Indiana, exceeded only by the Gary area. The rest of the state's residents were largely American born, but many of these small town and rural citizens moved to South Bend to find work also. The city's population grew, following industrial expansion, from 35,999 in 1900 to 70,983 in 1920 to 104,193 in 1930. In the 1930s South Bend workers led the way in the formation of the United Auto Workers as the local numbers for Studebaker (5) and Bendix (9) unions testify. The second national convention of the UAW was held in South Bend and the Bendix sit-down strike in late 1936 paved the way for the General Motors strikes of early 1937. World War II was the peak of South Bend's industrial strength, when Studebaker employed 17,000 workers and high school students worked after school and on vacations to meet the demand of military contracts held by South Bend's industries.

After the war things began to change. Singer's cabinet works, a local fixture since the 1860s left South Bend in 1954, the first of the big industries to begin the move south. Studebaker and Oliver employment declined throughout the 1950s, although Bendix continued to grow. Studebaker closed its South Bend plant in December, 1963, a date which has become a watershed in local history. Interestingly, the local unemployment rate fell to a very low figure within about a year's time as Studebaker workers moved, retired, or found employment at other still expanding local plants.

Industry has changed greatly in the past twenty-two years in South Bend. Manufacturing employment has decreased, especially in the past ten years, as corporations move manufacturing operations from the area. South Bend, like so many other northern cities, is working to re-establish its economy and its identity.

In the midst of this change, Discovery Hall Museum was established. In 1966, as Studebaker ceased auto manufacturing operations altogether, the company was approached about donating its collection of historic vehicles to the city. Studebaker agreed and the city took possession of over forty horsedrawn and motorized vehicles, all but five manufactured by Studebaker. Although the city had sought the collection, it had no plan for developing a museum to display them and for the next ten years virtually left control of the collection to the Studebaker Drivers' Club, a nationwide group of Studebaker enthusiasts. The club added vehicles to the original corporate donation and opened the museum to the public on a limited basis while the city provided a caretaker.

In 1974 the city began to make plans for construction of an arts/convention complex to be located in the downtown area. One of the planned features of the complex was space for a permanent home for the growing vehicle collection. The mayor appointed an advisory committee, including academic historians, businessmen, and other interested citizens, for the development of the museum. While this planning was going on, some businesses having been approached for contributions to the center, objected to a museum dedicated solely to Studebaker, which they said had left the city, while they remained--still providing jobs and supporting the economy. In response to these objections, the mayor's advisory committee proposed changing the purpose of the museum to cover all of the community's industrial history.

The purpose of the museum having been expanded, the first professional staff of the new museum was hired in 1976. They, and various consultants brought in to assist them, responded with enthusiasm to the concept of a community-based industrial history museum. Few museums existed anywhere in the country for this purpose and virtually none in the midwest. The staff began collecting artifacts and archival materials and applied for a planning grant from the National Endowment for the Humanities to begin studying ways of presenting this rich industrial history to the public. Many of the city's long established industries were very generous in donating material to the museum's collection and were excited that their contributions to the city's development would be preserved. Likewise workers, especially those retired and near retirement, donated many additional items.

In planning the exhibits, many segments of the community were invited to present their viewpoints on the history of industry in the area. These included: management representatives from both large and small industries, Chamber of Commerce people, elected officials, union leaders, retired workers, academic historians, teachers, and many others. From these discussions a consensus developed for a humanistic, rather than a technological, interpretation. There seemed to be at that time less interest in mechanical features of the products or in the process of manufacturing, than in the human resources: the expertise, the skills, the talents, and the pure hard work that made South Bend an industrial city. This group seemed to want to look at the forces which had shaped the city--the process which molded the city of South Bend rather than industrial technology. There was, of course, a diversity of opinion as to what to include and what to exclude in the exhibits, with a strong faction primarily interested in the Studebaker story.

Based on these meetings, the staff and the exhibit designers planned an interpretation which followed the history of industry in the area both thematically and chronologically. However, due to various delays the exhibits, constructed with the assistance of additional money from the National Endowment for the Humanities as well as appropriations from the South Bend Common Council, were not completed until the end of 1981. Before this, objects were exhibited in an open storage format, and interpretation was provided through tour guides, temporary exhibits, and special programs. Because of the lack of display cases, most of the objects exhibited were large and the Studebaker Vehicle Collection remained the center of the exhibits.

The new exhibits, when completed, provided a radical change in appearance as well as in general interpretation. There were six basic exhibit areas: Woodworks, Supply, Horses to Horsepower, South Bend - World Famed, Influence of Design, and Workers. An introductory slide/tape program points out the highlights in area industrial history and ends on a positive note--pointing out that even though things are changing radically in the manufacturing segment of the local economy, change in itself is nothing new. A second slide/tape program at the end of the exhibits, in the Workers area, focuses especially on the experiences of the people who have worked in industry.

Reactions to the exhibits have been generally positive. The combined chronological/thematic approach helps visitors see the patterns in local industrial history and tries to bring about a clearer understanding of "how we got here from there". The "Workers" slide show, which was largely based on oral interviews and included many photographs taken in factories in 1981, has been especially well received. The voices, with their faint Polish and Hungarian accents, are instantly perceived as "REAL".

These exhibits are now four years old. Two years ago we opened a second exhibit area in our storage building, about six blocks away, in order to exhibit more of the still growing Studebaker Historic Vehicle Collection. In 1986 some improvements and modifications will be made to the exhibits at Century Center including adding an exhibit on World's Fairs, especially the Worlds Columbian Exposition, and to make "South Bend--World Famed" a larger and more interpretive exhibit. Within the next five years we hope to consolidate all of the museum's exhibits and activities at a single location. In addition to consolidation, we will be adding new features to our interpretation. There seems to be a growing interest in "process and technology" type exhibits, as well as a renewed look at inventors and entrepreneurs. We have a greater collection of materials for the "workers' exhibit" than we did earlier and much outside research has been done in many areas.

In addition to the permanent exhibits, a temporary exhibit gallery makes space available for short term exhibits which can cover subjects more in depth than the permanent exhibit. The choice of topic for the first temporary exhibit, "Plowmakers for the World", a history of White Farm Equipment (Oliver), has set the pattern for most of the following exhibits. They have tended to be histories of a single company. While this may not be very innovative, it serves many purposes. Employees or former employees want to see the history of "their" company which they can feel very strongly attached to even many years after retirement or after the company closes. Because of our interest in focusing on the history that people can remember and because of our collection strengths, these temporary exhibits have been heavily oriented to the twentieth century. Other temporary exhibits have looked at South Bend's industrial contributions to World War I and at women workers in association with the SITES traveling exhibit, "Perfect in Her Place".

In addition to exhibits the museum is working in a number of other areas on local industrial history. The museum has a large archival collection which includes the Studebaker corporate archives and the Oliver (White Farm Equipment) photograph collection. These collections are heavily used for research, especially the Studebaker collection. The film archives provided much of the basis for the film "Studebaker: Less than they Promised" which was produced by the local PBS affiliate and which won a number of prizes including the Peabody Award. The authors of at least two books, one a management history of Studebaker and the other a study of auto workers in Indiana, are making use of the archives. Discovery Hall has published three booklets based on museum research: two exhibit catalogs and a walking/driving tour of industrial buildings. This last was produced by one of a number of interns who have worked at the museum. We sponsor school tour programs and make museum resources available to local students and teachers. We offer special tours and film programs for adults as well. The first Studebaker Festival in the spring of 1986 included a drivers' club meet, films, and other educational and entertainment events.

The museum has participated in a number of other community programs relating to industrial history. For several years Indiana University at South Bend (IUSB) operated an oral labor history project. The museum provided assistance and since the project ended has been the repository of the research material collected. We provided much of the research material for the Historic Preservation Commission's (HPC) industrial buildings survey and worked cooperatively with the HPC and IUSB's continuing education division to offer a historic industrial building tour program for the adult general public.

In 1984 the city of South Bend completed a long term project to re-open the East Mill Race for recreational uses. Although there is little historic interpretation at the Race, before Discovery Hall there probably would have been little interest in the East Race or in the industrial buildings surrounding it. Discovery Hall has been at the center of much of the public interest in South Bend's industrial history. The museum, its programs and activities--indeed its very existence--have sparked public discussion about South Bend, its industrial past and its less industrial future. Being in the center of this sensitive issue has frequently put the museum itself in some peculiar positions. For instance, we seem to get more coverage in the local paper from the city government writer than from the arts/cultural reporters. It seems that the controversies which sometimes surround the museum are not just concerned with our activities, but also serve as an outlet for the fears and frustrations over what is happening in our city. Overall the museum has asked the community to take notice of what is happening that it might not otherwise have considered. Since our industrial past so affects contemporary events, the museum has not been able to take refuge in the safe and comfortable past. Because of this, our interpretations of South Bend's industrial past will change as South Bend changes.

THE REMAKING OF LOWELL AND ITS HISTORIES: 1965-83

Loretta A. Ryan

This paper takes a long view of the transformation of Lowell and its histories between 1965 and 1982. As one of the most symbolically significant communities in the United States for over 150 years, Lowell provides rich material for an anthropologist concerned with the theory of ideology. One of the first manufacturing cities in the nation in the 1820s, it was also one of the first to face the devastating effect of "Runaway industries" in the 1920s. Much of what follows is based on an examination of the documentary record, but is selected with a view toward raising questions about directly observed contemporary debates.[1]

While others have concentrated on using Lowell's recent history as a practical model for economic "revitalization," I begin with the premise that Lowell's recent past sheds light on some crucial problems in the social science theory of ideology. Until recently, there have been two major scholarly approaches to "ideology." One follows from Karl Mannheim who stressed the use of ideas to mask and reinforce dominant interests in class-divided societies.[2] Adherents of this approach have often studied the various ways in which official educational programs tend to preserve the status quo; with respect to history, this school of thought tends to expect to find glorification of the past. The other tradition is reflected in the work of Edward Shils who saw "ideology" as a distorted or excessively coherent set of ideas which can be distinguished from scientific truth.[3] (1968). Members of this school have been known to dismiss radical critiques of educational programs as simplistic and incapable of dealing with complex realities.

My research, however, is built on the work of those in history, anthropology, sociology, and education who are concerned with long-term ideological processes and the ways in which complex pools of ideas - including partial truths - interact with material and social developments to support or oppose the powers that be.[4]   The result is an "uneven reproduction" of dominant structures which does not produce "totally subjected" persons.[5]   The interacting processes generate multiple, fragmented consciousness in people. Members of a society do not share a single understanding of events, but they do share in the social arguments touching their situations in life.

The theoretical work of Goran Therborn has done much to enrich a previously over-simplified view of ideology which assumed that official educational programs would glorify the existing order.   According to Therborn, ideological processes involve three lines of defense.   Where possible, "positives" such as "affluence, equality, and freedom" are celebrated and "poverty, exploitation, and oppression," ignored.   If "negatives" must be acknowledged, however, an attempt is made to blame the poor or oppressed for them.   Finally, if blaming the victims is recognized as unjust, then the feasibility of a just society is questioned for the time being.[6]   This sort of scheme suggests that activist challenges to official pronouncements can make a valuable contribution to honest social reports.

My study of the creation of a national park to interpret the Industrial Revolution in Lowell reveals additional complications that theoretical speculations do not anticipate.   In the case of Lowell, I have found a more and more complex history unfolding over the last twenty years.   It is broad enough to encompass both glorification and denunciation of conditions in the city's past.   What is theoretically interesting is that critical views of the past are not the sole property of social critics.   Although social activists have played an important role in protecting the public from overly sanitized presentations of history, the powerful have also used criticisms of the past to promote their interests.   In this paper, I will explore this theme by contrasting the failed attempt to save the Dutton Street Row Houses in 1965 and 1966 with the successful effort to create a national park in Lowell between 1966 and 1978.

The Row House Dispute

Like much of Lowell's historical record, the Dutton Street Row houses were the subject of much ideological debate in the past.   They were built to house workers for Lowell's first textile enterprise, the Merrimack Corporation.   After a visit to Lowell, Charles Dickens made the pianos in such Lowell boardinghouses famous as symbols of the early Lowell mill owners' "paternalism." Paternalistic measures and images have been recognized as devices to attract scarce labor to work in the new, unfamiliar industrial environments pioneered in Lowell.[7] It is less well known that Karl Marx challenged Dickens' view of Lowell corporation housing in the second volume of *Capital*. He scoffed at the pianos and interpreted the provision of housing, for which workers paid rent, as part of a dual process of turning workers into consumers and shelter into a commodity to be rented.[8]

As the *Factory Tracts* illustrated, Lowell women workers of the time also debunked the benevolence of the mill owners and attacked the crowding, discomfort, and unhealthful conditions in the boardinghouses.[9] Later, however, architectural historian John P. Coolidge would speak of the row houses as evidence of a "native tradition" in the United States which regarded decent housing as a "birthright." He did so to support federal legislation of the 1930s creating federal housing projects.[10]

Thus there was no single historical verdict on the significance of the row houses. It may not be surprising that it was the capitalist interpretation of the houses as benign provisions of saving the row houses in 1965-66. Their prior association with a "right" to decent housing or with turning housing into a commodity was not invoked. A look at the complete story of the circumstances in which the houses were torn down reveals that such invocations would have been particularly appropriate.

The destruction of this worker housing has been viewed by some as exemplary of the mistakes of urban renewal and as an inspiration to current preservation efforts in the city. The demolition of the Dutton Street boardinghouses has too often been discussed in terms of a general unwillingness of people to remember the hard times of the past. To the extent that there has been any effort to put such attitudes in their social context, the blame has been put on federal urban renewal funding policies which supported demolition, but not preservation. A thought-provoking piece by Mary Blewett, on the other hand, has depicted the demolition as a case of "working class revenge" in which working class city residents and officials defeated the efforts of a privileged preservationist group to present a glorified look at the "paternalistic" era in Lowell history.[11] The analysis is of special interest because of its recognition of the potential impact of images of the past. I would, however, propose still another approach to the controversy over the Dutton Street Row Houses prompted by my concern as an anthropologist not only with the power of contrasting images of the past, but also with the unexpected uses to which they may be put.

After examining press accounts of the extended debate over preserving these houses, I would suggest that the controversy was not just about the merits of historic preservation. It entailed a gradual process of separating middle class preservationists in Lowell from an emergent statewide and local coalition which was raising questions about growing federal intervention in local affairs and about the displacement of the poor and the elderly from housing in urban renewal neighborhoods. At the same time, the debate resulted in the formulation of economic arguments for preservation which many influential Lowellians came to accept by the time the houses were finally demolished in August 1966.

In the fall of 1965, in press coverage of the Row House issue and in letters to the editor of Lowell's daily newspaper, the defense of historical sites in the city was linked to a critique of federal policies which victimized the poor, the elderly, and their landlords.[12] The preservationists had neglected to act earlier to save the French Canadian neighborhood, Little Canada, which was leveled by the same urban renewal project which destroyed the Row Houses. As Mary Blewett has pointed out, the preservationists did invoke a version of Lowell's early history which would have warmed the hearts of the founding capitalists.[13] Yet the preservationists did, in the beginning, join with groups in Boston and other parts of the state which were belatedly raising questions about the effects of urban renewal.

In the early stages of debate over the row houses, the city's powerful daily paper stirred up feelings of "working class revenge." It did so to oppose preservation and to defend urban renewal demolition and highway expansion plans for the land on which the row houses stood. The newspaper joined a prominent city councillor in arguing that the row houses were "a part of our history that should be forgotten."[14] In an editorial position it would later reverse, the newspaper gave substance to the councillor's general remarks by stressing the "spartan, stern surroundings" in which early nineteenth century women workers worked in Lowell.[15]

But such paradoxes are not the end of the row house story.   Increasingly, Lowell preservationists worked with federal and state officials, area museums, and Boston real estate developers to present economic arguments about the tax producing potential of converting the houses to garden apartments in order to promote plans for saving the row houses.[16]   Although individual preservationists involved in the case have shown some continuing concern with the issue of displacement,[17] the group's earlier critique of profit and victimization of the poor and the elderly dropped out of public discussion about the fate of the row houses in 1966.   In fact, one early preservationist came around to supporting demolition on the grounds that some proposals for row house apartments merely supported displacement elsewhere in the city.[18]

By the time that a few row houses blocking highway expansion had been demolished in mid-July 1966, prominent Lowellians began to speak out in favor of preserving the surviving structures.[19] Some *Sun* columns, editorials, and letters to the editor (for the most part, from ex- and non-residents) offered support for preserving a few of the houses - in some cases if public funding could be found.[20] Still, some "man in the street" interviews revealed some continuing opposition to memorializing the past.[21] The School Committee also had plans to use land on which some of the row houses stood for high school expansion.[22] In the end, a last-minute suit (by a Lowell resident giving a Boston Federal Street address) which returned to the critique of profit-making and displacement originally associated with row house demolition, failed to delay the wrecking ball.[23] The destruction was expected to be over by the time the case was heard, and the houses were gone by August 18.[24]

Had new federal subsidies for housing programs or preservation legislation been in place by August 1966, the short-term outcome vis-a-vis the row houses might have been different but the long-term effects may have remained the same.   The controversy laid the groundwork for future preservation efforts.   It served to create a distinction in people's minds between urban renewal and historic preservation.   It effectively separated the interests of preservationists and those opposing federal intervention in local affairs and displacement of the poor. It suggested that preservation projects which worked with rather than against federal and state development programs had a chance to win powerful supporters. It also suggested that an uncritical view of Lowell's past could easily be opposed. Successful efforts to promote Lowell history would need to deal with the fact that the powerful had manipulated "negative" aspects of Lowell history when useful to do so, and so had helped to keep alive a complex picture of the city's past.

Lowell Park Planning

The row house controversy foreshadowed some critical developments in the subsequent transformation of the city and the creation of Lowell National Historical Park. Although different groups were involved, the process of creating a park involved a gradual realignment of persons concerned with education, social programs, and historic preservation to work with rather than against powerful business interests in the city. In the process, some of the more progressive elements of the planning process were edged out. Simultaneously, multiple views of Lowell history were produced by a changing matrix of individuals and organizations. Their work has been shaped by shifting federal and state funding policies as well as by academic trends and by national, regional, and local politics. The net result has been a contradictory historical record. By episodically incorporating critical perspectives on distant and recent exploitation, history has been used to defuse opposition to the economic and political changes underlying the park building process.

The row house defenders were not central in the original planning for the park. A different Lowell group was responsible for conceiving and spearheading the drive to memorialize the Industrial Revolution in Lowell. Their efforts began with education rather than history, but they would interact to a great extent with other economic and social planning processes in the city, each of which gave voice to a different view of Lowell's past. The Chamber of Commerce spoke reverentially of the "paternalism" of Lowell's founders.[25] A regional planning commission was more neutral. It made the process of the Industrial Revolution and physical structures associated with it central.[26] At approximately the same time, city planners prepared chronologies of the city's history which neither glorified nor denounced the past; they sought out various "firsts" and connections with the famous ranging from the first workers' "strike" to the first "soda fountain." The overwhelming image in this chronology is of a community in a constant state of social and technological change.[27] Organizations with different conceptions of the past might join together in temporary broker organizations such as the Blue Ribbon Committee and the Center Cities Committee to plan for the future.[28]

Recently, Lowell has been touted as a model for using history as a tool for urban change. Often overlooked, however, is the critical role played by Great Society Model Cities Program funding in supporting the original park planning. That a Model Cities group led by Lowell educator Pat Mogan came up with the idea of a national park in 1970 is often acknowledged.[29] The Model Cities concern with "cultural heritage" is sometimes mentioned. Yet the group's early emphasis, in contrast to that of the row house defenders, on Lowell's history of ethnic conflict and memories of the depression is sometimes neglected.[30]

Also neglected are their many distinct efforts to overhaul the educational system in Lowell dating back at least to 1966 when federal environmental education money was awarded to Mogan for planning a regional arts and science center in the Lowell Dracut State Forest.[31] These efforts were based on a need to transform the school system from one oriented toward producing largely unskilled labor for local industries to one equipped to train professionals for such new industries as "high technology" - known as "electronics" in 1966.[32] In the process, they spawned many creative, substantive ideas for using the entire city as a school. In so doing, they broke not only with conventional views on curriculum and Lowell history, but also with existing political structures controlling education in Lowell. The early educational plans which gave birth to the National Park idea were oriented toward attracting middle class residents to the city. They provided for intensive use of university consultants, state as opposed to local funding of education in Lowell, and bypassing, to some extent, the school committee and local political networks in control of the school system.[33]

The Model Cities Education Component was only one of several physical and social programs planned for the Acre, a low-income neighborhood near the edge of the downtown area. The Lowell Model Cities Program as a whole, moreover, with its attention to historic preservation and social programs represented only one of a number of competing development conceptions for the city.[34] Other visions continued to depend on demolition, construction of high rise buildings and parking facilities, and highway and commercial expansion in neighborhoods.[35]

The national park idea gradually evolved from an educational program into an economic development platform that facilitated some unity among the competing factions in the city. Funding received from the New England Regional Commission, another Great Society creation, enabled the Model Cities Education Component to implement some of the recommendations made by university consultants under contract to the Model Cities Education Component and the Acre Model Neighborhood Organization, the "community participation" parts of Lowell's Model Cities Program.[36] A core group around Pat Mogan set up a Human Services Corporation in 1971 which submitted still more substantive educational proposals to federal and state agencies, and also served as a broker organization harmonizing some of the conflicting interests in the city.

The early 1970s was a time of recession, high unemployment, plant closings and empty industrial parks,and considerable tension between downtown businesses and neighborhood groups, between industry and labor, between the city government and the Locks and Canals Company, and between landlords and tenants. It was also a time of financial trouble for the city's leading bank which was eventually taken over by a Boston-based financial institution. Relations with the Locks and Canals Company, said to include among its investors the leading businessmen of the city[37], were especially crucial in that the company controlled the canal system essential to park development.

The Park idea embraced educational innovation, environmental concerns, and a non-confrontational approach to the leading investors in the city. In fact, park supporters made a point to solicit business support.[38] Park backers offered a tourist and service-oriented economic development program at a time when conventional industrial development plans were going nowhere. The Park idea won audiences among city businessmen that it might not have achieved in more prosperous economic times. Simultaneously, the cutbacks in federal aid for social and educational programs fostered a receptivity among educators to economic development orientations. There would still be ongoing arguments between preservationists and demolitionists about the relative merits of buildings and parking lots (as in the case of the Wentworth Building).[39] Yet there was sufficient support for a city Historical Commission and two historic districts to be formed by August 1973. The commission was composed of two city residents, a lawyer, an architect, a realtor, and representatives of the Planning Board, the Lowell Historical Society, and the Acre Model Neighborhood Organization. The commission supervised the construction, alteration, and demolition of buildings within the historic districts.[40]

A coalition of disparate elements (not always in agreement) formed around supporting legislation to create a Lowell national park. A bill was submitted to Congress in 1972 and then resubmitted annually until Congress passed a bill at the end of 1974. The final bill did not create a park. It established a politically feasible federal-state-local commission to plan a historic preservation program for Lowell. The governor's commitment, won during the 1974 election campaign, to seek funds for a Lowell State Heritage Park has been seen as useful in convincing Congress to establish the commission. By 1974, there was sufficient consensus around creating a park so that the campaign issue was not whether or not to have a park, but who could do more to bring it into being. That this was so testifies to the success of the multiple, bipartisan strategies followed by the core group of park supporters.

As the coalition supporting Lowell national park legislation took shape, new versions of Lowell history emerged. By the time of Congressional hearings on the park idea in 1974, educators promoting the park had joined their concern with Lowell's ethnic history with the positive images of Lowell's founding fathers reinforced by some university-trained consultants as well as by the row house defenders. Thus a highly favorable view of early Lowell became politically acceptable even as some versions attributed the industrial greatness of Lowell to the ethnic groups rather than Yankee capitalists.[41] This concern with ethnicity is often viewed as a parochial concern, but it should be noted that national, state, and private agencies actively promoted ethnic consciousness in the early 1970s.[42] At the same time, some university specialists in women's and labor history were posing some radical questions about changing class relations in Lowell history. These appeared in Congressional testimony along with the more familiar positions of the Chamber of Commerce on the beneficence of Lowell's founders.[43] Consistency of historic interpretation was less important than the image of cooperation around the goal of establishing a national park. The Park umbrella accommodated many views of the past.

With the advent of the Bicentennial year and the renewed interest in Lowell history as a development vehicle, more detailed and complex pictures of Lowell's pasts proliferated. Attention to difficult issues surfaced in two major statements appearing in 1976: the Lowell

Museum exhibition and *Cotton Was King,* an anthology of essays on Lowell history published by the Lowell Historical Society.[44]   The anthology did not attempt to offer a single, coherent account of Lowell history, but did more than previously published works to deal with ethnic and labor history, the political activities of early mill owners and engineers, and the interplay of class and ethnicity in Lowell politics. The Museum exhibition, in which the Historical Society was also involved along with the Human Services Corporation, went even further by exploring the divisive impact of ethnic conflict on labor organizing.   The Museum presented some hard hitting views of the strikes and suffering of the 1930s. Some of the material in the Museum exhibition and *Cotton Was King* overlapped with material presented in the *Communicator,* a radical monthly newspaper which did more than any other source of the time to relate a critical view of contemporary economic circumstances to a questioning tradition in Lowell's past.   But negative approaches to Lowell's industrial history were also particularly useful to cite in the search for federal grants in the 1970s.   Coolidge's observation that the city's original planners made decisions at the expense of the town (or downtown) rather than the corporations was   invoked   in   fundraising   for   downtown revitalization.[45]

Increasingly critical views of Lowell's past, therefore, coexisted with the increasingly economic orientation in park planning.   For a time plans for a national park in Lowell were merged with proposals for an oil refinery, a monorail, and a hydroelectric project.[46] After the election of a new governor and congressman in 1974, refinery and monorail plans fell out of favor, and park-related economic projects centered more around downtown revitalization programs although the hydroelectric planning did not die.   Federal National Endowment for the Arts and Historic American Engineering projects supported some planning for the canal system and conversion of the Boott Mill.[47]

The Lowell City Council's creation of two city historic districts in 1973, and their placement on the National Register in 1975 and 1976 made some downtown buildings eligible for federal grants under the National Historic Preservation Act and for tax benefits under the Tax Reform Act of 1976.[48]   Facade work was also funded after some community opposition by Community Development Block Grants and by a consortium of Lowell Banks organized in 1975 as the Lowell Development and Financial Corporation.[49]   The city's tax title program facilitated the transfer at city

auction of tax-delinquent properties to new owners and,
in spite of considerable local competition for grants
federal "turnkey" and "Section 8" housing money also
supported historic preservation efforts, many of which
were centered in downtown buildings.[50] It should be
remembered, and often is not, that local labor
organizations also helped subsidize the process by
agreeing, at a time of drastically high unemployment, to
the federal Section 8 requirement that they accept below
scale rates for work on the projects.[51]

Some prominent residents attempted to attack a
mill restoration housing project which had won a grant
competition by arguing once again, as some had during
the row house dispute, that people did not want to
remember the hard times of the past. They argued that
workers who had "slaved" in the mills during their
working careers would not want to retire to apartments
for the elderly in a converted mill.[52] By 1977, such
arguments were countered effectively.[53] They could not
forestall preservation/development projects which had
garnered support from federal and state agencies as well
as labor unions.

Native American history, never central in most
Park proposals, was successfully invoked in the mid-
1970s to block a neighborhood development project and
a highway expansion program in the Lowell Dracut
State Forest.[54] Yet critical views of Lowell history were
generally used to protect Park planning and
development projects associated with it. To counter
National Park Service objections that too many of
Lowell's historic structures had been demolished to
create a national park in Lowell consultants to park
supporters argued that it was the full sweep of Lowell
history, including experiences with "exploitation" and
"demolition," not just its early paternalistic period, that
was nationally significant.[55]

At the same time, the consortium of consultants
hired by the Lowell Historic Canal District Commission
(established by Congress in 1974) to plan for a national
park concentrated most of its planning on downtown
structures, the majority of which were built before
1850.[56] As a result, although the consultants were
periodically reminded by Lowell residents to take note
of ethnic history, it did not provide for the inclusion of
structures in the park which would mandate
interpretation of the "immigrant experience." The
"tyranny of structure" which Mary Blewett would see in
National Park Service thinking about Lowell after
creation of the park in 1978 actually had its roots in the

work of the Lowell Historic Canal District Commission and their consultants.

Offered a choice among six alternative physical plans designed by the consultant team, the Commission selected an alternative that put the needs of downtown revitalization ahead of neighborhood, ethnic or school programs.[57] It was argued that downtown development would eventually spill over into other areas, but that the reverse process was unlikely.[58] To support this choice, the appeal of departing from a traditional Park Service concern with mansions of the elite in isolated neighborhoods and moving toward a concern with "working class" mill environments in the downtown was highlighted.[59] Nevertheless the version of Lowell history presented in the commission's final report to Congress, which would become known as the "Brown Book," although diverse in its elements and not lacking in attention to structure and hierarchy, had largely removed the conflict from Lowell history which the Historical Society, in its anthology, and Lowell Museum, in its exhibition, had begun to address.[60]

Prior to passage of the legislation creating Lowell National Historical Park in 1978, a number of Congresspersons raised the question of whether the bill was not really an "urban renewal" proposal in disguise.[61] In testimony, Lowell residents and the city's Congressperson countered such views by stressing a need to memorialize the immigrant worker along with the famous and the "firsts" connected with Lowell.[62] Interpretive issues were also invoked to defend the need for a commission. In view of the limited land acquisition provided for in the park legislation, interpretive coherence would suffer, it was argued, if there were no commission to promote its educational progress and make sure that incongruent fast-food restaurants did not appear next to properties acquired by the Park Service.[63] By April 1978, the director of the Park Service also affirmed that Lowell park plans did not constitute urban renewal.[64]

While the debate in Washington was phrased in terms of history versus urban renewal, there was a debate within Massachusetts over how to deal with the harsh working conditions of the past. It was testimony to the growing regional image of Lowell that the debates took place in the Boston *Globe* as well as in the Lowell *Sun*. Some letters to the editor protested that creating a national park around the mills would "enshrine" them while others wrote in to say that an honest presentation of working conditions could and would appear in the park.[65]

This debate began the process of putting the Park Service on notice that a glorified approach to Lowell's past which did not address the full complement of consequences of the Industrial Revolution would not be accepted in Lowell. There were of course many to whom history and historical interpretation mattered little. The creation of the national park in 1978 by no means guaranteed unanimous support for historic preservation in Lowell. The decision of Wang in the late 1970s to locate its international headquarters in the city and to expand in the Lowell area buoyed the spirits of those who backed industrial development rather than preservation and downtown revitalization as a development strategy. In a controversial move which disappointed many park supporters, the city did not approve funding needed to save the mansion once owned by controversial General, mill owner, worker "advocate," and Massachusetts Governor, Benjamin Butler. Some key owners of downtown properties ignored historic guidelines in facade renovation. Efforts to preserve a downtown movie theater for cultural programs eventually yielded to plans for a downtown hotel.

At the same time, some key elements of the original holistic park planning process - overhaul of the education system, concern with environmental issues, and social programs for the Acre - have become the province of other, distinct constituencies. Although the Park planning process succeeded in the long run in tempering some of the more extreme suggestions of the local "growth machine" (e.g. the refinery, the monorail, and highway expansion in the Lowell Dracut State Forest), it is tempting to suggest that economically it served the purpose of defusing opposition to public financial aid to new downtown investors. General invocations of history were useful in bringing federal and state money to property-owners and some educational and cultural organizations. The existence of national and state parks also serves to enhance the "quality of life" in the area and so make it attractive to industries seeking to relocate in Lowell. Thus the parks have supported a process of capitalist reclamation of a once abandoned region.

That the history invoked in the process was a complex one capable of giving attention to the mistakes as well as the purported magnanimity of the founding capitalists may be explained by looking at the effects of Lowell's long decline after the departure of the textile and shoe industries from New England. This long

decline produced a complicated historical and social
consciousness in Lowell. A single-faceted glorification
of Lowell's past was not realistic or politically viable.
The powerful and those who would oppose them have
each had to make at least partial acknowledgment of
exploitation in the past in order to win acceptance.

What is very striking in the period between 1966
and 1982 - as opposed to the time of the Row House
controversy - is the growth of oppositional voices,
including university historians, neighborhood activists,
community residents, community agencies, and
professionals. They have joined forces at different times
to put pressure on the city, and more recently the park,
to broaden the scope of historical interpretation. The
public library, the Lowell Museum, community activists,
and University of Lowell academics have done much to
insure that certain topics would be covered. Twentieth
century Lowell history, the common experiences of
ethnic groups from the Irish to the Indochinese, the life
of the worker, and Jack Kerouac as cultural rebel have
all received attention as the result of their efforts.[66]
Much as the *Communicator* did in the 1970s, community
activists have also raised questions about the
contribution made by recent changes in the city to
gentrification. Inspired more by the fate of Little
Canada than by the demolition of the Row Houses, they
have shown great sophistication in using the national
and regional media, fund-raising skills, and their own
MIT-trained consultants to develop alternative programs
to prevent displacement in the Acre.[67]

In such an atmosphere, it is not surprising that
the Park has developed a rich and varied interpretive
program. I have only occasionally heard glowing
accounts of the city's early years on park tours. They
are far less frequent than mixed portrayals. There are
also many, quite conscious efforts to point out the
deafening noise and other health hazards of mill work
such as the "kiss of death shuttle," which one public
critic of the park feared would not be included.[68] In
state and national park slide shows and in a play
sponsored by the Lowell Historic Preservation
Commission, a reflexive spirit, capable of confronting
different views of the past, is encouraged.

There were many complicated twists and turns in
the process of creating a national park in Lowell that
have been neglected in this paper. Hopefully, enough
has been said to indicate that the planning process was
a fluid one in which the persistence and adaptability of
park supporters were crucial. However, also essential,
and frequently receiving less attention than the will,

determination, spirit, concern with image, and community pride of park supporters were the economic incentives such as Great Society funding and the material circumstances of the recession of the 1970s which shaped the planning process. The utility of invoking negative aspects of Lowell's history, the consequences of its long decline, when development plans associated with the park faced political obstacles, should also be clear. The Park then is by no means a simple monument to the worker.

Many questions remain. Is the Park the piano in the boardinghouse? Is it the amenity that deflects attention from the social transformation taking place in the region? Is it the concession to "quality of life" concerns that will help lure the middle class worker into a high tech working environment? And will that industry prove as capable of intensification, deskilling, and relocation as the textile industry before it? Will the Park distract people from such issues, or, as originally conceived, be an educational vehicle to help them address them?

Notes

1   This paper is an opportunity for me as an anthropologist to share with a community studied some preliminary conclusions and to raise some questions for future discussion.   Although I am a Lowell native and a frequent visitor in the past, I grew up and have lived outside the city.   My research is that of a "blow-in" who has taken up the traditional anthropologist's role as an outside observer rather than a maker of events.
        Between 1979 and 1982, I gathered material on efforts to establish a national park in Lowell for a Ph.D. dissertation in Applied Anthropology.   I have taken Park programs in Lowell, attended public meetings, school events, and festivals, used census and directory data to write about nineteenth century Afro-Americans, and pored over the many documents and press articles related to the creation of the park which many individuals and agencies generously allowed me to use.
        Documents reviewed include: grant proposals to federal, regional, state and private agencies; city planning reports; the city's daily newspaper; an alternative monthly newspaper from the 1970s; Lowell Historical Society publications; materials on museum exhibits; state park plans; federal commission plans for the National Park; and its plans for tours, exhibits, and other programs for visitors.
        I also worked during field work as a plastic cup packer in the Mobil Chemical plant that used to be in the Boott Mill, as a waitress at Friendly's, as a "data enterer" in a University project funded by the Lowell Historic Preservation Commission, as a clerk in the Lowell Museum book store in the Park Visitor Center, as a part-time lecturer at the University of Lowell, and as an interviewer with a market research firm near Route 128.

2   Karl Mannheim, *Ideology and Utopia* (New York: Harcourt Brace and World, 1936).

3   Edward Shils, "Ideology" in *International Encyclopedia of the Social Sciences*, ed. D. Sills (New York: Macmillan, 1968).

4   P. Bourdieu and J.C. Passeron, *Reproduction in Education, Culture and Society* (London: Sage, 1977), vi; J. Karabel and A. Halsey, *Power and Ideology in Education* (New York: Oxford, 1977), 40; H. Lefebvre, "Ideology and the Sociology of Knowledge" in *Symbolic Anthropology: A Reader in the Study of Symbols and Meanings*, ed. Janet Dolgin et al. (New York: Columbia University Press, 1977), 268; T. Asad, "Anthropology and the Analysis of Ideology," *Man* 14 (1979): 607-27; J. Clarke et al. *Working Class Culture: Studies in History and Theory* (London: Hutchinson, 1979); M. Apple, *Ideology and Curriculum* (London: Routledge and Kegan Paul, 1979); M. Apple, "Ideology and Educational Reform," *Comparative Education Review* 22 (1980): 367-387; G. Therborn, *The Ideology of Power and the Power of Ideology* (London: Verso, 1980); S. Hall, "Notes on deconstructing the 'popular,'" in *People's History and Socialist Theory*, ed. R. Samuel (London: Routledge and Kegan Paul, 1981).

5   R. Johnson quoted in H.A. Giroux, *Theory and Resistance in Education: A Pedagogy for the Opposition* (Massachusetts: Bergin and Garvey, 1983), 199.

6   Therborn, 19.

7   T. Bender, *Toward an Urban Vision Ideas and Institutions in Nineteenth Century America* (Baltimore, Johns Hopkins Press, 1975), 33-35; T. Dublin *Women at Work: The Transformation of Work and Community in Lowell Massachusetts 1826-1860* (New York: Columbia, 1979), 77.

8   K. Marx, *Capital* (New York: International Publishers, 1977 [1893]), Vol. 2, 516.

9   *Factory Life as it Is* (Lowell: Lowell Publishing Company, 1982 [Lowell: Female Labor Reform Association, 1845]), 2, 3, 6.

10   J. Coolidge, *Mill and Mansion: A Study of Architecture and Society in Lowell, Massachusetts 1820-1865* (New York: Russell and Russell, 1976 [Columbia University Press, 1942]), 116.

11   M. Blewett, "The National Park Service Meets the Working People of Lowell," *Labor and Community Newsletter* 1 (1979):2-3.

12   See the *Lowell Sun*: 29 September 1965, 1; 1 October 1965, 1; 7 October 1965, 1; 14 October 1965, 6; 15 October, 6; 25 October 1965, 1.

13   *Lowell Sun*: 10 November 1965, 6; 13 December 1965, 1; 3 July 66, 8).

14   *Lowell Sun*, 15 December 1965, 72.

15   *Lowell Sun*, 18 December 1965, 4.

16   *Lowell Sun*: 16 May 1966. 4; 3 July 1966, 8.

17   *Lowell Sun*, 16 January 1981, 5.

18   *Lowell Sun*, 12 July 1966, 4.

19   *Lowell Sun*, 10 July 1966, 8.

20   *Lowell Sun*: 3 July 1966, 8; 6 July 1966, 6; 12 July 1966, 4; 16 July 1966, 7; 18 July 1966, 4; 21 July 1966, 6; 22 July 1966, 4; 25 July 1966, 4; 28 July 1966, 8; 2 August 1966, 5; 9 August 1966, 5.

21   *Lowell Sun*: 13 July 1966, 7; 14 July 1966, 7; 15 July 1966, 5; 3 August 2966, 4.

22   *Lowell Sun*, 7 July 1966, 1.

23   *Lowell Sun*, 5 August 1966, 1.

24   *Lowell Sun*: 7 August 1966, 44; 18 August 1966, 1.

25   *Lowell, Massachusetts U.S.: A City of Diversified Industries* (Lowell: Chamber of Commerce of Greater Lowell, 1969), 18-19.

26   Greater Lowell Area Planning Commission, *Volume I: Inventory: A Study of Natural Resources, Scenic and Historic Features and Existing Public Recreation and Open Space Lands in the Greater Lowell Region* (Lowell: Greater Lowell Area Planning Commission, 1969), 48-52.

27   Lowell: City Development Authority, October 1968, 1-13.

28   *Central City Study* (Lowell: City Development Authority, March 1971), 113, 116; Center City Advisory Committee, "Statement of Goals," unpublished manuscript, Human Services Corporation files.

29   e.g., *Lowell National Historical Park: General Management Plan* (United States Department of the Interior, National Park Service, August 1981), 1.

30   Acre Model Neighborhood Organization (AMNO), "The Development of Educational Opportunities for the Public Schools - A Proposal" in "Special Opportunities Facilities Grant Report" (Phase II), unpublished manuscript, Human Services Corporation files, Appendix 5: pp. 1, 2.

31   *Lowell Sun*, 16 July 1966, 1.

32   Lowell Public Schools, "Guidelines for Educational and Urban Change in Lowell," unpublished Title III proposal, Human Services Corporation files, 27 December 1967, 15.

96   Loretta A. Ryan

33   Lowell State College, "Special Opportunities Facilities Planning Grant Report to Higher Educational Facilities Commission," unpublished manuscript, Human Services Corporation files, pp. 20, 28; Acre Model Neighborhood Organization, 1-3; Lowell Public Schools, 10, 26.

34   "Lowell Model Cities Plan," unpublished manuscript, City of Lowell Division of Planning and Development files, 1969. See also the Lowell Sun: 23 February 1967, 1; 8 May 1967, 5; 19 November 1967, 12; 11 May 1969, 1, 18.

35   D. Frenchman, Connecting the Past to the Present: A Planning Strategy for Urban National Historical Parks. Masters thesis in city planning and architecture. Massachusetts Institute of Technology, 1976, 159. See also the Lowell Sun: 27 May 1973, F41; 8 February 1976, b1.

36   See Acre Model Neighborhood Organization; Lowell Sun 14 June 1972: 26; "The Lowell Exploratorium," unpublished proposal, Human Services Corporation files, 14 March 1973, pp.3-4; M. Southworth et al., "Ideas for Developing the Public City of Lowell for Education," unpublished manuscript, Human Services Corporation files, 11 January 1971.

37   Lowell Sun, 27 April 1980, A5.

38   "List Sent to F. Bradford Morse of Persons Advocating the Urban National Cultural Park," unpublished manuscript, Human Services Corporation files, 31 May 1972.

39   See the Lowell Sun: 10 August 1975, B3; 2 August 1976, 13; 14 September 1976: 13.

40   Lowell Sun, 29 August 1979, 14.

41   See unpublished documents prepared by the Model Cities Education Component in Human Services Corporation files: "The Human Services Corporation: Design and Negotiation," September 1971, 1; "The Center for Human Development, A Proposal to the Board of Education, Commonwealth of Massachusetts, Experimental School," 25 April, 1972, 1; "Proposal to New England Program in Teacher Education: Environmental Curriculum Team Involving Community School Partnership," 18 May 1972.

42   See documents in Human Services Corporation files: "EMPAC! Newsletter of the Ethnic Millions Political Action Committee," January 1977, 1; "The Ethnic Parish and Your Community," June 1974, 1-2; and National Center for Urban Ethnic Affairs, "Fact Sheet."

43   See unpublished papers in Human Services Corporation files: Statement of Greater Lowell Chamber of Commerce for the Record in support of H. R. 14689," 19 August 1974; and T. Dublin, "Lowell: The Early Years: 1822-1840."

44   A. L. Eno, Jr., ed., Cotton Was King: A History of Lowell, Massachusetts. (New Hampshire Publishing Company in Collaboration with the Lowell Historical Society, 1976).

45   City Development Authority, Land Use Plan (Lowell: City Development Authority, September 1972), 3.

46   See documents in Human Services Corporation files: 1) Raytheon Corporation, Transit Plan for the City of Lowell, July 1973, p.2; 2) Human Services Corporation, "Progress Report, #10230486" 13 August 1973, 6; and 3) Human Services Corporation, "Canal Waterpower Electrical Generation Program." 30 November 1973, 1-2. See also the Lowell Sun: 1 February 1974, 4; 4 February 1974, 9; 1 December 1974, 13.

47   P. Mogan, Letter to William Lacy, 14 February 1972, 1-2; Lowell Sun: 23 April 1973, 10; 29 March 1974, 9.

48   Historic Preservation, September/October 1980, 57. Lowell Sun: 10 August 1975, B1; 14 September 1976, 13; 8 April 1977, 11.

49   *Lowell Sun*, 20 February 1975, 9; *Communicator* February 1976, 2.

50   *Lowell Sun*: 10 August 1975, B4; 29 October 1975, 13; 9 January 1977, B4; 29 April 1980, 1.

51   *Lowell Sun*: 9 December 1976, 10; 20 January 1977, 1; 1 February 1977, 13; 10 April 1977, B1; 1 May 1977, Bi.

52   *Lowell Sun* 24 March 1977: 9.

53   *Lowell Sun* 30 March 1977, 11; 31 March 1977, 7.

54   *Lowell Sun*: 6 March 1975, 10; 17 August 1975, B3; 18 September 1975, 10.

55   See documents in Lowell National Historical Park files: 1) "Statement of the Witness of the Department of the Interior Before the Subcommittee on National Parks and Recreation, House Committee on Interior and Insular Affairs on H.R. 14689, Lowell Historic Canal District, Massachusetts." 19 August 1974, 3 and 2) Lowell Team, "Draft Phase I Report," 1976, pp. 7-8.

56   Lowell Historic Canal District Commission, *Report* (Washington: U.S. Government Printing Office, 1977), 140-1.

57   Lowell Historic Canal District Commission, Minutes, 2 August 1976, Federal Archives, Waltham, Massachusetts, pp. 53-56.

58   *Ibid.*, 55.

59   *Ibid.*, 64-65.

60   Lowell Historic Canal District Commission, *Report*, 16-17.

61   95th Congress Second Session House of Representatives Report No. 95-1023, Lowell National Historical Park files, 30 March 1978, p. 24. See also the *Lowell Sun*: 27 January 1977, 1; 9 March 1977, 10; 7 April 1977, 9.

62   P. Stamas, "Testimony for Lowell National Cultural Park," Human Services Corporation files, 2-4; *Congressional Record*, 3 April 1978, pp.H2386-7.

63   Transcript of Senate Hearing, Lowell National Historical Park files, 6 April 1978, 26-27.

64   W. Whalen, letter to Paul Tsongas, Lowell National Historical Park files, 10 April 1978, 1.

65   See the *Boston Globe*: 23 March 1978, 30; 27 March 1978, 9; 15 April 1978, 14; 4 May 1978, 7; 11 May 1978, 7.

66   e.g., M. Blewett, *Surviving Hard Times* (Lowell: Lowell Museum, 1982); *Kerouac's Lowell Places* (Lowell: Lowell City Library); Pollard Memorial Library, "The Immigrant Experience" exhibition, Summer 1983.

67   e.g., *Newsweek* 28 September 1981, 38.

68   M. Blewett, "The National Park Service," 2.

COMMENT: INDUSTRIAL MUSEUMS AND THE HISTORY OF DEINDUSTRIALIZATION

Mike Wallace

The past ten years have seen dramatic changes in the world of industrial museums. The focus of attention has shifted from industrial objects, processes, and entrepreneurs to the universe of the working class: its experience, its culture and cultural creativity, its forms of economic and, to a lesser degree, political organization. In North Carolina, many public historians now tell the story of the region's mill towns largely from the point of view of the workers. They examine the experience of paternalism, the nature of textile workers' culture, and the story of the populist movement, recalling especially its attempts to transcend racism in the south. In New Jersey, Paterson's Botto House chronicles silk workers' lives in the mills, in their homes, and on the picket lines. In Massachusetts, Lowell's National Historical Park chronicles the world of labor from the mill girls through the ethnic workers of the twentieth century. In Indiana, South Bend's Discovery Hall, a city-sponsored museum of industry, presents reminiscences of Polish and Hungarian autoworkers and recalls the sitdown strikes. Some years ago I decried the thinness of museums' attention to working-class life and their tendency to avoid conflict in the past. Times have changed. This is clearly due to the efforts and the struggles and the courage of public historians, and I think it is a splendid development.

For all the progress, possibilities for creative new approaches still exist. I would like to suggest some pathways that public historians might consider worthy of exploration. Let me first state them abstractly, and then give an example of a specific interpretive project that might both serve as a vehicle for the theoretical propositions and yet be of practical interest to industrial museum designers.

First, we need to strive for a still better connection of past, present, and future in our exhibitry, to overcome the tendency many Americans have of seeing the past as something that is over and done with, and of merely nostalgic, academic, or entertainment value. This has, of course, become something of a ritual piety in our profession. The difficult question, really, is how to accomplish this. One clue might lie in my second abstract point: we need to stress that our museums treat moments in larger processes, processes which are still in operation. Exhibits should be analogous not to snapshots, but to frames from an ongoing movie. Third, our presentations should be set in a larger spatial as well as temporal context: even the most "local" of exhibits would benefit from a more global perspective. Fourth, we should pay considerably greater attention to the role of the state in the histories we are relating. We need to recall, for example, that industrial workers (and, for that matter, industrial capitalists) were citizens...and still are.

As a way of illustrating how these concerns might be brought to bear on a particular historical problem, I will focus on "deindustrialization," a contemporary issue that is of enormous relevance to museums that treat the history of industrialization. Indeed the very creation of an industrial museum is often a *response* by a community to the collapse of its manufacturing base, part of an attempt to transform defunct plants into marketable historical commodities and thus generate jobs. But the value to museums of telling the story of "deindustrialization" goes deeper than institutional self-reflection: the issue is a matter of considerable public concern and an accessible treatment of it might attract visitors. Guides who lead tours around industrial museums tell me that people repeatedly ask: "Why did the factories leave?" and "Where did they go?" Yet it seems to me that most industrial museums deal with this matter at best tangentially. There are many institutions I haven't seen, and I would be delighted to be corrected on this, but it appears to me that an opportunity is being lost to inform visitors about great historical processes which have drastically affected their lives, and thus to empower them, by enhancing their capacity to understand, and perhaps to change, their world.

But before we can tackle the matter of "*de*industrialization," we have to talk about "*in*dustrialization"--the concept around which most industrial museums organize their interpretive structure. I have problems with the word as it is commonly used to describe the course of American economic history. It sidesteps the fact that industrialization in the United States was of a particular variety: it was carried out under capitalist auspices. And capitalism is only one of a variety of possible roads a society may travel down if it chooses or feels itself impelled to embark on industrialization.

There are a host of reasons why adding the word "capitalist" is not merely a nominalogical quibble but makes a great deal of difference for interpretive strategies. It forces a shift of attention, not only from technology to the social relations of production, but then beyond (and to some degree behind) those relations, to the way in which participants of all classes find their actions profoundly constrained (though not determined) by the rules of the capitalist game, by the logic of the capitalist system.

Take Lowell. Nineteenth-century Boston capitalists dreamed they could avoid the European experience, and build capitalism without class conflict. They thought they could step outside of history, and in this, of course, they were typical Americans. But they soon enough found that competition in a context of unequal class power led to old-world results. The Lowell museum's introductory slide show demonstrates this quite nicely. It notes that "ironically, success led to competition"; that competition forced employers to push wages down in order to keep profits up; and that this engendered working-class resistance, which shattered the utopian vision of harmony. What happened, in other words, was a textbook case of the increasing exploitation of labor (at least if Volume 1 of *Capital* is the text), not because the mill owners were bad guys, but because the nature of the capitalist game circumscribed the choices individual entrepreneurs faced. Rationality at the level of the firm led to a larger social irrationality. This was not the first time such a thing happened. Nor would it be the last. Museum goers benefit from having it pointed out, as Lowell does with inventiveness and economy, that there were large systemic issues at stake in the mill girls' story.

A quick caution here: obviously, telling the full story of a local situation requires close attention to the specific historical context. One cannot deduce the nature of particular events from an abstract analysis of capital-labor relations. A full presentation of the Lowell case, for instance, would have to consider the crucial role of gender, the existence of a regional and

international labor mobility, the role of the state, the
nature of capitalist development elsewhere on the
planet--and many other matters.

But keeping such abstract (and seemingly less
relevant) issues in the front of our minds begins to
remind us of several things. First, that before
capitalism could be fully constituted in this country (as
elsewhere), it required not just factories and workplaces,
but an entire supporting body of laws, major spacial
reorganizations, and profound political and cultural
transformations. Second, that capitalism did not come
in on the first ships nor grow spontaneously out of the
American soil. It was, rather, merely one of a variety
of contending modes of organizing an economy and
society. It was resisted by artisans, small farmers, and
slave planters as well as by native and immigrant
laborers. Most of these people (together constituting the
overwhelming majority of Americans) rejected
capitalism. They saw the industrialists and "moneyed
aristocrats" it engendered as potential usurpers of the
Republic, and they considered the spread of wage labor
and the growth of the urban poor as degrading and
dangerous reversals of the gains achieved for working
people by the American Revolution. The nineteenth
century was, accordingly, marked by clashes not only
over wages and hours, but over tariffs, immigration
policy, slavery, the gender order, the judicial and
financial systems, and, indeed, the overall future course
of the United States--a future that, at the time, without
the benefit of hindsight, seemed very much up for
grabs. Capitalism's opponents would repeatedly
propose a variety of other systemic paths for American
society to follow, from a slave republic to an agrarian
freeholders' democracy to the Cooperative
Commonwealth to socialism.

A third and closely related point: workers were
citizens, not just workers. Museums have insufficiently
explored this fact, not only at the grand level of
systemic social choices, but even in the recounting of
local situations. It is splendid that so much attention is
now paid to social and labor history, but I am
beginning to fear that the old tyrannies of artifact and
place may have been replaced by the new tyrannies of
the shop floor and the boarding house. To thicken the
Lowell story, for instance, it would be good to know
who ran the town, who ran the state. What was the
impact of the emerging Irish machine on the nature of
work life? How did the struggle over social welfare
and labor reforms affect workplace matters? Where did
working-class voters stand on issues of labor or capital

mobility, in the debates, for instance, over immigration restriction? What stance did workers and businessmen take on presidential politics and the battles over the banking system? Most broadly, what difference did the possession of political liberty and the exercise of political power make to the people whose lives the museums have taken to chronicling?

Fourthly, continuing along from the last point, attention to capital-labor relations, in the sphere of politics as well as production, might draw our attention to the complexity of those relations, and even force us to note that despite their enmity in the factory they were often allies in the legislature. One issue that occasionally brought them together was foreign affairs. Where workers did accept the larger capitalist rules of the game they were open to being persuaded that improving their own position required them to support their employers' attempts to obtain tariffs (and stand with them against free trade opponents). Or that workers' self-interest (or cultural identity) might incline them to backing nationalist or imperialist policies that could afford access to raw materials or new markets. Even if they rejected capitalism, they might be led to form political alliances with it, against still less acceptable socio-political economies, such as those based on slavery. All these issues might create cross-cutting pressures that could weaken workplace solidarities. An attention to these complexities would help us overcome the occasional tendency to present romanticized images of working people.

*   *   *

My next point is that we should make clear to visitors that these capitalist rules of the game are in fact still operative, that the system instituted in the nineteenth century is fundamentally intact. To be sure, capitalism has survived only by making major adjustments. Over the intervening century, capitalism came to terms with changing local, national, and international conditions; with new technologies of production, distribution, and communication; with the legacy of struggles over the rules of the games themselves by contestants whose relative balance of power fluctuated over the years; and with the far greater centrality of the state to the workings of the economy. For all that, the fundamental imperatives and tendencies of the "free enterprise" system continue profoundly to affect life in the United States, and its impact on American industry over the last fifty years has been decisive and devastating.

Which brings us to "deindustrialization."

As I object to "industrialization," so I object to "deindustrialization" as a concept. It obfuscates what is happening in the United States today. As usually employed, the word implies a stages-of-development theory. Pre-industrial gives way to industrial, which then moves on to a service (or, as it is often called, a post-industrial) economy. There are several difficulties here. For one thing, this approach generates banal and vacuous categories. Such terms as "pre-industrial" or "post-industrial" fail, I submit, to illuminate the key characteristics of the epochs they seek to describe, other than by reference to some other period.

Secondly, the notion of historical process implied is teleological. The movement from "pre" to "post" has no subject; it just happens, presumably as the result of the working out of imminent tendencies. In this it resembles that other triumph of tautology, modernization theory, which tracks a similarly inevitable and unidirectional march from pre-modern through modern to post-modern society. In neither theory are we drawn toward considering human agency (much less human conflict) to be a crucial variable.

Thirdly, as historical development is imminent, so too is it ineluctable. To some this inevitability is sad, a Spenglerian saga of decline. To others it is a source of Spencerian self-satisfaction: despite the anguish and cost, it is all a manifestation of "progress".

A fourth and more particular reason to balk at the concept of deindustrialization is that to the degree we accept it, we automatically relegate "industrial" museums to the dustbin of history. Their object, by definition, is a now superseded historical period. Studying the industrial era becomes perhaps an interesting but essentially an antiquarian exercise. Certainly the experience of the women and men who labored in sooty or linty nineteenth-century factories can tell us little about life in the new tertiary economy. The definition dooms the industrial museum to being, willy nilly, a purveyor of nostalgia.

But see how different matters become if we think not about "deindustrialization" but about the global reorganization of capitalism in the twentieth century. Industry, after all, has not been surpassed; it has just *moved*. Why not call a spade a spade, and re-conceptualize our subject not as de-industrialization but as capital flight--the story of how corporations have sidestepped organized labor, and pressures to pay their share of social costs, by moving to more quiescent pastures, first to the United States South and then abroad, in a restless search for areas willing to provide tax breaks, cheap land, or the muscle needed to repress the economic and political organization of labor. What has emerged--seen in a planetary perspective--is not a de-industrialized society, but a global assembly line.

Such an approach situates deindustrialization not in some mystical urge toward a "service" economy inherent in the industrial order, but in the recent history and current logic of contemporary capitalism. It helps us see capital flight as yet another case of short-term private rationality producing long-term social insanity. The point of industrial production under capitalism is to make a profit for the firm, not simply to produce socially useful items. It would be absurd for managers to pass up the opportunity to make higher profits through relocation (or shifting out of production altogether into financial speculation) simply because doing so would wreck communities and lives in the towns, cities, or regions being deserted. Indeed, to the extent that global mobility allows managers to play off regional or national workforces one against the other, the way they once played off ethnic, gender, and racial groups *within* communities, it would be a virtual dereliction of duty for them not to do so. Corporate directors, after all, when they act in their corporate capacity, see this country, indeed the planet, not as a society or a human community, but as an economy, a grid of opportunities. Nor, according to capitalist ethics, is capital flight immoral (much less illegal). The factories, the means of production are, after all, privately owned. Their proprietors can do with them as they wish. Understanding this explodes in a flash the illusions generated by the massive structures of the industrial plants themselves. What is remarkable about capitalism is that behind the facade of solidity lies the quicksilver reality of mobility and relentless transformation, a phenomenon Marshal Berman brilliantly explored in his book, the title of which (*All That Is Solid Melts into Air*), is taken from Marx.

Finally, if only by implication (though preferably through assertion), attributing "deindustrialization" not to the working of invisible hands, but to the very visible decisions taken by governments and businesses, prompts the realization that it is possible to *contest* the social irrationality of capital flight--though only by shifting to an entirely different (i.e. social) system of cost-accounting and ethical standards. Museums cannot facilitate this realization, if their attention is restricted to the kinds of tactical considerations that dominate activities of workers (and businessmen) at the point of production or even the surrounding social community.

*   *   *

Assuming for the moment the validity of this analysis, let me return to my original concern with how industrial museums might incorporate new perspectives, and try to sketch out what an exhibit on deindustrialization might look like. Let me begin by confessing, if it is not already apparent, that I am not a practitioner, but merely a critic, of public history presentations. Exhibit designers are experts, trained in a craft, and the possessors of a considerable body of practical experience which I do not have. I would be, I suspect, about as good a designer as most drama critics are playwrights, and I am all too aware of the insufficiencies of what follows as a guide to practical action. But perhaps, nevertheless, professionals may find these musings useful as they go about the difficult task of making economic history accessible to popular audiences.

*   *   *

One way to confront the central issues involved in "deindustrialization" might be: head on. When I attended a conference at Paterson, New Jersey, awhile back, I was told that the designers who put the museum together faced a fundamental problem. Many in the community believed that the great strike of 1913 had caused the collapse of Paterson, that the worker demands for higher wages led the silk mills to depart to more exploitable climes, thus bringing on the "deindustrialization" process. Given these bitter memories of the strike, the museum avoided confronting the question, and dealt instead with the social history of the contemporary working-class communities. An alternate approach--easy enough for *me* to suggest-- would be to mount a special exhibition on it, devoted precisely to the central question: Did labor militancy drive the silk industry out of Paterson? I wouldn't want to prejudge the findings, but it is certainly conceivable that the answer would be yes. This in turn might force visitors to confront not just the limitations of struggles at the workplace, which of course today's workers confront every day of their lives, but also help them to imagine alternative political and economic strategies.

This approach need not be restricted to towns like Paterson. Any museum that focuses on industrial history has a great opportunity to more fully connect past and present, to demonstrate the lines that run from the institution of capitalist industrial relations in the nineteenth century, down to the condition of the host town in the twentieth century. An exhibit that boldly focused on the history of capital mobility and its consequences would not be easy to put together. To present the complex story in all its richness might require demonstrating, for instance, how the process was aided mightily by the state. In the United States, for example, the decline of the frostbelt was related to the construction of the sunbelt. That enterprise, in turn, depended in large measure on federal fiscal transfers of money from the north to the south, spurred by the disproportionate power of southern and western Congressmen, by military sponsorship of the textile industry in the south during the Second World War, and by postwar federal support for the aerospace and electronic complexes. In addition, governmental underwriting of the cost of constructing highways, water projects, and natural gas pipelines laid the basis of sunbelt metropolitan development. This made it easy and feasible for northern capital to flee to antiunion climates.

"Deindustrialization" was also rooted in the formation of a growth coalition--Alan Wolfe and John Mollenkopf have written most illuminatingly on this--that promoted both urban "renewal" and suburbanization, processes that eroded industrial cities.

Deindustrialization had a foreign-policy dimension, too. Staunchly (if shortsightedly) supported by the AFL-CIO, the U.S. installed or propped up regimes that maintained low-wage export platforms to which multinational capital could move. An exhibit investigating the emergence of industrial competitors in the American, Mediterranean, and East Asian borderlands might examine the role played by U.S. investment capital (and union pension funds), the World Bank, the IMF, the CIA, and the U.S. Marines--in short, the nature of contemporary imperialism.

This in turn would provide the chance to inject the global dimension I referred to earlier. It might, for example, be interesting to trace where local factories went when they left, either in the U.S. or abroad. It would be illuminating to examine the conditions under which their new employees work--in Taiwan, Korea, the Dominican Republic, and Singapore. An innovative exhibit might explore parallels between nineteenth-century American conditions and those prevailing in the new sweatshops of New York City and Hong Kong. As we now have sister cities, so we might have sister museums. Why not a comparative exhibit on "Farm to Factory in Puerto Rico and Massachusetts"?

We might also pay attention to the way that expansion of U.S. multinationals abroad creates and precipitates new flows of immigrants back to the United States. Some wonderful recent work has studied the reflexive impact on the U.S. of the establishment of export platforms in Latin America and Southeast Asia: the displacement of peasants to urban factories; their relocation from Third World shantytowns to U.S. cities; the deployment and exploitation of their labor to help "re-industrialize" America by reviving such debased manufacturing institutions as sweatshops. These are events for which the theory of deindustrialization can hardly account. To bring such a trajectory to life, could we not, perhaps through use of videotaped interviews and narration, trace the story of a young woman or an entire family as they moved, say, from the Malaysian countryside, to electronic assembly plants in Penang "free trade zones," to Queens or Los Angeles? The family saga seems to be a form that works spectacularly well for historical novels or TV docudramas; might there not be a way to put such a form to museum uses? Video cannot and should not substitute for exhibits that draw upon authentic artifacts, but might assist in setting local stories in global context.

A capital flight exhibit might also attempt to connect the collapse of the productive sector with the shift of capital into financial circuits--with the consequent spectacular rise in levels of debt, of currency and stock speculations and manipulations, of takeovers and mergers, of assorted swindles and scams all too reminiscent of the late 1920s--and might go on to muse about the possible relation between "deindustrialization" and a conceivable collapse of the American economy in the 1980s.

Finally, it would be helpful to present the current debates over the responses which have been proposed to deindustrialization, ranging from accelerating it via deregulation (the Reagan plan), to hindering it by erecting tariff walls (the AFL-CIO plan), or reversing it through federal investment support (the Rohatyn/Iacocca plan). Our hypothetical exhibit might *analyze* these options--discussing   critically,   for   example,   such

conventional axioms as "high-tech jobs can replace
departed manufacturing ones" (a notion that is, in my
opinion, largely illusory; witness Wang's recent lay-offs
in Lowell and the sad state of Silicon Valley). It might
be interesting for such a Solutions Section to assess
whether worker-ownership takeovers of ailing plants is a
way ahead or a device for leaving workers holding the
unprofitable bag, to discuss the feasibility of municipal
or state ownership, to discuss the desirability of altering
U.S. foreign and interregional policies, to ponder placing
legal constraints on the mobility of capital--to think,
that is, about wide variety of experimental possibilities.
Involving museum-goers as citizens might enhance their
capacity to make historically informed decisions and
thus strengthen the democratic process.

Here, again, visual presentations of such complex
matters might seem beyond a museum's capabilities, but
again short video presentations, perhaps in a debate
format of the sort currently popular on TV, might be
one way. Or we could (had we the money) draw upon
immensely successful practices developed at Disney
World.   One exhibit there brilliantly presents a
discussion between animated cartoon spokespeople for
and against various alternative energy sources for
tomorrow's automobiles.   One after another speaker
presents, in remarkably few words, his or her preferred
choice--a Yuppie lady promotes nuclear power, a hard-
hatted miner pushes coal, a mad dwarf Japanese
scientist with a Peter Lorre accent suggests inventing a
water engine--and each is in turn ridiculed or dismissed
(this is, after all, a General Motors presentation) until
the field is left to "Tex," the lanky GM persona whose
drawling conclusion favors the "good ol' reliable
internal combustion engine." I raise this not to promote
either gasoline, GM stock, or the hard-sell approach, but
to note that in the business and commercial world,
extremely complex matters are, routinely, made
accessible to audiences numbering in the millions.
Surely there are some pointers to be picked up there, as
well as a compendium of things to be avoided.

*   *   *

But even if we were to design a presentation that
treated these difficult matters in a popularly appealing
way, a host of obstacles would remain to obstruct our
presenting such an interpretation of deindustrialization.
The most obvious one stems from the likely resistance
of conventional sponsors: who would *fund* such a show?

(Animation isn't cheap, though video is eminently affordable.) This sober question brings us to the realities of power (something I've avoided so far) and to the very real constraints imposed upon public history producers. Asking the question, in fact, should be an integral part of exhibit designing. It might be a salutary exercise for all public history programmers to prepare, as a matter of course, a "political impact statement." Doing so would direct attention to the necessity of lining up political support for any given interpretive strategy.
In this case, a plausible first assumption might be that business funders would not be interested in helping explicate the "downside" of a capitalist economy. But the experience of a South Bend, Indiana, museum suggests that even businessmen might not be quite as antagonistic to such an exhibit as might be thought. There were certainly some entrepreneur-funders who wanted Discovery Hall Museum to avoid even the mention of old strikes from the 1930s. They feared discouraging outside investors thinking of bringing in new businesses to South Bend by making them aware of a history of unionism. They proposed instead a celebratory saga centered on the history of the largest auto firm, the Studebaker company. But other businessmen in South Bend rejected a narrow-gauged focus on antique cars, in large part because they were enraged at Studebaker, a capital-flight company they perceived as having left the city in the lurch.
Despite the Indiana case, it's probably more likely that support for a "deindustrialization" exhibit would be forthcoming from labor groups. Some unions are more open to such approaches in this current time of crisis, when old analyses and practices seem to be of little service. Conceivably there might also be sources of public funding in frost-belt states, from outraged communities who are interested in understanding what has happened to them and where they might go from here. Working people and ordinary citizens might be drawn to supporting museums' work if they believed such institutions could help make sense of their world.

Supporters might be more readily attracted to a deindustrialization show if they were persuaded that a range of analytic points of view would be presented. Perhaps the videotaped debates mentioned above could be a way to integrate multiple perspectives. It would, for instance, be most illuminating to let a spokesperson from the Heritage Foundation try to convince working-class and small-business audiences in shattered rustbelt towns that deindustrialization and the workings of the "free market" are in their long-term interest.

*   *   *

Whether or not such an exhibit ever gets mounted, thinking about its merits and demerits may be of use to industrial museum designers. Deindustrialization is only one topic they might consider; the history of depressions and the story of automation are others that come to mind. And the larger principles--that public historians can situate today's world in a temporal continuum, locate their subjects within still evolving processes, set their local stories in a global context, and emphasize that historical actors and contemporary visitors were and are political actors--might be helpful guides to continuing the exciting transformations of the past decade.

THE NEW SOCIAL HISTORY AND THE CAPTAINS OF INDUSTRY: WILL THE REAL NATHAN APPLETON PLEASE STAND UP?

Michael Brewster Folsom

The remarks I make today are not the conclusions of profound research. There is a great deal more I should like to know about the character and career of Nathan Appleton and the class of men he represented. I rely tentatively on the research of others to raise questions and propose strategies for further research and interpretation. What follows is a museum director's instructions to his exhibit and education staff, at the outset of their effort to design a program on the early period of American industry. I imagine myself at the end of a long day of discussion, during which we have wrestled with still problematic questions about technology and innovation, shop floor experience and the relations of production, the home life and social structure of the new industrial working class. Long about 4:30 in the afternoon someone asks, "What about the owners of the mills? Aren't we going to interpret them, too?" The meeting breaks up in exasperation, and I go home and draft this memo to circulate before the next staff meeting.

THE CHARLES RIVER MUSEUM OF INDUSTRY

MEMO

To: Exhibit and Education Staff
From: Mike
Re: The Role of Owners and Managers of Industry in Our Interpretive Programs
Date: The mid-1980s

113

QUOTE: "Wealth is power" Nathan Appleton

ASSUMPTION: We all agree that the New
Social History, so called, has succeeded. Working class
history, black history, feminist history, urban history,
ethnic history, American Studies, material culture
studies, community studies--with the help of the
Marxists and the anthropologists--all these have taught
us that history is the study of ordinary people, history
"from the bottom up."
The New Social History has triumphed because it
has taught us *how* to study ordinary people.   Despite
the excesses of the cliometricians--who employ the
methodology of the Cuisinart to process raw human
data into a bland statistical paste--despite the
cliometricians, over the recent quarter-century we have
learned, to our credit and delight, how to entice, invent,
and cajole from the wealth of public records the lives of
our multitudinous, humble, and unlettered forebears.
No historian dare say anymore that the inarticulate are
unknowable, and that we must rely upon the literary
relics of elites and the public careers of prominent men
to define what happened in history.

QUESTION: But, now that the New Social
History *has* succeeded, **what are we to do with the
great men whose sedulously preserved testimony we
no longer take for gospel?** Is their history but a great
warehouse crammed with two-dimensional stageprops
and costumes, self-serving myths, mendacities, and
apologetics? No. Obviously not. But what then? How
do we conceive a place in an interpretive public
program for the men who owned and governed the
institutions of industrializing America?

ARGUMENT: The New Social History is
suggestively described as "history from the bottom up."
That does not mean it is only the history *of the bottom.*
It should offer a perspective on the roles and meanings
of *all* the principal social actors, not neglecting elite
white males.   Workers know they have real bosses.
Blacks take whites very seriously.   Women understand
fathers, brothers, husbands, sons excruciatingly well.
Historians should be so smart.
The last thing we need, however, is a simplistic
righting of the balance, a swinging back of the
historiographical pendulum, giving equal time for the
white male elite, rescuing the two-dimensional giants
from the warehouse and remounting them on foamcore
instead of cardboard.   What we need is a way to

comprehend the role of the elite as an integral function of the real history of ordinary people.

Scott Fitzgerald and Ernest Hemingway offered us an avenue to understanding. Fitzgerald is supposed to have asked if Hemingway realized that "the rich are different from you and me." And Hemingway is supposed to have replied plainly, "Yes, they have more money." I think we need to take seriously both assumptions--Fitzgerald's that the rich are qualitatively different from ordinary people, and Hemingway's that the rich are just ordinary people like you and me, who happen to have more money.

Take Nathan Appleton, for example. For most of the first fifty years of corporate industrial capitalism in the United States, he was undisputedly (though he disliked the term), our greatest manufacturer. Our interpretation of his life may serve as a model.

The rich, like Nathan Appleton, are different from you and me and from the multitude of women and men he employed, not because the rich have more money, but because they have more power--vastly more power. The vastness makes that power qualitatively different from any power that you and I and other ordinary people may share and exercise. Theirs is the power to *initiate*--to establish and mold major institutions, to decree that the mills shall be erected, and to determine the terms and conditions of work, and in large measure to shape the structure of the society in which they and their employees shall live.

The working class did not invent the integrated cotton mill, or the industrial corporation, the company town or manufacturing city, mass-production with interchangeable parts, the moving assembly line, the vertically integrated trust, the conglomerate, the multinational, the automated factory or robotic manufacturing. The working class did not invent "deindustrialization." Nor, for that matter did the working class invent the working class.

The infinitesimal fraction of the American public, the men of great wealth who could command the power of capital to create these fundamental institutions, have had to observe certain limiting conditions, to be sure, both material and cultural. You can't turn a mill wheel where there is no head of water. Nor can you, in a nominal democracy, press-gang a workforce to tend your machines. And you can't buy machines that haven't been invented. But the power of money will buy you the mill privileges where they exist, entice workers enough, and encourage the kinds of technological

innovation that serve your interests--if you choose to
spend your money that way.   Within the given
framework of history, economy, topography, and
culture--the rich make the decisions, sometimes even to
alter that framework.   Ordinary people react, and make
do.   The initiatives they do take are proscribed by
institutions they did not create, and even their
rebelliousness is a response to conditions imposed on
them by others in charge.

Ralph Waldo Emerson's whimsical
characterization of the New England industrial capitalist
as a Paul-Bunyonesque giant does not exaggerate the
power of the class in dominating the landscape and in
surmounting cultural inhibitions:

> An American in this ardent climate gets up
> early some morning and buys a river; and
> advertises for twelve or fifteen hundred
> Irishmen; digs a new channel for it, brings
> it to his mills, and has a head of twenty-
> four feet of water, then to give him an
> appetite for his breakfast, he raises a
> house; then carves out within doors, a
> quarter township into streets and building
> lots, tavern, school and the Methodist
> meeting-house--sends up an engineer into
> New Hampshire, to see where his water
> comes from, and after advising with him,
> sends a trusty man of business to buy of
> all the farmers such mill privileges as will
> serve him among their waste hill and
> pasture lots, and comes home with great
> glee announcing that he is now owner of
> the great Lake Winipeseogee, as reservoir
> for his Lowell mills at midsummer.   They
> are an ardent race, and are fully possessed
> with that hatred of labor, which is the
> principle of progress in the human race....
> They must and will have the enjoyment
> without the sweat.   So they buy slaves,
> where the women will permit it; where
> they will not, they make the wind, the
> tide, the waterfall, the stream, the cloud,
> the lightning, do the work, by every ant
> and device their cunningest brain can
> achieve.

Look what Nathan Appleton could do, in addition
to just about everything Emerson described: Although
Appleton was pleased to emphasize his origins in

agrarian poverty, his family was in fact among the elite
of rural New Ipswitch, New Hampshire, in the economic
upper 5%. He was born to a strong family tradition of
leadership in public affairs. A university education at
Dartmouth was open to him, though he chose a place in
his brother Samuel's then modest mercantile firm in
Boston instead.

In our interpretive program we should make
graphically clear the structure of economic inequality
Appleton was born to in New Ipswitch and grew up
benefitting from.   At the same time we need to
emphasize how dramatically mercantile capitalism upped
the stakes and exaggerated the imbalance of inequality
in the early decades of American independence.

Appleton's father died in 1807 leaving a
substantial farmer's estate valued at $7500--in an age
when a farm laborer might hope for a wage of $.50 a
day. Two years later--fifteen years after Appleton had
started as a bookkeeper with his brother--his own assets
were valued at $87,500. That year (1809) the firm of S.
and N. Appleton had a profit of almost $30,000. In
1812 the firm's ten ships grossed $119,700, with a profit
of 88%. Appleton was pleased to contemplate retiring
from business in 1814 with a competence of $200,000.

The opportunities of industrial capitalism, which
opened up that same year to Appleton, proved even
more exceedingly lucrative.   He was to become the
largest single investor in American textiles, with stock
valued at as much as $700,000, in an industry worth a
billion dollars by 1860, when a woman's wage in the
mills was still under $3 a week.

Just how such wealth might grow, with what
shrewd mingling of prudence and swashbuckling
bravado, is absolutely necessary for public programs in
industrial history to explain, and the career of a
prominent individual like Appleton is a ready vehicle
for enlightenment. There is a heuristic value in treating
him as a "great man," outsized, and "mythic" in
proportions.   What he was able and allowed to
accomplish with his wits and his capital is so far
beyond the prospects of almost everyone in this land of
opportunity that our first task is to allow our visitors to
define for themselves the distance between themselves
and such a representative of industrial capitalism, as a
first step to understanding what that difference means.

The "mechanics," the mathematics, the stratagems
and tactics of such an economic life as Nathan
Appleton's have never been made evident in any
interpretive program I've ever seen, and just how we

might do so is not simple to imagine. Certainly we are not going to take Appleton and his apologists at their word, though their "mythmaking" has to be taken into account. (Successful myths have great power which mere facts do not vitiate.) And I frankly believe that the method of the "expose," revealing the disreputable, debunking the "myths," will not gain the confidence of our audience. Among other things debunking is too easy. Every assumption about what was wrong with nineteenth-century industrial capitalism, leaves unanswered a host of questions about why it worked so well, why it succeeded, whatever the costs.

Before we go much further with this project, I suggest that everyone read Theodore Dreiser's novels, *The Financier* and *The Titan*, based on the life of Chicago street railway "baron," Thomas Yerkes, to learn how both to be fascinated with the exploits of the ascending rich in industrial America and at the same time to be deadpan in the presentation of their acts and character-- how to imagine them larger than life and also--with no contradiction--very, very ordinary.

Which leads to the second half of my argument. How and why do we want to see the rich as people who are very much like us, just with more money?

Certainly we do not want to add to the "myth" of the great man by convincing our audience that Appleton was not really a "captain of industry," but rather just a humble pious businessman and loving family man. But we do want our audience to be able to understand him, to find him credible and comprehensible *in their own terms*. He was, after all, a person with a known, finite set of responsibilities, with no more hours in the day than you and I have in which to acquit them. There certainly was a hum-drum, or at least a methodical procedure to his work life, however huge the sums were he dealt in. He did have a family which was no more large and complex than those of many of his corporations' employees. Having defined how exceedingly different such a man was from the rest of us, how privileged and powerful, I think we need to help our audience see his whole life matter-of-factly.

The records of his life appear to be detailed enough that we can reconstruct the pattern of a day, a week, a year in his business career. Given the facts of attending to business, what were his assumptions about ordinary behavior? What about his procedures for making a living? He is known to popular history for his investment in early textiles. What else was he doing during 1814 when he put a mere $5000 of discretionary capital into Frank Lowell's "risky venture" in Waltham?

How did that stock fit into his portfolio in a reasonable and responsible way?   An exercise in double-entry bookkeeping might enable our audience to imagine what industrial capitalism is all about.   (Appleton gets credit, recall, for introducing that form of precise accounting into the industrial economy.)

The   ways   in   which   the   Boston   mill   rich intertwined the mundane and the grandiose is evoked by J.P. Marquand in *The Late George Apley*, in a letter to the young George from his uncle, who was a man of Appleton's generation:

> My dear George: I find the order for the Number 4117 tickings. . . will require two hundred bales additional "Strict Middling" good body and staple.   I am therefore asking you to inquire around the Boston market with a view to picking up these two hundred bales at a reasonable price . . . . .The last price we paid for this variety of cotton was 6 7/16 cents.   From my estimate of present market conditions, I am of the distinct impression that this figure may be shaded 6 13/32 cents. . . .
>
> Should you see Mr. Salter in the office of the Boston Waifs' Society, you may tell him to count on me for my usual contribution of fifteen thousand dollars. . .
> .

Can we find Appleton documents which suggest the same cast of mind as crisply?

Crucial concepts in recent historiography of labor and technology may be well worth employing in our study of the industrial elite.   The culture of the workplace may be found in the counting house and boardroom and on the floor of the stock exchange, as well as on the shop floor.   Why is our respect for the precision   and   finesse   of   the   machinist   shading thousandths of an inch from a piece of steel on a lathe more profound than our appreciation of a textile lord building his power of noblesse oblige by shading 32nds of a cent from the price of cotton?   Innovation in the "mechanics" of management and the transfer of financial expertise are analogous to innovation in and transfer of technology.

But in no arena of life have the insights and methods of the New Social History wielded greater explanatory power than in the study of the family, and in no aspect of the life of the mill rich can those same insights and methods, worked out to study the multitudes, be more fruitfully applied. I urge you to follow up on the argument of Anthony Wallace in *Rockdale.* Among the peoples of the nineteenth-century textile villages along the Brandywine south of Philadelphia, he observed that

> . . . [T]he working-class family style and the managerial-class family style, however different in some ways, were precise complements to one another. The managers, in order to make the profits required to support their own extended family alliances, needed a stable and contented work force, composed of nuclear family partnerships and unmarried boarders in households that provided the proper mix of males and females of various ages.

For heuristic purposes, I think it might be useful first to address the Appletons as we would any family, relying on public records and the study of material culture, not literary evidence. What do these people look like in the manuscript census, city directories, tax records, vital statistics, probate records? What can the style and organization of their housing reveal? What is the economic function and structure of the extended Appleton family as we may reconstitute it from these records? What was the "proper mix of males and females of various ages" in that household, and who decided what was "proper"?

Nathan Appleton and his brothers relied heavily on each other to conduct their economic affairs over great distances. Brother Eben settled in England to represent the family interests. At one point fourteen Appletons owned 208 shares of stock in the Hamilton Company. As many as ten Appletons owned shares in the Boston Manufacturing Company.

Extended families of industrial workers also operated as far-flung integrated economic systems of mutual support stretching from mill town to farmstead, and New World port to peasant sod.

Nathan Appleton was a patriarch in a patriarchy, but so were the fathers of the mill women and their husbands to be. Females had well-defined economic roles within the households of rich and poor alike. Appleton bestowed shares in five textile corporations and in the Essex Company on his daughter Fanny's husband, Henry Wadsworth Longfellow, as part of her dowry. How exactly is such largesse different in its social role in that family from the few dollars a mill employee might bring home with her to help her find a husband and a stable family life? Seen in similar terms and with similar historiographical methods, the complementarity of structure and pattern between a family like Appleton's and the families of corporate employees suggests a larger pattern of belief and behaviour in a rapidly industrializing society, a pattern which may rest latent if we emphasize only the differences between the rich and the poor.

Having stressed the possibility of finding common grounds for defining and studying the interrelated kinds of lives led by the very rich and the working poor in early industrial America--or in America today, for that matter--I do not mean at all to abandon the point of view inherent in the New Social History, the view *from the bottom up.*   Anthony Wallace's definition of the complementary nature of industrial families, rich and poor, suggests why they were so very different. It was not just that the rich had more money and might enjoy the benefits of affluence unequally distributed. It was that the rich had the power, not only of distributing wealth, but also of shaping the most intimate experiences of their workers, defining what kinds of families they should have and who should reside within the bosoms thereof--"the proper mix of males and females of various ages."

The New Social History, it seems to me, is inherently an ever more sophisticated critique of inequality in the land of the free. Public interpretations of our common past which build on the plain facts which the New Social History reveals should also build on this critique. My argument in this memo is that the New Social History can wield even more explanatory power if its methods comprehend *everyone,* from the bottom up.

THE HEROIC THEORY
OF TECHNOLOGICAL
CHANGE:
THE CONTINUING MYTH
OF ELI WHITNEY

Frances Robb

Michael Workman

As we have seen in this conference there are a variety of factors that shape popular perceptions of industrial history. Unfortunately, we historians have not played as an important part in this process as we would like. Part of the reason for our ineffectiveness is that our basic understanding of industrial history differs so greatly from that of the public. The purpose of this paper is to explain how this difference in understanding and perception has come about and to show how historians in one particular case--Eli Whitney and the rise of the American system of manufactures--can play a more constructive role in shaping public perceptions.

In the last twenty-five years there has been a tremendous increase both in the number of historians practicing industrial history and the number of sites and museums where industrial history is a primary focus. We now have historians of technology, public historians, industrial and historical archaeologists, and practitioners of what Thomas Schlereth has called "material culture perspectives,"[1] working in the field. These professionals have produced a vast body of scholarly literature dealing with industrial history. Despite some limited attempts by leading industrial sites and museums, this body of scholarly literature has not been translated--via exhibits or interpretive programs--into terms comprehensible by the public, and as a result there is a major gap between scholarly and public perception of industrial history.

Part of the reason for this gap is that popular perceptions of industrial history are based in part on a deeply felt system of beliefs--an ideology--that has as a key tenet the belief in the inevitability of progress through technology. On the contrary, industrial historians, as a general rule, do not give allegiance to this traditional ideology of progress.[2] Instead, partially because of the reflective nature of their discipline, industrial historians have developed a paradigm that is anthropological in nature, and antagonistic to this dominant ideology.   Thus, the division in perception between historians and the public has deeper roots than what may appear on the surface. The real challenge to public historians interpreting industrial history is to transcend this ideological division and develop interpretations based on scholarly knowledge, yet at the same time to be sympathetic to the values of the public.

To make the problem concrete we propose to look at one of the most important episodes in American industrial history: the rise of the American system of manufacturing from 1800 to 1834.   In this period, the technology of small arms manufacture was transformed. Our questions are these: who was responsible for this technological breakthrough?   how did it occur?   and how can this information be brought to public knowledge?

Compounding this problem of interpretation is the fact that popular knowledge is often built around myths and cultural images that perpetuate the dominant ideology. One popular myth is that Eli Whitney single-handedly invented the American system at his gun factory near New Haven, Connecticut.   Born in 1765 to a New England farm family, Whitney's life as an inventor, public figure and promoter of the American system encouraged the heroic portrayal of him first made by Denison Olmsted in the 1832 *Memoir of Eli Whitney*.[3] Olmsted's narrative was essentially a eulogy of Whitney, lauding him not only for his inventiveness, but for his Yankee yeoman background, his optimism, perseverance, his "industry and frugality" and other all-American qualities.

Looking at the life of Thomas Edison, Wyn Wachhorst[4] explained the role the mythical hero plays in American culture.   Like Edison, Whitney expresses several important American cultural themes: the gospel of technological success, the rural Protestant virtues (hard work, initiative, perseverance, honesty, frugality and industry), the success mythology of the self-made man, optimism and the belief in democracy.

Olmsted's *Memoir* served as the standard interpretation of Whitney's life until the 1950s when several new works[5] were written about the man and his contributions to the American industrial revolution. Reflecting the Cold War fear of America's loss of technological superiority, the authors of these works looked into America's past to illustrate the great inventions that had been nurtured.   In doing this, they shaped the Eli Whitney story around their ideological bias, portraying him as the Yankee inventor with the perfect solution to America's technological problems. This perspective bolstered national patriotism and confidence, but it left untouched many important issues regarding the origins and development of the American system of manufactures.

The 1960s saw something of an intellectual revolution as many American historians left the narrow minded nationalism of the fifties and became more critical of traditional standards and beliefs.   The discipline of the history of technology was born in 1958, as a child of this revolution.   Coming out of this new discipline was Robert Woodbury's seminal 1960 article "The Legend of Eli Whitney and Interchangeable Parts."[6] Woodbury reevaluated Whitney's contribution to the development of the American system.   He concluded that Whitney's factory never had interchangeable parts, thus challenging the most sacred aspects of the Whitney myth.   Edwin Battison's 1966 article "Eli Whitney and the Milling Machine"[7] further substantiated Woodbury's position through the evaluation of artifacts from the Whitney works.   Both of these studies concluded that Whitney deserved little or no credit as the founder of the American system of manufacturing.

In 1977, Merritt Roe Smith's award winning book, *Harpers Ferry and the New Technology*[8] focused on technological development at the National Armory at Harpers Ferry.   Putting technology into its political and social context, Smith showed how John H. Hall was the first to put into place the American system at his rifle works.   In related articles,[9] Smith recognized that Whitney devised a more rational division of labor that was a prerequisite to the development of the American system.   He also recognizes Whitney's role as an advocate of interchangeable parts, but gives him little credit as an inventor.

The concept of interchangeable parts was not unique to Americans.   Design experiments took place in at least three European countries during the eighteenth century.   In the 1720s the Swedish engineer Christopher Polhem produced wooden clock gears that were uniform in size.   In the 1790s Samuel Benthem of England patented a technique for using the circular saw to produce identical pieces.[10]   However, designers in France came the closest to perfecting a system of uniform parts in the eighteenth century.   As David Hounshell pointed out in his book *From the American System to Mass Production 1800-1932*,[11] the inspiration of the armament industry was General Jean-Baptiste de Gribeauval. Working under Gribeauval, Honore Blanc perfected dies, moulds, and gauges that produced uniform lock plates. Blanc also mechanized some aspects of the process, in particular the cutting of tumblers and hammers. However, hand filing was still required as the final step.

Americans had won their independence with French arms, so it is not surprising that the French armament industry provided a model to aspiring Americans. In 1785 Thomas Jefferson visited Blanc's workshop and personally disassembled one of his locks. Soon after this demonstration, Jefferson made arrangements for six of the muskets to be sent to the United States. In 1788 Blanc's report on his manufacturing technique was received in the United States. The shipment of Blanc's muskets and plans to the United States provided the physical transfer of technology. With war threatening on the horizon in the 1790s, and both the federal and state governments suffering a shortage of arms, private companies were engaged to manufacture muskets. In 1798 Eli Whitney, who had failed in his attempt to manufacture cotton gins, turned his attention to guns. He and twenty-seven other private manufacturers were awarded federal government contracts to build muskets. Whitney was awarded his contract in part because of his reputation as the inventor of the cotton gin. Whitney not only agreed to manufacture the largest number of muskets, he also promised quick delivery: 4,000 to be delivered by September 1799 with the remaining 6,000 due in 1800.

There were strong economic reasons for Whitney and other gun manufacturers to pursue the system of interchangeable parts. The ability to use unskilled labor and the faster manufacturing rates could result in substantial savings to the owner.[12] The larger the contract, the more cost efficient the machines necessary could be. Whitney, with the largest private contract was in a position to use this economy of scale. It was the combination of private manufacturers trying to minimize their costs, and the support of the Ordinance Department that led to the eventual development of interchangeable parts. The military was interested in interchangeable parts because of their practical advantages in battle.

Eli Whitney faced some enormous problems in starting his gun production. In time, however, his factory at Whitneyville, Connecticut was hailed as a modern shop.   It is now clear, (through the work of Woodbury, Battison, Smith and others) that Whitney's factory was more of a fitting plant and less of a craftshop.   Whitney subcontracted production of gunstocks and barrels to others, while the more complicated lock mechanisms were manufactured on site.   All of these components were brought together and fit together into muskets in the Whitneyville shop. This process relied heavily on jigs that guided the unskilled or semi-skilled laborers in their filing. Whitney's inventories show no precision machine tools, though his factory did use hollow mills for machine shaping rough forgings, and machines to mill screws, but Battison clearly demonstrated that the milling machine cannot be credited to Eli Whitney.   Eli Whitney was a private contractor to the government who manufactured guns from 1798-1825, but his guns did not have the high degree of uniformity that he advocated.

Other American contractors were also interested in interchangeable parts, particularly Simeon North and John Hall.   North's pistol factory in Connecticut also received federal government contracts.   While his contract of 1813 specifically required interchangeable parts he was not able to achieve this.   His 1816 contracts no longer required overall interchangeability, but the lock plates were to be uniform.   Before 1818 North's factory was using the earliest known American milling machine.   This reduced the costs of filing.   He also achieved success in his manufacturing techniques with the gun barrel turning machine and later turning gun stocks.   North invented and adapted various machines for his factory, but he was only partially successful in achieving interchangeable parts.[13]

John Hall was granted a patent in 1811 for his rifle, and by 1817 his production methods were in place at Harpers Ferry.   In an 1827 Ordinance Department report to a congressional committee, Hall's methods and rifles were acclaimed for their interchangeable parts, and the machines he used in manufacturing them.   Hall's Rifle Works included a self-acting milling machine, metal cutting engine, die forging through drop hammers and metal trimming machines.   Hall was able to bring together the right combination of skill, invention, machinery and men at his factory.   By 1834 his rifles were being produced at both Harpers Ferry and North's armory in Middletown, Connecticut.   The gauges, machines, as well as close inspections allowed the rifle parts from either place to be interchangeable with parts from the other factory.[14]   While it would take another ten years for the entire industry to adopt such precise uniform standards, the technological barrier to interchangeable parts had been broken.   Smith and Woodbury agree that the American system of manufacturing was a direct outgrowth of Hall's work at Harpers Ferry not Whitney's work in Connecticut.

So, where does all of this put Eli Whitney? Woodbury and Battison have both demonstrated that Whitney's muskets were not made of interchangeable parts: the lock pieces were carefully marked, unnecessary if they had been uniform, lock plates had irregularly spaced holes--precluding uniformity, and modern attempts to exchange parts do not work.   Nor did Whitney invent the milling machine or other machines needed for precision work.   However, he did have a role in the evolution of interchangeable parts. Whitney was one of many to recognize the desirability of interchangeable parts, and should be considered a part of what Nathan Rosenberg calls "technological convergence."[15]   Whitney used his reputation to promote the possibilities and potential of the technique.   As an inventor of repute Whitney was able to convince politicians to support standardization.   This support would eventually find its way into government contract specifications, and is an important factor in the technological development.

Perhaps Whitney's other contribution to American industry should be considered his division of labor. Smith considers Whitneyville to be a transitional place. It stood between the craft gun shop and the large factory.   As in the craft shops there was still much hand work, but the use of jigs allowed labor tasks to be divided and less skilled labor to be used.   By looking at the muskets in parts, and not as a whole unit, Whitney divided his labor work force, and also his cost analysis procedure.   This system required more management coordination of the workers, and a new cost accounting method to deal with the divisions of his system.   In both of these areas Whitney was an innovator.[16]   He was also a part of the early-nineteenth-century gun manufacturers "network" that allowed him to pass on his own ideas, as well as utilize the ideas of others.   As a vocal advocate of the desirability of interchangeable parts he persuaded politicians of the advantages.   Eli Whitney was a well known American inventor who set out to solve the problem of interchangeable parts, both mechanically and politically.   He made few, if any, innovations mechanically, but his political influence and labor division made a lasting impact on the American scene.

Since Whitney did not develop the American system, who should be given credit for this? Rather than a one man project, the development of interchangeable parts came from the "technological convergence" of many men and the support of the Ordinance Department. Some of these men like Eli Whitney, Simeon North and John Hall continue to be remembered for their specific ideas or innovations. Other men, particularly the mechanics who moved from factory to factory, are likely to remain anonymous, but still significant. The group effort does not diminish the achievement of interchangeability, rather it reminds us that successful technological change is a social process.[17] As historians we must now decide how to convey our understanding to the larger public perception.

Despite the scholarly destruction of the Whitney myth, it endures in our society. It continues to crop up in textbooks, as well as popular and scholarly articles. A group of articles written in New Haven for a 1978 Connecticut Humanities Council program[18] shows how people living close by retain their heroic image of Whitney. They discount as merely "technical" the scholarship of professional historians and favor the more traditionally oriented views of the 1950s.

Working through a historical site, a different medium than the printed page, we believe the history of the development of the American system can be better brought to public awareness. Historic sites offer several advantages over the scholarly article: larger audiences, the ability to use artifacts, the opportunity to interpret the whole picture of how technology fits into society, and the personal interaction of guides with visitors. We have chosen Harpers Ferry National Historical Park to illustrate how, in one park, this aspect of history can be interpreted to the public. This significant innovation can also be interpreted, with a different perspective, at other historical sites, including the Whitney Museum. Harpers Ferry has been selected for several reasons: first is its link to the technological developments through John Hall and the Federal Armory. Second, as a whole town, and not just one building, the industrial changes can be presented to the visitor together as a part of nineteenth-century culture.

Industry is one of Harpers Ferry's four interpretive themes. (The others are Black History, the Civil War, and of course John Brown.) At the present time the industry theme at Harpers Ferry is underdeveloped. The current approach hardly illustrates the complexity of technology or specifically, of interchangeable parts. One blacksmith shop and a small exhibit on guns comprise the industry section. This is supplemented with general guided tours that may or may not discuss the town's industry. The work of John Hall is represented in the gun exhibit by one paragraph.

While the historical events at Harpers Ferry lend themselves to this theme, time has not been so generous to the site. Paul Lee, the park's Chief of Interpretation summed it up when he said, "We are limited by what we don't have."[19] Not only was Hall's factory destroyed in the Civil War, but it suffered further indignities when a paper mill was built on its foundations in the 1880s. Physical limitations are further compounded by an acute shortage of artifacts--there are few of Hall's rifles around, few drawings of his machines and no other known artifacts from his factory. Despite these limitations there are still ways Harpers Ferry can show the technological development of the early nineteenth century.

Working through stationary exhibits (perhaps in the Master Armorer's House, the current location of the gun display), the proposed exhibit can demonstrate some of the leaders behind interchangeable parts--John Hall, Simeon North and Eli Whitney. By showing how various ideas "converged" in John Hall's work the visitor can be exposed to the complexities of this development. We are not advocating a new John Hall myth, but we do believe that Hall is a logical person on which to center Harpers Ferry's interpretation of industry.

This exhibit can flow into one showing the continuum of innovation. By starting with the acceptance of interchangeable parts, it can show how precision improved, and standards were raised, so that parts considered interchangeable in 1820 would not be acceptable in the 1850s. Other technological developments, particularly in the armament industry can also be illustrated.

A third section of the exhibit could illustrate the role of laborers. This was a transitional period for workers as manufacturing moved from a craftsman tradition to the mechanized factory method. How these changes impacted the workers needs to be explained. As a part of this display, it would also be appropriate to show the movement of laborers. At one point the superintendent of Springfield complained of his workers' "Harpers Ferry Fever." As the men relocated between factories they became a part of the convergence of ideas and techniques. Further illustrating that the American system developed from a synthesis of many people's work.

Finally, as an industrial village, Harpers Ferry, like Lowell, can allow visitors to put the technological development into the proper nineteenth-century social perspective. As they wander through the old town, and as the society is explained and illustrated to them, the visitor can place Hall, Whitney and others into their historical period. This social perspective (and therefore also political) is what is excluded with the heroic myth.

Harpers Ferry is not the only place that this type of interpretation can be given, nor is this the only scenario for Harpers Ferry to follow. Each historic site can tailor its interpretation to fit its specific requirements, but these general themes and concepts can remain the same: social context of technological change; the convergence of ideas and men; the evolution of technology; and the continuum of ideas. This broader, social approach to technology is important to convey to the general public. Few visitors will remember the specific information about Hall or his machines, but they are apt to remember the more general themes behind technological innovation. This perspective can help mold how we view our own technology. Harpers Ferry is not only a place to integrate popular with elite perceptions in regard to the development of the American system of manufactures, but also to convey an attitude about the social aspect of technological development. Right now, heroic myths, including Eli Whitney's, are clouding the popular understanding of technological development. These distortions foster a view of technology that is romantic. They focus on the individual rather than the group, portraying change as revolutionary and not evolutionary. Heroic myths encourage us to wait for the new deliverer who will solve our twentieth-century problems as heroes in the past have done. This precludes us from recognizing that technology is a social, and not heroic, endeavor.

(Editor's note: Since this paper was presented, the exhibit at Harpers Ferry has undergone renovation and now reflects the complexity, as well as the impact of, the development of interchangeable parts.)

Notes

1   Thomas J. Schlereth (Editor), *Material Culture Studies in America* (Nashville, Tennessee, 1981).

2   John F. Kasson, "The Invention of the Past: Technology, History and Nostalgia," an unpublished lecture presented at the West Virginia University Humanities Seminar. We are indebted to Kasson for drawing attention to the "heroic school" of interpretation in the history of technology.

3   Denison Olmsted, *Memoir of Eli Whitney, Esq.* (New Haven, American Journal of Science, 1832). Olmsted was Professor of Natural Philosophy and Astronomy at Yale.

4   Wyn Wachhorst, *Thomas Alva Edison, An American Myth* (Cambridge, Massachusetts, 1981), 3.

5   Jeannette Mirsky and Allan Nevins, *The World of Eli Whitney* (New York, 1952) is by far the best of the lot. Constance Green, *Eli Whitney and the Birth of American Technology* (Boston, 1956) is a popularization. Two children's books that perpetuate the Whitney myth are Miriam Gilbert's *Eli Whitney, Master Craftsman* (New York, 1956), and Jean Latham *The Story of Eli Whitney: Invention and Progress in the Young Nation* (New York, 1953).

6   Robert S. Woodbury, "The Legend of Eli Whitney and Interchangeable Parts," *Technology and Culture* 1 (Summer, 1960), 235-253.

7   Edwin A. Battison, "Eli Whitney and the Milling Machine," *Smithsonian Journal of History* 1(1966), 9-34. Also see his later article "A New Look at the 'Whitney' Milling Machine," *Technology and Culture* 14(October, 1973), 592-598.

8   Merritt Roe Smith, *Harpers Ferry and the New Technology* (Ithaca, 1977), chapter eight is particularly relevant.

9   Merritt Roe Smith, "Eli Whitney and the American System of Manufacturing," *Technology in America*, Carroll W. Pursell, Jr, ed. (Cambridge, MA, 1982), 45-61. Smith briefly mentions this in *Harpers Ferry and the New Technology*, 81.

10   Battison, "Eli Whitney and the Milling Machine," explains the personal achievements of each of these three in depth.

11   David A. Hounshell, *From the American System to Mass Production 1800-1932: The Development of Manufacturing Technology in the United States.* (Baltimore, MD, 1984).   While Hounshell moves quickly through the armament industry, he adds several interesting points about French influence.

12   Robert A. Howard, "Interchangeable Parts Reexamined: The Private Sector of the American Arms Industry on the Eve of the Civil War," *Technology and Culture* 19(October, 1978), 633-649. Also see Paul Uselding, "Elisha K. Root, Forging and the American System," *Technology and Culture* 15(October, 1975), 543-568.

13   Smith, *Harpers Ferry and the New Technology*, chapter seven. From a very different but still helpful perspective is Arcadi Gluckman, *United States Muskets, Rifles and Carbines.* (Harrisburg, PA, 1959).

14   Smith, *Harpers Ferry and the New Technology*, chapter eight.

15   Nathan Rosenberg, *Technology and American Economic Growth*, (New York, 1972), 16.

16   Smith, "Eli Whitney and the American System of Manufacturing."

17   Anthony F.C. Wallace, *The Social Context of Innovation*, (Princeton, NJ, 1982).   In this work Wallace considers the role society and its institutions have in technology.

18   University of New Haven, *Essays In Arts and Sciences: Nineteenth Century American Industry and Culture: Eli Whitney Issue.* 10 (March, 1982). For other examples of the myth's appearance in articles see Kent Gilbreath, "From Fruited Plain to Industrial State" *Baylor Business Studies* 124(May, 1980), 81-96, and also John S. Hekman and John S. Strong, "The Evolution of New England Industry" *New England Economic Review* (March/April 1981), 35-46. There are many other examples including college textbooks and Mark Paul's "When Cotton Became King," *Senior Scholastic* 114(November, 1981), 18-21.

19   Paul Lee, interview with Frances Robb, Harpers Ferry, WV September 20, 1985.

COMMENT: THE HERO
IN INDUSTRIAL HISTORY

Gary Kulik

Francis Bacon's utopia on the archipelago of New Atlantis contained two galleries, one devoted to the most important inventions in the world, the other to the most important inventors. It took an extraordinary leap of imagination to envision such honors for common artisans in the England of Charles I. Yet within three decades, a Royal Society would exist, within a century English scientists would become knights, while another fifty years later, a portly barber with dubious claims to inventive originality would step out into the world as Sir Richard Arkwright.[1]

By the middle of the nineteenth century, Samuel Smiles had established a firm place for the industrial hero. He was self-taught and self-made, a risk taking visionary, a benefactor of mankind. He was practical, impatient of theory, a doer. Smiles' idealization of the heroic inventor is still very much with us, though certain aspects of Smiles' ideology may appear anachronistic today, living as we do in a culture that values the making of deals more than the making of things. Smiles, like virtually all his contemporaries, was firmly wedded to the labor theory of value, to a producer ethic which honored farmers, laborers, and manufacturers and held non-producers in contempt. Who were the non-producers? In republican America, they included the non-working poor certainly, but also the military, and political "jobbers." They included lawyers, bankers, even merchants. And, of course, they included European royalty. All but the poor have had their revenge.

The city of Washington in the fall of 1985 is shivering in an unprecedented fever of Anglophilia--a fascination with English royalty and their stately homes that only awaits its satirist. How ironic, how perverse even, that in an age of supply-side economics we should see this fawning over men and women that the great

American inventor-entrepreneurs would have regarded as non-producers, contributing nothing to the fund of labor, skill, and inventiveness that marked the nineteenth century. How much more perverse is it that the closest analogue we currently have to a nineteenth-century industrial hero--Lee Iacocca--owes his prominence to the effective management of a quasi-public corporation whose potential losses, contrary to the heroic image of entrepreneurship, had been effectively "socialized" by government loan guarantees.

As historians who care about uncovering the truth of nineteenth-century industrial society, perhaps we should be grateful for such perversity. Supply-side economics and right-wing politics have not yet yielded a new and ideologically charged entrepreneurial history. Yet it may be only a matter of time before far-sighted, industrial statesmen stride across the pages of our textbooks once again wreathed in glory.

That is why the public history programs that Michael Brewster Folsom and Frances Robb and Michael Workman offer are so important. Both papers seek to place inventor-entrepreneurs Nathan Appleton and Eli Whitney in historical context. Both are aware that part of that context is the history of workers and artisans. Both seek to build on the achievements of the "new" social history and, in particular, on the way in which social history has begun to inform history exhibits. Yet both papers display a certain smugness about the triumph of the new social history--an assumption that the gains in historical understanding over the last twenty years are not reversible, that the social history of business and technology has won and that historians now need to be more attentive to businessmen. I hope that they are right, but there are reasons to be skeptical. A "new" history of inventor-entrepreneurs could easily bring with it the morally and intellectually stultifying notion that only their history mattered.

In this light, I have some disagreement with Michael Folsom. It is a half-truth to imply, as Folsom does, that recent social historians of industrial America have written exclusively about the relatively powerless and thus neglected "elite white males." Some of the best recent work, in particular that of Paul Faler and Jonathan Prude, has successfully blended the histories of workers and manufacturers. Folsom goes to some length to stress the power of Nathan Appleton and the relative lack of power of those who worked for him. "Ordinary people react, and make do," he tells us, "even their rebelliousness is a response." Yet if the new labor history has taught us anything it is that workers do more than "react, and make do."   The degree of working-class agency in any given period is a proper subject for debate, but Folsom's language legitimates the neglect of working-class history, and inadvertently undermines his own argument.   If workers had no power over their fate, then their history can have only an anthropological interest, and there is no need to qualify, as Folsom does, the importance of the elite, for theirs is the history that really matters.[2]

Yet Folsom's main point is an intriguing one.   He urges us to employ the methods and perspective of social history to understand the likes of Nathan Appleton--to see him in his everyday life, at work, with his family, making business decisions and to see him through the lens offered by probate records, the census, and city directories.   In the wrong hands such an approach could degenerate into a lifestyles of history's rich and famous.   But Folsom's intent is serious.   He wants to comprehend the power of Nathan Appleton and the social effects of his power, and he believes that a social-history approach will assist him.

If Folsom succeeds, he will have done something rare in historical writing and even rarer in industrial museums.   Few historians study business decisions and their social effects in a way that comprehends both the social forces that led to such decisions and the consequences of them.   We know far more about liberal reformers and disaffected intellectuals than we do about the real wielders of power in American society. Industrial museums have offered little help, preferring to present the past through the eyes of inventors and engineers, oblivious not just to workers, but often to the captains of industry as well.

Robb and Workman urge us to deconstruct the myth of the heroic inventor.   Although no serious scholar any longer credits Eli Whitney with "discovering" the principle of interchangeable parts, the myth endures.   Historic sites offer better teaching possibilities than books the authors believe, and they propose several improvements to the National Park Service's interpretation at Harpers Ferry.   They seek to bring to the public a more complex view of technological change, one that sees invention as a social and a cumulative process, one that is properly attentive to the role of working people.   Many curators of industrial museums share their goals, but few have yet succeeded.

Both papers, though vague about specifics, mark a measure of progress.   A decade ago, such proposals

would have seemed radical indeed.   Most museum
curators would have scorned them, committed as they
were to an ideology of technical progress and to a belief
in the historical importance of engineers that was little
more than an extension of the simplicities of Samuel
Smiles.   Now such arguments seem tame, in the
mainstream.   Several museums have broken new ground
in recent years, both in their exhibits and in the
interpretation of those exhibits.   Slater Mill Historic Site,
the Hagley Museum, Lowell National Historical Park,
the Museum of American Textile History come clearly to
mind.   There are hopeful signs at other industrial
museums.   But skeptical curators and museum directors
remain, and the conservative pressures that obstruct
probing presentations of industrial history have certainly
not abated.   We have a great deal more work to do
before we can feel satisfied, and we have a great deal
more to learn about the effective museum presentation
of industrial history.   If today's papers can bring us
closer to more critical, more contextual industrial-history
exhibits, exhibits that offer intellectual meat rather than
piety, exhibits that present the tough questions about
power and authority in industrial America, then they
will have served a useful purpose.

Notes

1   Anthony F.C. Wallace, *The Social Context of Innovation* (Princeton, N.J., 1982), 103-106.

2   Jonathan Prude, *The Coming of Industrial Order: Town and Factory Life in Rural Massachusetts, 1810-1860* (New York, 1983); Paul G. Faler, *Mechanics and Manufacturers in the Early Industrial Revolution: Lynn, Massachusetts, 1780-1860* (Albany, New York, 1981).

SELLING AN IMAGE:
VIEWS OF LOWELL
1825-1876

Helena E. Wright

For decades after independence, there was serious debate about whether the United States should permit a factory system to be established.[1] But material welfare and improvement came to be embodied in technical progress or industrialization, rather than in agrarian democracy, and the Industrial Revolution brought many changes to the American landscape.

How these changes were perceived was due in no small part to their interpretation in paintings and prints. Prints had the advantage of wider distribution at lower cost and therefore reached a larger public. They helped inform American attitudes about the process of industrialization.

One specific instance, the success of the Lowell "Experiment," depended upon favorable public perception of industrial capitalism, and one way to influence people was to provide images carrying a positive picture of the city's development. In this paper I want to look at the ways that works of art and advertising were commissioned and published for the specific purpose of selling a positive image of Lowell.

Following the founding of Lowell, Massachusetts, in 1822, a succession of images was created to document its growth. These changes were recorded in numerous paintings, printed views, book and periodical illustrations, and details on advertising and printed ephemera of all kinds.

In the beginning, the fledgling community was shown as a basically rural environment surrounding the nucleus of a new concept, an entire town created expressly for textile manufacturing. Benjamin Mather, a little known local artist, painted the earliest known view of Lowell in 1825 <Figure 1>. He presented it as the factory-in-the-forest concept idealized in early writing.[2] On his canvas, the setting is still pastoral; there are few houses to interrupt the rural simplicity of what could be any factory village. But meadows and pastures at the river's edge were giving ground to clusters of red brick and frame buildings which rapidly accumulated, changing forever the farms of East Chelmsford into an industrial landscape.

Fifty years later, the bird's eye view of 1876 shows a mature developed city, and the Lowell "Experiment" has been incorporated into the American experience. No vestige of the rural landscape remains <Figure 2>.

Views of Lowell executed between 1825 and 1876 carried particular messages about nineteenth-century American industry. Lowell was planned from the beginning as a manufacturing center. This set it apart from the more casual development of other towns and made it an experiment to be observed closely. Solidity, substance, and power were conveyed, yet the rural quality of the surrounding landscape was not impinged upon--at first. These images told the new city's story as commissioned by the incorporators, almost as if issued along with the shares of stock. The way such views were commissioned and published is related to the production of advertising and product identification. In picturing the locus of their operations, the corporations had both motive and opportunity to present the city's image to their best advantage.

There is no need to recount the litany of American industrial development; a brief outline of the chronology should suffice. Alexander Hamilton encouraged manufacturing, and in the 1790s the Society for Useful Manufactures developed several establishments in Paterson, New Jersey. The textile industry was among the first to reach maturity. Samuel Slater first spun cotton yarn by powered machinery in Rhode Island in the 1790s. The Boston Manufacturing Company, begun in 1813 on the banks of the Charles River in Waltham, Massachusetts, was the first integrated textile manufacturing plant in the United States to turn raw cotton to finished cloth under one roof by powered machinery.

Two paintings of the Boston Manufacturing Company introduce the concept of recording industry as art in the mid-1820s. One, an oil on panel, is signed and dated "Elijah Smith 1824"; the other, oil on canvas, has been attributed to Smith and tentatively dated between 1826 and 1830. They document the factories at Waltham with clarity, presenting an attractive portrait of a new industrial complex.

These paintings are the direct precedent of a whole line of Lowell images, just as the Boston

*Figure 1. **Lowell in 1825**. Oil on canvas by Benjamin Mather. Lowell Art Association. This early view of Lowell shows a pastoral setting that could be any factory village.*

Manufacturing Company factory buildings served as models for New England textile mill development, and the concept of employing significant numbers of women represented the Waltham system as enlarged upon at Lowell.[3]

In 1821 Boston investors turned from Waltham to the Pawtucket Falls on the Merrimack River, where an existing transportation canal gave them a head start on building power canals, and later, an entire community planned and developed as a textile manufacturing center. Named for Francis Cabot Lowell (1775-1817), one of the prime movers behind the Waltham endeavor, the town grew from farmland into an industrial landscape in a few short years. The Merrimack Manufacturing Company was soon joined by a number of textile manufacturing companies, all of whom needed corporate "images" almost as soon as they had walls.

The first major print of Lowell was a lithograph of 1830, drawn by James Kidder and lithographed by the Senefelder Company of Boston, an early firm named for the German inventor of the process. Lithography was a medium well-suited to the distribution of multiple works of art within the range of many pocketbooks, and in fact the development and popularity of the lithographic process were contemporary with Lowell itself.

Lithography was introduced in America about 1820, just about the time the Boston Associates were planning their venture at the Pawtucket Falls. Boston's first lithographic firm, that of the Pendleton brothers, was established in 1825--the same year that Benjamin Mather painted Lowell. Boston was a center of this new art form, and it is not surprising that by 1830 the Kidder view appeared, the first of many Lowell lithographs to be issued over the next half-century.

Lithographs of other towns and individual factories appeared about this time. The Senefelder firm produced views of the Crown and Eagle cotton mill in North Uxbridge, Massachusetts, and the Dover Manufacturing Company in Dover, New Hampshire. Without hard data from either patron or lithographer, neither of whose records have survived, we can only speculate, but it is easy to imagine a proud group of stockholders commissioning prints of such impressive new ventures.

The Senefelder Lithographic Company was a logical choice to produce the first lithographic view of Lowell. George C. Smith, associated with the engraving firm of Annin, Smith, & Co., was a principal in the Senefelder shop as well. Annin & Smith engraved and

Figure 2. Lowell, Mass. 1876. Lithograph by Bailey & Hazen. Museum of American Textile History. Within fifty years of its founding, Lowell had developed into a mature city filling the boundaries of the bird's eye view.

printed the labels used to market Merrimack Manufacturing Company cloth.[4] Both engraving and lithography were used for Lowell city views and for factory advertising, and the firms as well as the images, were closely inter-related.

Merrimack Manufacturing Company accounts document that first Annin & Smith and then the Pendleton shop produced their cloth labels. Both firms produced both engravings and lithographs, and after 1831, Pendleton absorbed the Senefelder operation.[5] Annin & Smith was employed by the Merrimack Company from 1825 through 1829; the Pendletons, and their successor, Thomas Moore, were employed from 1830 through 1838. The chronology of the firms' employment by the Merrimack Company, bracketing the 1830 date of the Lowell lithograph, in addition to their mutual involvement in the Senefelder enterprise, indicates to me that the 1830 view was made for the corporation, even if it does not appear in any existing corporate accounts. Due to inconsistencies in bookkeeping in Lowell's first decade, it simply may not have been recorded, or the data may have not survived, or one individual director may have paid the bill.

In 1839, a new engraver, P.A. O'Neill, appeared in the Merrimack Company's journal, and he was paid specifically for "designing a view of Lowell," engraving the plate, and printing tickets or labels.[6] I regard this later view as an overt marketing effort, but I feel it is linked in intent to the 1830 Kidder lithograph, an earlier, more subtle image-maker.

In the case of two oil paintings of Lowell, records of a direct corporate commission do survive. Kirk Boott, the irascible agent of the Merrimack Manufacturing Company and prime mover of early Lowell, purchased two canvases from artist Alvan Fisher in 1833. *Falls in the Merrimack River Near Lowell* and *Merrimack River, Lowell* show the river in its natural state, the activities of men secondary to the landscape of lush greenery and rushing water. The building of Lowell is very much a background theme, although granite quarrying and river traffic are shown. The mood is wistful, almost retrospective in both canvases, as if the irrevocability of industrialization had been sensed by the artist, and he wished to evoke an earlier time. Boott no doubt wished to have a visible record of the powerful river which was to make his fortune and those of other Lowell investors.[7]

Corporate connections appear in contemporary prints about this time. The Pendleton lithographic shop produced a view in 1834, drawn by E.A. Farrar <Figure

Figure 3. View of Lowell, Mass. Lithograph by Pendleton., 1834. Museum of American Textile History. Drawn by E.A. Farrar from the Dracut shore of the Merrimack, this view is the first taken from this perspective. It shows the new industrial city rising amidst its rural environs.

3>. The perspective shifted from Tewksbury to Dracut, from which vantage point several other successive views were taken. Shifting the vantage point seems quite deliberate when we consider what was at stake. The row of brick mill buildings, soon to become known as the "mile of mills," was Lowell's *raison d'etre*, and it only made sense for that aspect to be featured over the landscape emphasis of the previous prints and paintings. By this time, too, the need to balance agriculture and manufacturing was mitigated by the rising power of industrialization.

Even though construction was by no means over, the row of brick mill buildings as seen from across the Merrimack was beginning to be quite an impressive sight. This print is particularly interesting, because at this point neither the Boott Mills nor the Massachusetts Mills had yet been started. Therefore, we have an open view into the heart of the city, exposing the Hamilton, Appleton, and Lowell Manufacturing Company mills, which in later prints would be hidden behind the Boott and the Massachusetts. Dead center along the Merrimack Canal, the Dutton Street housing of the Merrimack Corporation formed an even row behind St. Anne's Church.

The 1834 Pendleton lithograph, long thought to be only a framing print, recently turned up in the format of a sample folder <Figure 4>. The print is backed with the same stiff embossed paper covering the engraved "Merrimack Prints" sample folders. I am convinced that this Lowell view, too, was used to sell cloth. The chronology of the two lithographs is unclear as to whether or not the commercial version was issued simultaneously with the framing print.

The textiles for which Lowell was famous were sold with pictorial sales aids as well as on the basis of the cloth's design and inherent physical characteristics. Point-of-sale advertising consisted of a pictorial label attached to the cloth. These labels were used on cuts of cloth sold both retail and wholesale <Figure 5>. Attractive folders of cloth samples for the wholesale trade came with views of the city featuring the Merrimack Manufacturing Company factory. A number of versions of these survive, cut to size to be used as framing prints, testimony to the appeal of the picture.

That appeal is due largely to the skill of the artist, David Claypool Johnston (1798-1865). An ink drawing, the basis for this plate, is attributed to him. Johnston, one of the few American artists who produced

Figure 4. Merrimack Prints. Lithograph [by Pendleton, ca 1834] Museum of American Textile History. The same view as shown in Figure 3, but here Farrar's lithograph has been overprinted as a selling device for the Merrimack Corporation. It appears to have been redrawn.

Figure 5. Merrimack Prints/Fast Colors. Engraving, ca 1840. American Antiquarian Society. This uncut sheet of labels for Merrimack Company cloth represents four scenes, Boston, Philadelphia, New Haven, and Maine. In this case, none of the images is Lowell, indicating an appeal to the buyer's interests and an attempt to show a wide marketing area.

Figure 6. *Merrimack Prints/Lowell, Mass. Engraving, ca 1848 [after D.C. Johnston]. Museum of American Textile History. Images of Lowell and its mills appeared on labels used for retail sales and on sample folders of cloth like this one intended for the wholesale trade.*

etchings in the mid-nineteenth century, is best known
for his wonderfully humorous and satirical caricatures
and theatrical portraits. He exhibited regularly in Boston
from the late 1820s to 1861 and published his own
series of caricatures called *Scraps*, modeled after George
Cruikshank's *Scraps and Sketches*, in nine volumes
between 1828 and 1849. Commercial work like the
"Merrimack Prints," Lowell views, and sheet music
covers also issued forth from his prolific hand[8] <Figure
6>.

The majority of these sample folders were
engraved and printed from steel or copper plates, not
the easiest or cheapest method available at the time, but
one which gave a long run of good quality impressions.
The plate could be altered and reprinted, as the
surviving images indicate, giving a fashionable new look
to the sample folder, or a bolder brand name. The
surviving copper plate in the collection of the Lowell
Art Association shows evidence of the plate's reworking
on the reverse, where the metal has been hammered out
so that the front could be re-engraved.

P.A. O'Neill, the engraver paid for designing a
view of Lowell in 1839 <Figure 7>, published a very
similar reduced version in the 1845 book, *Lowell As It
Was and As It Is* <Figure 8>. Here is essentially the same
view used on a sample folder also appearing to
illustrate a book touting Lowell's achievements during
its first twenty years. I doubt that this similarity is a
coincidence, although the sameness reflects the rather
limited conventions of landscape depiction by
commercial artists. The corporate image may resemble
the municipal portrait because there are only so many
ways to show the same city, after all. But it is no
coincidence that the approved corporate image found its
way into a book of Lowell boosterism.

These examples shed new light on the role of the
city itself as a promotional concept. Lowell, unlike other
"products," was conceived as a total systems approach.
Specific companies may have had their individual
advertising images, but in the main, it was the city and
the new idea of industrial capitalism that were being
marketed. As the city developed, the views produced
conveyed a sense of growth and power helping to put
Lowell ahead of its rivals in the market place. In the
period before the Civil War, the number of Lowell
views--and revenues--far outdid the newer competitors,
towns like Manchester, Holyoke, and Lawrence.

This is not to say that other cities didn't try the
same sort of promotion, or that there is any difference
in the way Lowell was depicted. It became common

Figure 7. Merrimack Prints. Engraving [by O'Neill, ca 1840] Museum of American Textile History. P.A. O'Neill designed and engraved a view of Lowell for the Merrimack corporation. This engraving, although unsigned, is very similar to O'Neill's view published in Lowell As It Was and As It Is (1845). This view definitely carried the Merrimack Company's message.

practice, as John Reps has said: "Land speculators, townsite promoters, and civic leaders all used urban views to attract people and industry to their communities, often subsidizing the publication of the views to make wider distribution possible."[9] But they started early in Lowell to publish views of all varieties, and the incorporators had a vested interest in selling a new system about which there was some controversy, as well as in marketing cloth, house lots, and shares of stock.

Several Lowell views appeared in the 1840s and 1850s. With the growth and success of the city, outside publishers appeared to get in on the action. The later lithographs were produced either as commissions or by subscription, a practice that grew increasingly popular as the lithographic trade flourished. The artist or publisher made known his intention to produce a view and invited subscriptions through ads in the local papers or samples placed in shops as announcements. These often took the form of a painting or drawing to show prospective customers the view they could order. Publication was contingent upon enlisting a number of subscribers sufficient to pay for the costs.[10]

The experience of an artist who produced a view of nearby Lawrence may well represent the pattern for producing Lowell views in this period. The artist, Albert Conant, drew a view of Lawrence published in 1848 by the Boston lithographic firm of J. W. A. Scott, *View of the Town of Lawrence (From the East) April 1848.* By July of that year, Conant dejectedly wrote to Charles Storrow, Treasurer of Lawrence's Essex Company, to say that the views were not selling well, either in Lawrence or up river in Lowell:

> The time you mentioned regarding the sale of my views of Lawrence has expired. I left 50 copies with Mr. Bixby of Lowell and received a letter from him tonight stating that they had not sold one. The sale in Lawrence too has been small, as large however in either place as I should have expected had it not been a view of so new a town....I am certain there have not been more than forty sold. The remainder of the 300 shall be delivered to you as soon as you say, and I can collect them from the different places they are now in.[11]

Conant asked Storrow to pay him $231 to cover the expense of making the views, some 232 colored by

Figure 8. View of Lowell. Engraving by P.A. O'Neill. Museum of American Textile History. Published in Lowell As It Was and As It Is (1845), this view bears a strong resemblance to a larger engraving used to market Merrimack Manufacturing Company printed cloth. Its appearance in this book shows an important link between the desired image of the city and its major corporation's marketing efforts.

hand at $.90 and 30 uncolored at $.75.[12] It is easy to imagine why the Company would get involved: they happened to employ Conant, a talented artist, who had drawn and published four views of other Massachusetts towns; the new city was beginning to take shape, and there were tangible results of building to show prospective buyers of land and investors in the manufacturing companies. What better way to indicate the nature of the investment than to produce a lithographic view? Photography was still in its infancy, not yet a decade old, and at this point, in the United States, limited to daguerreotypes. A handsome lithograph, colored to show the extensive use of brick in the new city, was just the thing to attract capital to Lawrence and to provide a positive impression of the value of industrialism.

Even in a more established city like Lowell, the impact of a lithographic view showing industrial development was bound to be felt on potential investors and customers for the mills' products. Conant worked on other views with another artist, Fitz Hugh Lane, who about 1840 had lithographed a view of Lowell.

Fitz Hugh Lane (1804-1865) was a prolific artist in the media of oil painting, water color, and lithography. His view of Lowell executed about 1840 is the first to portray a solid wall of brick mills following the river bank. This dates it definitely after the building of the Boott and the Massachusetts corporations. A companion print by Lane, a lithograph of the Middlesex Company Woolen Mill, appeared about the same time <Figure 9>.

The Middlesex Company treasurer was Samuel Lawrence, one of the family of investors and merchants of that name whose capital funded the Lawrence, Tremont, Suffolk, and Middlesex corporations in Lowell, and who were major financiers of the "new city on the Merrimack," Lawrence, in 1845. A large lithograph of the city of Lawrence, published in 1854, was dedicated to Samuel Lawrence, seeming to indicate that he was the chief subscriber to the publisher's effort, if not the outright commissioner of the print.

A handsome oil painting of the Middlesex Company survives <Figure 10>, along with the Fitz Hugh Lane lithograph, and engraved business stationery incorporating a view of the mill. It is tempting to attribute the painting to Lane on the evidence of the signed lithograph and stylistic similarities to his other work and to link all three images to the patronage of Samuel Lawrence.[13]

Figure 9. Middlesex Mills, Lowell, Mass. Lithograph by Sharp after Fitz Hugh Lane, ca 1845. Lowell Historical Society. As lithography became more widespread, views of factories proliferated, to be used as both framing prints and advertising. Lane did not execute many such images, however, and this print is a rare survivor.

Lowell images in other media and other formats also appeared, with messages both subtle and direct. Wood engraving, which had the advantage of being printed directly with type rather than requiring a separate press, was also used for images issued along with text. One of the first of this type, *The People's Magazine* of 1834, ran a story about Lowell, touting its novelty and promise, and illustrating it with a wood engraving, by a Mr. Martins, looking up Dutton Street. John Warner Barber's "East View of Lowell, Mass." appeared as an illustration in the *Historical Collections. . . relating to the history and antiquities of every town in Massachusetts,* published in 1839. Lowell was one of the places selected to be shown in a full-page wood engraving. This was due no doubt to the interest and curiosity that attended the city's reputation as the fastest-growing town in New England. It is not impossible that a stipend was paid to the publisher for the privilege, either.

Dozens of images were issued before the Civil War, showing mills and machinery, city views, and residences. Special-purpose illustrations used as cloth labels and folders, magazine and book illustrations, letterheads, advertising, and bank notes carried images of Lowell and its technology throughout the land. The success of this industrial experiment was well known, and no doubt many people wished to see just how the city appeared. Visitors flocked to the city during its first two decades, travelers from home and abroad, from Davy Crockett to Charles Dickens. Even after the novelty of the Lowell experiment diminished, the growth of the city itself supplied numerous customers for the views.

These speculations about relationships and corporate involvement in making Lowell's image tell us much about the role of the arts in forming popular attitudes toward industrialization. We know that a picture is worth a thousand words; maybe it's worth $1,000 in sales or capital investment or public opinion, too. Advertising lithographs, including builders' drawings of machines, sold many types of products such as locomotives and textile machinery.[14] Why not consider city views as sales agents for what the city had to sell?

Accounts for engraving and lithographing labels and sample folders (including at least one identified as a "View of Lowell"), along with records of the paintings Kirk Boott commissioned, provide evidence of direct corporate involvement in making Lowell's image.

Figure 10. [Middlesex Mills, Lowell, Mass.] Oil on canvas. [Provisionally attributed to Fitz Hugh Lane, ca 1845]. Museum of American Textile History. Frequently artists painted scenes which then were lithographed or engraved for wider distribution. This painting has been attributed to Lane in part on its similarity to the signed lithograph.

O'Neill's 1839 view of Lowell for the Merrimack Company's sample folder reappeared in *Lowell As It Was and As It Is*. Essex Company records show corporate support for the 1848 Conant view of Lawrence. These examples prove the creation of a body of graphic work to market the concept of the city. Specific images, such as those found on cloth labels for individual mills, of course, provide more direct evidence, but the city views are an important component as well.

The comprehensive printed Statistics of Lowell Manufactures indicate a corporate idea and image not limited to one factory or product, but rather directed to a system representing a radical change in the American way of life. Industrial capitalism, as represented by Lowell, was perceived as a threat to agrarian democracy (*vide* note 1), and the investors had to show its best face in order to convince philosophical opponents of their position. I do not want to open the question of primacy of place as an image-maker in the American Industrial Revolution, but I do not know of a more dense paper trail than that leading to Lowell. It may have been that the most concerted public relations effort was at work there, or simply that more pictorial and business ephemera has survived for Lowell than for Paterson, the Brandywine, or Lehigh Valleys, or other contenders.

The surviving evidence, in the form of both framing prints and advertising, shows the degree to which industrialization became accepted not only as a business system but as an attraction, a positive element to be celebrated in paintings and prints, even in the home. Factory and town views became positive icons, celebrated in a place of honor on the parlor wall.

Despite the warnings and pessimism of some critics, the view of technological and industrial progress has been, in the main, a celebratory one, especially before 1860. Industry was represented by the cornucopia, a symbol of plenty. Subtle influences are at work in early images of industrialization. Overlaid on the familiar landscape are the hallmarks of the new age of the factory, presented as an integral part of the scene. They represent changes in the old order, implicitly assuming that industrialization is grand, glorious, and here to stay.

We know how the tale comes out in the end, or at least up to this point in the story. Graffiti on factory facades proclaims "Mills are a Kurse." Now we are caught up in the midst of another type of revolution, high-tech communications, but it does not picture or sell itself in quite the same way as the Lowell of 150 years ago. Then, the product, the city's corporate image, sold itself and perpetuated the system that produced it, despite earlier negative attitudes about industrialization.

Notes

1   Michael B. Folsom and Steven Lubar, eds., *The Philosophy of Manufactures* (Cambridge, MA, 1982), xix.

2   Thomas Bender, *Toward an Urban Vision* (Lexington, 1975), considers Lowell in this context.

3   Richard Candee has examined historical assumptions regarding the Waltham precedents for Lowell. He presents important new evidence from buildings and census records that changes Waltham's role in subsequent New England textile corporation town development in "Architecture and Corporate Planning in the Early Waltham System," *Essays from the Lowell Conference on Industrial History, 1982 and 1983* (North Andover, MA, 1985).

4   Merrimack Manufacturing Co.: Agent's Journal (1822-37), Journals 14-20, (1825-45), Manuscripts Dept., Baker Library, Harvard University.

5   Pamela Hoyle, "The Senefelder Press, 1828-1838," unpublished exhibition notes, Boston Athenaeum, *ca*1977; David Tatham, "The Pendleton-Moore Shop, Lithographic Artists in Boston, 1825-1840," *Old Time New England*, LXII, 2 (October-December 1971), 29-46.

6   Merrimack Manufacturing Co. Journal 19, entry for October 1839. Baker Library.

7   Boott's purchases are recorded in the manuscript notebooks of Alvan Fisher, which are privately owned.
    Thomas Doughty (1793-1856) showed the factories much more prominently in his painting, *Mill Pond and Mills, Lowell, Massachusetts*. Frank H. Goodyear Jr., *Thomas Doughty: An American Pioneer in Landscape Painting* (Philadelphia, 1973), dated the painting about 1833, making it exactly contemporary with Fisher's two canvases. Doughty lived in Boston in the 1830s, and he and Fisher made many sketching trips together to the surrounding countryside. According to the National Museum of American Art's art exhibition index based on catalogues published prior to 1877, this canvas does not appear to have been exhibited in the Boston galleries where Doughty's other work for sale was hung, and it is possible that Boott commissioned it from him as he did the Fisher paintings.
    However, the facade of the mill building shown, although not identifiable as a particular corporation, looks like a building of later than 1833, and the large smokestack at the left would not have appeared so early. Doughty visited Boston again in 1843, and it is possible that he painted Lowell following that trip, which fits the details of the painting more accurately. Doughty is not known for representational accuracy, however.
    If the Doughty painting was executed later, it was not done for Boott, who died in 1837. However, all three paintings descended together from the Merrimack Corporation through the Saco-Lowell Shops to a private collection. No evidence has yet come to light to document when and from whom the Doughty canvas originated.
    See Jadviga da Costa Nunes, "The Industrial Landscape in America, 1800-1840: Ideology into Art" in IA in Art, a special thematic issue of *IA: The Journal of the Society for Industrial Archeology*, Vol.12, No. 2 (1986).

8   For more on the career of this talented and versatile artist, see Malcolm Johnson, *David Claypool Johnston: American Graphic Humorist, 1798-1865* (Boston, 1970), catalogue of an exhibition shown in several New England locations. David Tatham of Syracuse University has written several articles on various aspects of Johnston's work.

9   John W. Reps, *Views and Viewmakers of Urban America... 1825-1925* (Columbia, MO, 1984), 4.

10   In about 1850 and again in 1876, Edwin Whitefield (1816-1892) produced fully finished pen and wash drawings of Lowell. With these two examples, Whitefield probably tried subscription efforts to cover publication costs of the views, but no printed version of either view has come to light. The Bailey and Hazen bird's eye view of Lowell also appeared in 1876 which perhaps depleted the potential market for Whitefield's second attempt. For a comprehensive and sympathetic treatment of Whitefield's career, see Bettina A. Norton, *Edwin Whitefield: 19th-Century North American Scenery* (Barre, MA, 1977).

11   A. Conant to Charles Storrow, 15 July 1848, MS 69, Museum of American Textile History (MATH).

12   A. Conant to Charles Storrow, July 25, 1848, MS 69, MATH.

13   John Wilmerding, author of *Fitz Hugh Lane* (New York, 1971) and acknowledged expert on Lane's paintings, provisionally attributed the Middlesex Mills oil to Lane, subject to further inspection and documentation. Albert Conant and Fitz Hugh Lane worked in partnership on half-a-dozen town views, including a painting and print of the city of Baltimore. Lane's painting was produced as a lithograph by Conant, and sold on subscription in 1850. The two men began to work together after Lane's Lowell projects, and Conant's Lawrence view was printed by Lane's former partner, J. W. A. Scott. John Reps lists each known town view produced by Lane and Conant.

14   On the use of lithographs to aid in the sale of locomotives, see the *Railroad Advocate*, Nov. 8, 1856, and John H. White, Jr., "Locomotives on Stone," *Smithsonian Journal of History* I, 1 (1966), 49-60.

Note:

In 1985, the Lowell Historical Society published a catalogue, *Lowell Views: A Collection of Nineteenth-Century Prints, Paintings, and Drawings*, containing reproductions of many of the views discussed above. Copies are available from the Society or from the bookstore at the Lowell National Historical Park Visitor Center.

"OUR MEN BUILD THEIR SOULS INTO STUDEBAKER CARS": A COMPANY'S EFFORTS TO CREATE AN IMAGE OF ITS WORKERS

Patrick J. Furlong

For many years the Studebaker Corporation endeavored to portray itself to the public as a firm which employed craftsmen rather than ordinary assembly line workers and treated them as men rather than human machines. In its automobile advertising, as well as its internal publications, Studebaker claimed to be the company that cared, the company which stood by its workers in good times and in bad. According to the company's unique advertising theme, Studebaker cars were built by highly skilled craftsmen who passed on their tradition of careful workmanship from father to son. This theme of families of craftsmen working together in the Studebaker factory was a pervasive one in the company's advertising for almost thirty years, and it remains a strong element of South Bend folklore.

During the 1930s when General Motors called for the Michigan National Guard to break the sit-down strikes and Ford's company goon squad beat the union organizers at the "Battle of the Overpass," Studebaker calmly accepted United Auto Workers Local No. 5. For many years, a strike was "unthinkable" at Studebaker, but by the 1950s its workers had a reputation for generous pay and miserable productivity. After heated arguments in 1954, Local 5 agreed to a revised contract and accepted reduced wages in order to save the company. Piece-work rates gave way to the straight time rates used by all other automobile manufacturers, and work standards were tightened, but not to industry norms. Studebaker survived, but it did not prosper, and early in 1962 there was a bitter six-week strike.[1]

Little more than a year later, after its new models failed dismally in the marketplace, Studebaker announced the permanent shutdown of automobile manufacturing at South Bend and left its once-faithful workers unemployed and in many instances unpensioned as well. December 9, 1963, is remembered as the darkest day in South Bend's history. The Studebaker work force had already declined from its 1951 peak of 23,000 to about 7,000, and those who remained on the job until the end were chiefly men above fifty years of age with better than twenty years of seniority. Was the company's carefully nourished image over so many years nothing more than an advertising slogan, or had Studebaker really been a different sort of automobile company?

Henry and Clement Studebaker opened their blacksmith shop in South Bend in 1852, with a total capital of $68. They built wagons as a sideline, common practice for blacksmiths of the time. Their business grew slowly at first, and then rapidly with wagons and gun carriages for the Union Army during the Civil War. When the Studebaker Brothers Manufacturing Company incorporated in 1868, it had assets of almost $250,000 and employed 190 men and boys. The company continued to expand, rebuilding quickly after a disastrous fire in 1874 which almost destroyed the factory. Studebaker was the largest employer in South Bend, with 890 workers by 1880. Many of the men came from the growing stream of immigrants from eastern Europe, particularly Poland and Hungary. Although other local factories employed large numbers of young workers, fewer than ten per cent of Studebaker's employees were boys, and there were only half a dozen women on the payroll in 1880. Working conditions and labor relations were in keeping with the familiar late-nineteenth-century American pattern. The Studebaker brothers were typical industrialists of their era, Republican in their politics and high tariff in their economics. A Studebaker banner at a Republican rally in 1884 emphasized the theme: "Protection protects the laborer, and the laborer supports the world." In fact the company motto in those days was "Labor omnia vincit."[2] In an era when violent strikes were commonplace, there was very little trouble at Studebaker. According to company lore, Clem Studebaker proclaimed in 1887: "The interests of employer and employee are identical. Capital can't succeed without labor; nor can labor expect its reward without capital."[3]

As it celebrated its centennial in 1952, the company sponsored an elaborate technicolor film called

The Studebaker Story.   In a dramatic scene of the disastrous fire in 1874, a disheartened Clem Studebaker says that the firm would have to close.   His brother John M. Studebaker replies immediately: "But what about our men.   Most of them never worked for anyone but us.   They helped us to build a tradition of fine craftsmanship.   We had sons working at benches beside their fathers."   So of course Studebaker rebuilt, bigger and better than before, and its faithful employees returned to their jobs.   This indeed is the way the company wanted its workers and other viewers to think of it during its centennial year, an everlasting pillar of the community.

By the end of the nineteenth century Studebaker advertised itself as the world's largest vehicle manufacturer, with an annual capacity of 75,000 vehicles and sales of more than $3,000,000.   Studebaker and its home town grew up together.   By 1900 South Bend was a bustling city of 36,000, with one out of every four residents born in Europe.   The Studebaker vehicle factory was the largest employer in town, with nearly 3,000 men and boys on the payroll, together with a few women in the office and the upholstery shop.

Studebaker continued as a family-owned company until 1911, when it was reorganized as the Studebaker Corporation and listed on the New York Stock Exchange.   By that time it had become an important manufacturer of the new horseless carriages, beginning with an electric automobile in 1902 and expanding to gasoline-powered models two years later.   Studebaker was the only carriage and wagon manufacturer among the 6,200 which were operating at the turn of the century to survive the transition to the automobile age. The last of the five Studebaker brothers retired in 1915, and the dynamic salesman Albert R. Erskine took over as president.   Erskine decided that the company should concentrate on automobiles, and John M. Studebaker's last reported intervention in the company's affairs was his advice to locate its new automobile factory in South Bend rather than Detroit.[4]

President Albert R. Erskine took great pride in the company's good relations with its growing labor force, which reached nearly ten thousand workers by 1929.   During the 1920s, Studebaker built several housing developments for the company's production workers and sold the homes below their construction cost.   Studebaker also began to provide paid vacations, a pension plan, life insurance, and a special bonus paid on the anniversary of a worker's joining the company.

There was a company-paid chaplain at the factory to advise troubled workers, but strangely enough, management hired a Presbyterian minister to counsel the largely Catholic work force. Some outside observers were of the opinion that the chaplain's chief duty was to undermine any efforts toward organizing a union, and Erskine explained candidly in an interview that "Since Dr. Lippincott came with us . . . we have never had any labor troubles." Erskine boasted extravagantly to *Forbes* magazine in 1924 that "Our men build their very souls into the Studebaker cars." The Studebaker work force was "a happy family" where management was both generous and caring; where, in Erskine's words, "Every man eats and thinks and dreams Studebaker."[5]

Of course Erskine exaggerated his personal and corporate generosity, just as he exaggerated the pay scale and the importance of the old carriage-building craftsmanship. But the point is that this was the impression that Studebaker management wanted the American public to share. Would Henry Ford ever have dreamed of saying such things?

Unlike so many other famous automobile manufacturers of the 1920s, Studebaker did not disappear during the Depression. It was the only automobile company successfully reorganized under the bankruptcy laws, thanks to the exceptional efforts of a new leadership team. Erskine, who probably had put his soul into the business, was forced out in March, 1933, and a few months later put a bullet through his heart. Paul Hoffman and Harold Vance had each worked for Studebaker more than twenty years, and they knew the business and the company well. They understood the importance of continuing production when the situation was most desperate in order to persuade both suppliers and customers that Studebaker was in business to stay. Hoffman telephoned the bankruptcy judge at one o'clock in the morning to ask permission to spend $100,000 of the firm's scarce supply of cash for a special advertising campaign. "Studebaker Carries On," the nationwide advertisements read, and the South Bend factory resumed limited production only three days after the company "failed." Employment was far below normal, and the plant was open only two or three days a week, but at least some Studebaker workers had jobs, a true joy to cherish in March of 1933.[6]

Studebaker survived, but it was not the same as it had been, and neither was the world in which it competed. The workers were not the same either, at least not in their way of thinking. Harold Vance was

an old automobile production boss, and his door was
open to any man from the assembly line who had a
complaint. Workingmen were no longer willing to rely
on the good will of a few company officers, however.
They wanted protection from abusive foremen, and they
wanted a formal contract to spell out their wages,
hours, and working conditions. In other words, they
wanted a union. The National Industrial Recovery Act
of 1933 offered the Roosevelt administration's
encouragement for union organizing as part of the New
Deal program for the revival of the American economy.
Most of the existing unions were narrow groups of
skilled workers organized according to their particular
trades, gathered under the loose structure of the
American Federation of Labor. During June and July of
1933, seventeen Studebaker workers joined together and
became the charter members of a new and unspecialized
A.F. of L. union, called Federal Labor Union No. 18310.
The A.F. of L. had no understanding of the needs of
large groups of assembly line workers, and long-
established unions such as machinists, electricians,
millwrights, and foundry molders argued that
automobile workers should join a dozen or more
separate unions according to their various crafts. Wages
were not an issue in 1933, when twenty-five per cent of
American workers were unemployed and many of the
remainder were on short hours and reduced wages.
What mattered was job security and working conditions,
and the A.F. of L. craft structure offered little or
nothing to the semi-skilled workers of such industries as
automobiles and steel.

Paul Hoffman and Harold Vance, struggling to
reorganize the company under court supervision, did
not oppose the union movement, and Studebaker
workers faced none of the stern opposition which
characterized General Motors or the violent oppression
of Ford. Federal Labor Union No. 18310 had more
difficulty with the A.F. of L. leadership than it did with
Studebaker management, and late in 1934 the company
was able to increase wages by five cents per hour. The
following year in Detroit, representatives from the
Studebaker plant in South Bend formed the largest
delegation at the convention which organized the United
Automobile Workers of America. The Studebaker
workers became UAW Local No. 5, which signed a
formal contract with the company on May 21, 1937. The
contract provided for a plant-wide seniority system,
systematic job classifications, vacation pay, a forty hour
week, and time-and-a-half for overtime. There were

disagreements and arguments enough, but Studebaker maintained its proud record of never having had a strike.   Local No. 5 had more than seven thousand members, representing all Studebaker employees, except those classified as management, receiving an average wage of about ninety cents an hour.[7]

In the midst of its reorganization and labor turmoil, Studebaker launched a new advertising campaign in 1935 on a theme unheard of among American automobile manufacturers. The company now boasted of its dedicated work force of skilled craftsmen whose skills guaranteed the quality of Studebaker cars:

> Many of the men who construct these Studebaker Champions are descendants of men who started this business with the Studebaker brothers in the year 1852. The average length of employment at Studebaker exceeds ten years. The craftsmen whose fine work goes into every Studebaker car are as interested and devoted to Studebaker's maintenance of leadership . . . as Studebaker executives . . . .
>
> Not since the days of the medieval guilds has there been anything comparable to the spirit that pervades the great Studebaker factories where all take pride in the Studebaker tradition of excellence.[8]

Of course this was advertising hyperbole. Of course it was too good to be true. But why did Studebaker choose to advertise itself in this fashion in 1935, why not Packard or Chrysler? And this was not an occasional theme; the craftsmanship tradition was advertised regularly in both trade and consumer publications, in popular magazines such as *Time* and the *Saturday Evening Post* and in expensive business publications such as *Fortune*. I do not say that Studebaker executives believed that they were the masters of a giant medieval guild, but they did believe that advertising the claim of dedicated craftsmen building Studebaker cars was an appropriate method to reach a broad range of customers in a highly competitive market. And Studebaker did sell cars with this type of advertising, enough to lift it out of bankruptcy by March of 1935.

Studebaker published a well-illustrated promotional pamphlet in 1936, showing some of its employees at work in the factory. The pervasive theme was simple and direct: "Only Champion Craftsmen Can Build Champion Motor Cars." The workers in the pictures were identified by name and craft and they were real enough. The text was carefully polished, and it proclaimed a view of automobile manufacturing which would have caused turmoil in Detroit:

> Many motorists assume that cars today are built almost entirely by automatic machinery and that the human element counts for little in car construction. * * * Despite the marvels of machinery, the determinant of quality is still the human element. * * * Studebaker with the greatest group of understanding, scrupulous, experienced artisans to be found in any one automobile factory, can and does build better cars. * * * There isn't a transient in the company's employ . . . most Studebaker workers are long acquainted, friendly neighbors. * * * That a young man should grow up to be a fine automobile craftsman in such an environment is only natural. * * * Most of them are home-owning, vote-casting, tax-paying citizens of South Bend. And they like to work in a factory which still obeys the injunction of old John M. Studebaker: "Always give a little more than you promise."[9]

During the Second World War, when there were no new cars on the market, Studebaker advertised how its craftsmen were making a magnificent contribution to the war effort. A very popular series of advertisements in such magazines as *Life* and *Saturday Evening Post* showed young Studebaker workers on the war fronts of the world, admiring aircraft engines and trucks proudly manufactured by their fathers back in South Bend. When automobile production resumed in 1946, the public was so desperate to buy new cars that advertising was scarcely necessary. Still Studebaker occasionally featured its father-and-son teams of craftsmen, and in its internal publications, it strongly promoted the company spirit, expressed by the usual softball teams as well as a most unusual company glee club. After a splurge of historical and father-and-son craftsmen publicity during its centennial celebrations in 1952, Studebaker attempted to emphasize style, then economy, and in final desperation, the idea that

Studebaker cars were "Different by Design." Labor troubles, falling sales and constantly declining employment characterized the company during the 1950s. The compact Lark provided one year of profit in 1959, but increasing competition doomed Studebaker in the early 1960s.

To see the company as its executives wanted it to be seen, it is better to return to 1952 when Studebaker celebrated its 100th year as a vehicle manufacturer. As part of its centennial celebration Studebaker collectively looked back with pride upon the company's real and imagined regard for its workers. This is most clearly seen in a black-and-white film called *A Family of Craftsmen.* As idealized as it may seem to modern viewers, the film featured a real family of Studebaker workers, father, sons, daughters, and sons-in-law. In 1983, as part of a television project called *Studebaker: Less Than They Promised,* the surviving members of the Bokon family came together to talk about their memories of Studebaker. There was nothing of the resentment sometimes said to be characteristic of assembly line workers. Studebaker was never a model of managerial skill, and its cars were frankly no better made than Fords or Chevrolets, but there was a different feeling about the place.[10]

The most telling remark was that of a tearful Evelyn Bokon, in answer to a question about the happiest days of her life. She answered without hesitation, "When everybody was working at Studie's." Or as Rudy Bokon told an interviewer, "I enjoyed going through that gate and going to work. It was a glamorous place to work. That was my life." Or as his sister Thelma Bokon explained, "I worked other places, and I don't have that bond with the other places like I do with Studebaker's." The Studebaker Corporation survived because its leaders had the courage to leave the automobile business and use its capital to produce other products. It has since disappeared in a series of mergers, but its shareholders were well compensated. As for its employees, those already retired continued to draw their pensions, and the remaining seven thousand or so workers were simply out of a job. We hear much today about the secrets of Japanese automobile manufacturers and the extraordinary loyalty of Toyota or Honda workers. Perhaps the concluding scene of *A Family of Craftsmen* makes the point most effectively, as the Bokons joined a large group of Studebaker faithful to sing the company's centennial song, *Rolling Along for a 100 Years.* In 1952 both executives and assembly line workers were confident that Studebaker would flourish

for another century.   This is how the Studebaker
Corporation wanted to be seen.   The reality was
something else.

174   Patrick J. Furlong

Notes

1   There is not yet a comprehensive business history of Studebaker, only short company-sponsored works, a 1942 family-centered study, and illustrated guides to the automobiles.   The most recent survey is a brief work by Michael Beatty, Patrick J. Furlong and Loren E. Pennington, *Studebaker: Less Than They Promised* (South Bend, 1984).   For a brief scholarly view of the company's labor policy see Robert M. MacDonald, *Collective Bargaining in the Automobile Industry* (New Haven, 1963), esp. 259-284, 357-367.

2   Kathleen A. Smallzried and Dorothy J. Roberts, *More Than You Promise: A Business at Work in Society* (New York, 1942), 92-105.

3   *Ibid.*, 129-136; the unattributed quotation appeared in a 1952 centennial publication, *100 Years on the Road*, 89.

4   Smallzried and Roberts, *More Than You Promise*, 171-266 *passim.*

5   A beautifully printed 230 page volume was issued by Studebaker in 1924, purportedly written by Erskine and called *History of the Studebaker Corporation*; see especially Chapter 9, "Profit-Sharing and Co-operative Plans." The Erskine interview appeared in *Forbes*, (April 26, 1924).

6   Smallzried and Roberts, *More Than You Promise*, 280-301.

7   The story of organized labor at Studebaker was told by one of the founding members of Local No. 5, James D. Hill, *U. A. W.'s Frontier* (Indianapolis, 1971).

8   *Studebaker Champions 1935*, pamphlet in Studebaker Corporate Archives.

9   *So You Think All Automobiles Are Pretty Much Alike*, 1936 pamphlet in Studebaker Corporate Archives.

10   There is an extensive literature on the subject of worker alienation and dissatisfaction with repetitive assembly line work.   See, for example, Walter A. Weisskopf, *Alienation and Economics* (New York, 1971), a rather theoretical survey which scarcely mentions the automotive industry although auto assembly lines are a classic example of bored and hostile labor.   More specific studies are those of Jon M. Shephard, *Automation and Alienation: A Study of Office and Factory Workers* (Cambridge, 1971) and Michael Aiken, Louis A. Ferman and Harold L. Sheppard, *Economic Failure, Alienation, and Extremism* (Ann Arbor, 1968), an examination of the impact of the closing of the Packard plant in Detroit in 1956.   Ironically Packard had just merged with Studebaker, and production of Packard cars was shifted to South Bend for about a year until the Packard nameplate was eliminated completely.   In 1963 it was a former Packard executive recently named president of Studebaker who ordered the closing of the South Bend plant.   There is a thorough review of the literature in the monumental *Handbook of Industrial and Organizational Psychology*, edited by Marvin D. Dunnette (Chicago, 1976) especially Chapter 30, "The Nature and Causes of Job Satisfaction," by Edwin A. Locke, 1297-1349.
     There are few studies of individual corporations' efforts to shape their public images, but a recent work provides a model of what can be achieved in this field, David E. Nye, *Image Worlds: Corporate Identities at General Electric, 1890-1930* (Cambridge, 1985).

ADVERTISING'S SMOKY PAST: THEMES OF PROGRESS IN NINETEENTH-CENTURY AMERICAN ADVERTISEMENTS

Pamela Walker Lurito

Introduction: Visions of Industry

Billowing smokestacks and puffing engines dominated the landscapes of industrializing America in the second half of the nineteenth century. From the aesthetic perspective of William Cullen Bryant's *Picturesque America*, the shift from rural to urban and industrial scenery weighed on the cost side of industry's balance. In one instance, this popular and prestigious travelogue of the mid-1870s described the change in Cleveland's industrial valley, the Flat:

> Not long ago it (the Flat) was a marshy meadow, where the river meandered in peace, with nothing to disturb its sedgy margin save the cows and water-birds. Now it is a dense mass of iron-mills, lumberyards, and oil-refineries--a seething basin of life, movement, noise, and smoke.[1]

This is, of course, but one example from the wide range of Americans' reactions to the dramatic industrialization and urbanization of the nineteenth century.[2] Mid-way between the extremes, *Picturesque America* recognized both the costs and the benefits of the changes. Returning to the description of Cleveland, we find that the city's pleasantness and material prosperity were happily depicted. But,

> step to the verge of the hill, and everything is different. Down on the Flat we see Cleveland at work, Cleveland grimy, Cleveland toiling in the sweat of

175

her brow. Slowly through the oily river...
wind the heavily laden boats, bringing
work for all those puffing engines, and
taking away the product in its new shape
as fast as the engines let it go.[3]

Was "the product in its new shape" worth "those puffing
engines" that changed the "marshy meadow" into "a
seething basin of life, movement, noise, and smoke"?
Picturesque America was not quite sure that it was.

In *Picturesque America's* descriptions of
Cleveland's industry, as with many other descriptions of
other industrial towns, two dominating images were
repeated: billowing clouds of smoke over factory
smokestacks and puffing steam engines.
Contemporaneous with Bryant's aesthetic evaluations,
but originating from a very different perspective,
another genre of communication actively represented
smokestacks and puffing engines to the public as
exciting, positive symbols of a valuable progress. This
symbolism arose early in the iconography of pictorial
advertising and gave a distinctively Victorian character
to countless commercial messages sent into the
marketplace by nineteenth-century entrepreneurs. How
was this symbolism related to the systems of incentives
that propelled Victorian Americans through their century
of changes?   How did this symbolism of enterprise
relate to Horace Greeley's expectation that industry was
the means to an era of progress that would secure "to
each individual the largest liberty for his personal
endeavors, and for society at large the greatest amount
of material for its collective comfort and well-being?"[4]

Marketing and Technological Background
In the middle of the nineteenth century, world trade
expanded dramatically, and the Industrial Revolution
entered its second stage.   The first stage of the
Industrial Revolution, from the late eighteenth century
to mid-nineteenth century, had increased the volume of
traditional goods in the marketplace.   These goods
included foodstuffs, textiles, shoes, table ware, and
ironware.   The surge of invention and industrial
production of the second stage combined to add
immeasurably to the types as well as the quantities of
worldly goods available in the marketplace.   The
innovations resulted in a vast array of new products
that included sewing machines, spool thread, clocks,
polishes, packaged foods and drinks, and infinite
varieties of tools and devices for everyone in every type
of work, including housework.

This expansion of goods into the marketplace set the context for the emergence of modern marketing and its tool, advertising. Entrepreneurs began learning how to introduce their products to the public and how to generate demand for them. As remarkable as the manifestations of material progress might have been, people could not very well want to buy what they did not know existed, did not understand, or did not perceive as a need. Advertisements were a primary means by which the public became aware of the fruits of inventions, industry, and world exploration. With promises and threats, with vitality and powerful imagery, advertising messages helped to define the rewards of the Victorian lifestyle. It was, therefore, entirely appropriate that one of the most potent and important motifs of advertising's new iconography was the symbolism of progress, including images of billowing smoke above towering smokestacks and engines.

Before *any* advertising images could be introduced to the public, however, significant changes in the technologies of communication were necessary. Prior to the nineteenth century, printed advertisements were primitive both in their styles and their technologies. With few exceptions, advertisements were little more than announcements of whatever goods a merchant had to sell or whatever services someone desired or offered. The simple announcement format sufficed for sellers and consumers alike at this stage of marketing because the goods and services offered before 1800 were traditional ones. There was no perceived need to educate the public about their uses or desirability; the presumption was that people already knew what they wanted.

The limitations of communications technologies before 1800 narrowly defined the potential media for advertisements as well. The relatively primitive capabilities of printing and paper making precluded anything but short announcements with rare, simple woodcuts in newspapers and broadsides. Engravings were costly and therefore rare in early American advertising. Still, as barren as this setting was by our standards, there was little else for people to read that was new each week, and so the merchants' lists of goods received at least as much attention as they were due.

At the same time that new products entered the marketplace because of invention and industrialization, developments in the communications technologies added to the means by which advertising messages could reach the public.   Advances in printing and paper-making technologies contributed to competitive advertising by expanding the number and size of periodicals as well as by making possible posters and a wide variety of other media such as packaging, tradecards, and a wide range of give-away items.   The old broadside looked tired indeed once the multi-colored chromolithograph became a   viable   advertising   medium.   In   addition,   the concurrent   advances   in   steam   transportation   vastly expanded the distribution of all printed media.

Advertisers   quickly   exploited   these   new possibilities for sending visual messages out to their markets.   Furthermore,   as   nineteenth-century businessmen competed for market attention and stature, they   supported   and   encouraged   advances   in communications technologies.   Like their counterparts today,   they   sought   a   competitive   advantage   through state of the art advertising media.   At the same time, the printers competed among themselves to attract the advertisers'   patronage   with   ever   more   sophisticated technologies.   For example, chromolithography was the first high volume, multicolored printing technology.   It was   the   nineteenth-century's   state   of   the   art   visual medium and, therefore, a favorite forum for advertisers. Printers, in turn, relied on advertisers' commissions to support   their   investments   in   this   new   technology. Symbiotic relationships like this between advertising businessmen   and   communications   professionals   have been   critical   to   the   organizational   and   technological development of all modern media.

In discussing the significance of images in the advertisements of another era, the question of how those images were selected is of paramount importance.   In this   regard,   several   important   conditions   prevailed during the nineteenth century that caused advertising images to be determined in a manner quite different from   the   patterns   of   today.   For   example,   most nineteenth-century enterprises, whether manufacturing or retailing, were quite small by today's standards, or even by the standards of the end of the century, when corporate consolidation was well underway.   Therefore, few companies had specialized personnel to make their advertising and marketing decisions.   As a rule, these decisions were made by an officer of the firm, often the owner himself, working with the people who would produce   the   advertisement,   either   in   a   lithography establishment or a newspaper or a magazine.   While the advertising   client   initiated   the   relationship, communicated his expectations, and held final control over the creative decisions, how precisely his expectations were defined depended on the particular relationship between the two parties. In many cases, the printers and artists had considerable freedom within general guidelines. Still the final approval of an advertisement's medium and message always belonged to someone keenly interested in the public image of his firm and its products. Most importantly, neither the representatives of the firm that commissioned an advertisement nor the "media" personnel were advertising professionals in the modern sense of the term; they were industrialists and printers.

Secondly, because American advertising agents before the twentieth century were primarily brokers of newspaper and magazine space, they were rarely involved in creative decisions.[5] Indeed, when George P. Rowell, one of America's most important early agents decided to experiment with the creative aspects of advertising, he had to buy his own patent medicine company. Without advertising agents acting as creative middlemen, and without the benefit of market research, advertising businessmen worked directly with their printers in deciding on the content of their work. Because of these conditions, the advertising images that have come down from this early period were the results of intuitive judgments by people whose primary occupations were outside of the field of advertising.

For historians, this combination of circumstances has had the advantage of making the advertisements highly reflective of the values and ideas that the businessmen and printers thought were important to communicate. The images sometimes portrayed the values of the creators and at other times those values that the creators thought would appeal to the appropriate audiences of consumers or even the undifferentiated public. Sometimes their notions about the purpose and styles of advertisements were idiosyncratic, and sometimes they followed several widely accepted conventions about advertising. Whether or not these practices were optimal strategies for selling, they accurately represented the cultural perspectives of their creators as they also shaped the perspectives of the society that was their audience.

There are also disadvantages for the historian in the directness of the pre-modern advertising techniques. Because the messages were largely the results of intuition and convention, we must be careful about submitting them to analysis in terms of modern advertising strategies. A greater difficulty for the historian, however, is the paucity of information about the decision processes. Because there were no professionals to direct the decision-making and then to mediate between their clients and the media personnel, two or three layers of "internal" communications that might well have been recorded simply never existed. Still, patterns there were, and these do yield valuable insights about the perceptions and judgments of those who selected the images.

Themes of Progress in Nineteenth-Century Advertisements
In the context of the nineteenth-century's vast changes and the demands that these changes made on Americans' lifestyles and values, it was only natural that the notion of progress should become an important, albeit not universal, world view. It defined the context, glorified the changes, and offered Americans a supportive perspective for their own contributions, goals, and burdens. This theme of progress allowed a self-fulfilling, self-congratulatory claim of success for any effort that moved away from the past. As James Russell Lowell wrote:

> New occasions teach new duties,
> Time makes ancient good uncouth;
> They must upward still on onward,
> Who would keep abreast of truth.

Accordingly, whether a change added knowledge, complexity, technique, productivity, territory, power, or grandeur, it qualified as progress, and therefore success. Anyone who participated in or partook of such progress qualified as a valued Victorian.[6] The Victorians' creed of material progress was an essential factor in their complex system of incentives. It helped define the rewards, and it justified, indeed, sometimes glorified, the costs.

How then could people of this century of changes share in the fruits of their progress and at the same time justify whatever costs that progress required of them? Or, to phrase the question in a more practical way, could such an abstract world view as the glorification of progress be translated into desirable lifestyles and commodities for individual Victorians and their families? Without question, the strength and credibility of the Victorians' positive evaluation of progress in the abstract depended greatly on its adherents' opportunities to bolster their faith by taking home or sharing in some concrete evidence of progress.

In this lay the beginnings of the American consumer culture. Ever since, Americans have judged themselves according to their abilities and styles in accumulating the manifestations of progress. The advertisements of entrepreneurs promoting those manifestations have therefore been a major force in defining both the nature and the rewards of success in American culture for the past one-hundred-fifty years.

What sorts of messages did the entrepreneurs of the Industrial Revolution's second stage send out into the marketplace while promoting their own contributions to progress?[7] Many advertisers used strategies that deliberately promoted the technological advances embodied in their products. Just as today, any product with a significant, demonstrable differential or benefit to the consumer was an easy subject for an advertisement. Victorian businessmen conveyed, even exaggerated, the unique advantages of their products to the marketplace. Consequently, many of the products new to the nineteenth-century public were advertised by showing or describing how they improved upon other alternatives. One style of pioneering a product compared its performance or benefits to "old-fashioned" alternatives. Another popular technique proclaimed the superiority of a product over its contemporary competition, often with a rather heavy handed self-righteousness.

Ever since the advent of illustrated advertisements, promoters have used advertisements that show the potential consumer how a product can solve a problem. Furthermore, it seems that neither Victorian nor modern advertisers have felt constrained to depict realistic or practical problems that might be solved by their products. Indeed, advertisers all too often create or exaggerate trivial or social problems in order to generate anxieties while they offer their products for relief. Popular in Victorian advertisements, storylines often claimed rather exaggerated solutions for life's problems, such as showing how a family's fortunes might depend on a purchase decision as seemingly trivial as stove polish. Outright fantasy was another advertising device that illustrated a product's claims. Thus, an advertisement for one thread company showed how its product could replace the cables of the Brooklyn Bridge, while another company pictured the popular circus elephant Jumbo held in check by its thread.

In the context of the Victorians' enthusiasm for progress and its various manifestations, many businessmen of the era featured some of those qualities in their public images. As discussed above, manufacturers often advertised by showing how their particular products could bring the benefits of modernity to the consumer. Two other styles of advertising messages also glorified industry, technology, and science, but only *indirectly* promoted the products. In both styles, advertisers between 1850 and 1910 used symbols and images that associated themselves and their products with important aspects of the progress of their era. By doing so, they set the advertised products in a context broader than the consumers' own needs or personal experiences. Instead, these messages often made a grand statement about the period and its most significant cultural and economic achievements and values.

Advertisements in the first of these two styles were characterized by the use of symbols and images that explicitly referred to something modern about the product itself, either something about its sources, its invention, or its manufacture. Some of the loveliest of Victorian advertisements featured the exotic origins of a product or its ingredients. Oftentimes, the means of transporting these ingredients were either shown or implied. Some advertisements of this genre showed the face of the founder, proprietor, or inventor, portraying him, or occasionally her as in some patent medicines, as a stalwart, sincere person of wisdom and good will. This attempt to create a sense of respectability and confidence is similar to the thinking behind the recent fad of prominent businessmen hoping to inspire confidence in their companies by appearing in television advertising as commercial spokesmen.

While the above advertisements explicitly reflected their products' ties with modernization, the advertisements of a second nineteenth-century style *implicitly* associated their products with the industrial and scientific development of the Victorian period. In this genre, the symbols of science, technology, or industry were entirely irrelevant to the product itself. Examples of this advertising style abound, but it is interesting to note that they were most prevalent in marketing products with dubious usefulness or insubstantial differentials, such as tobacco, patent medicines, cosmetics, and alcohol. Often these symbolic associations were dramatic, but they said nothing about the products other than that their marketers felt strongly about the positive connotations of progress.[8]

A very exciting example of this phenomenon was the popularity of electricity-related motifs as symbols in Victorian advertising. There were all varieties of products that used sparks or lightning bolts or the word "electric" in their promotions without making the least claim to the realistic application of electrical energy or technology. Among the types of products that used this imagery in their promotional material were cigars, plug tobacco, cough drops, magnetized hair pins for curing headaches, bitters (a species of medicine with high alcohol content), and even foods such as canned pumpkin.[9]

The Smoky Past of American Advertising

Of all the symbols of progress that were commissioned by nineteenth-century businessmen for their advertisements, none were so pervasive or so impressive as the smoke of chimneys and engines. Of course, smoke was part of the reality of the power sources in both industry itself and in the engines that industry produced for other people to use. Still, the extravagance of the smoke that was portrayed in advertisements indicated a greater enthusiasm for the symbolism of smoke than realistic portrayal demanded. It also showed an insensitivity to the ecological costs and the burdens on labor that the technologies of nineteenth-century industry imposed. If today's frustrated ambivalence towards industry had been a pervasive feeling a century ago, no advertiser would have dared to feature a smoky sky above his towering smokestacks and equipment. This was definitely a different era than ours, and it requires a different perspective to appreciate the messages of these images.

Like the other uses of progress motifs that were briefly reviewed above, smoke associated a product with the Victorian idealization of progress both explicitly and implicitly. That is, images of smoke and its sources in nineteenth-century advertisements sometimes explicitly represented some aspect of the production or transport of the produce being promoted. At other times, these images reflected the industrial or transportation activities of the era implicitly, with pictures of smoky progress that were not directly relevant to the particular product being promoted.

There were two major sources of smoke that were important for nineteenth-century businessmen: factories and engines of transportation. Victorian factories were architectural wonders, impressive not only for their sizes relative to contemporary buildings, but often also for their complexity. Occasionally an advertisement showed a manufactory's interior, but the factory portraiture style typically glorified the exterior with its tall, puffing smokestacks. Additionally, factory scenes almost always included examples of steam-powered transportation.   Both trains and steamships were essential to nineteenth-century production and marketing.   Accordingly, these engines of progress shared the factories' smoky glory.   Manufacturers of power equipment, such as steam agricultural implements, often added a third source of smoke to Victorian advertising images.   This group of advertisers demonstrated their place in the modern world by portraying the capacity of their products to produce smoke.

In many nineteenth-century advertisements, steamships or railroad trains appeared alone, sufficient symbols of progress unto themselves.   As the historian of technology and culture, Leo Marx, has described it, "The 'iron horse' embodied virtually all of the prominent sensuous attributes of the machine technology--iron, fire, steam, smoke, noise... the railroad was the industrial revolution incarnate."[10]   Together and singly, then, images of factories and steam equipment and steam transportation communicated many messages that were important to the manufacturers themselves, nineteenth-century business as a whole, and the dominant Victorian culture.   One might even suggest that there may be Freudian implications as well in the Victorians' use of this variety of smokestacks as the embodiment of power.

The advertisements that explicitly carried the images of a manufacturer's establishment into the public's view expressed his pride in his buildings, the array of modern devices within them, the massive transportation system at his command, and the accomplishments embodied in his final products. Furthermore, an imposing structure demonstrated the entrepreneur's success in building up his business. Interestingly, factory portrayals originated in the early years of the Industrial Revolution when factory owners commissioned paintings of their properties to hang in their homes, reception halls, and board rooms.   This would indicate that when the factory image was later commissioned for advertisements, it was as much a self-congratulatory expression of pride as a sales device.   In one stroke, then, the manufacturers promoted their products, their own accomplishments, and the salient technologies of their times when they showed their contributions to the progress of industrial production and transportation.   The smoke motif, therefore, associated the products of industry with all the excitement and the benefits of progress as that more optimistic society perceived them.

Thus, to those who could afford to buy the products while avoiding working in the factories, this motif was a symbol of inspiration reminding Victorians of the sources of their prosperity.   This is the overall message of the Diamond Wine Champagne Company in its poster showing two beautiful young women, hatless and therefore at home, entertaining a guest with a cheery mid-day party <Figure 1>.   The women are elaborately dressed, sitting in an elegant room, all in the highest fashion of the 1890s.   Clearly the beneficiaries of other people's worldly labors and successes, they could enjoy a luxurious, leisurely visit, appropriately oblivious to the source of their wealth and pleasant lifestyles. The advertiser who commissioned this image, however, ensured that his audience saw not only the rewards of his success, but the means as well, namely the factory and shipping technologies just outside his daughters' window.

The factory's symbolism in advertising for industrial goods also provided consumers with a way to share in the progress that was at the center of the nation's attention.   Virtually everyone could take home *some* example of industrial achievement.   Showing a factory on a package or advertisement also proved that the goods had been manufactured in modern facilities, under standardized controls.   This was a much more attractive sales pitch a century ago than it is today. Therefore, any purchase that carried a smoking factory on its packaging, or which was associated with this symbol through other advertising, was an ambassador of industry and modernization.   Certainly it appears that the American Cutlery Company intended to communicate these messages on its boxes which always paired the company's factory with the American eagle <Figure 2>.

This factory motif was used in advertisements for almost everything, including medicine, sewing machines, thread, alcoholic and non-alcoholic beverages, watches, tobacco, clothing, spices, chocolate, food products, and so on.   This was an appropriate advertising strategy for its day, giving the owner an opportunity to boast while inspiring the consumers' confidence.   The factory presumably testified to the product's efficacy, for only a good, successful product could justify and support such an impressive edifice.   Interestingly, in many of these advertisements, the factory image alone carried the advertiser's message.   The view of the August Wolf Milling Company on a large poster made such a dramatic statement about this tooling company that no other message was deemed necessary <Figure 3>. This night scene of the manufactory at work illustrated the impressive size of the establishment, its state of the art electric lighting, and the implied demand for the products that required that the factory run throughout the night. Smoke seemed a very natural element in this dramatic scene of heroic industriousness.

In appealing to professionals through a trade journal, the American Varnish Company saw fit to indicate the quality of its product by showing that it was made in a substantial, modern establishment, with materials brought to it with all due haste <Figure 4>. Thus we see trains and steamships around the factory adding their smoky contributions, even while they sit at their terminals.

Clearly the Victorians who designed these advertisements had ideas of beauty that did not preclude polluting smokestacks. On one paper sign, for example, The Dixon Pencil Company included its factory's portrait as a decoration in a very proper Victorian parlor <Figure 5>. The image of industry here not only carries the usual message of the smokestack genre, but also the implication that the factory scene was judged tasteful by a woman of artistic aspirations. The child, the woman, and the home setting were all symbolic of the greatest propriety. In this context, the factory too appears quite proper.

The factory and its products could be objects of artistic creativity in themselves as a beautiful poster for Fairbanks Scales demonstrates <Figure 6>. Furthermore, as if the smoking chimneys were not sufficient signs of activity and prosperity, two trains steamed their way through both the main scene and a vignette. This advertisement illustrates the uses of the product in a variety of settings as an additional promotional device.

Not all representations of the smoke motif were artistic. Indeed some of them were quite exaggerated and bizarre. A tradecard for the Willimantic Spool Thread Company used any number of advertising devices with little regard for credibility <Figure 7>. Clearly the associations with strength and productivity had precedence over reliable claims. The Brooklyn Bridge is shown to be made up of shipping boxes, and the cables are made of the thread itself. While the factory floating in the sky has no smoke coming from its smokestacks, the real, down-to-earth factories are actively puffing. One of the smokestacks is so prolific, in fact, that there is sufficient smoke to spell out the name and description of the product.

A strange example of the explicitly positive association of smoke with industry dominated an image used on both tradecards and posters for Babbitt's Best Soap <Figure 8>. No advertisement could possibly express a greater difference between Victorian attitudes towards smokestacks and our concerns today. In fact, it embodies such a remarkable paradox that it is difficult to imagine even the Victorians' accepting this presentation. There are actually several significant messages in this ad. The dominant message, of course, is that of the modern factory complex, covering many city blocks. The second message is that civilization will come to the rest of the world as Babbitt's Best Soap arrives on foreign shores to clean everything, including sundry savages. Yet, how could an advertisement promote cleanliness while showing these smoking factories? Likewise, how could the blessings of civilization be so blithely counted without considering the consequences of industrial-urban blight portrayed in the very same image? Only an American Victorian could have failed to see the paradox.

The motif of smoke had another form of expression in this advertising genre. Nineteenth-century images that promoted steamship and rail transportation invariably added generous amounts of smoke billowing from state of the art vehicles as part of their promotions. These examples illustrate the strength of the smoke motif as a positive symbol of progress because smoke and the soot it carried were in reality significant inconveniences to passengers. The Stateline Steamship Company, for example, demonstrated the superiority of its steamships over sailing ships in a large, colorful poster that shows puffing smokestacks out performing the quiet sales <Figure 9>. The several peripheral images also show the comfort and safety of this "modern" transport.

Another type of equipment that was frequently advertised with the smoke motif was agricultural machinery. The C. Aultman Company, for example, shared the Victorians' penchant to imbue their advertisements with what we see as a paradox <Figure 10>. Only in Victorian times would an advertiser juxtapose such smoky equipment with a beautiful guardian-goddess of fertility in the loveliest of rural settings.

A larger poster for Gaar, Scott and Company portrayed a remarkably busy assortment of important elements of the Industrial Revolution and its perceived benefits <Figure 11>. Presiding over the several scenes

is an impressive factory from whence came the
machinery. As in the C. Aultman advertisement, the
rural scenes illustrate the uses of the products. But
more significantly, they also fed the ambitions of any
farmer who might be a customer. On the one hand, a
pioneering family works the equipment outside a
cottage. On the other, a team of workers uses other
equipment on the property of an impressively large
home. This was a powerful appeal, for what would
have been more typical of the Victorian ideals than each
individual's hope to profit and prosper from industry
and progress? With all of the belching smokestacks and
hard labor portrayed, the overall beauty of this image
certainly has nothing of the idyllic pastoral about it.

The above examples of Victorian advertisements
promoted their products by associating them with
industrial and transportation achievements that were
explicitly relevant to the production, distribution, or
benefits of the products. The second type of advertising
technique to use smoke as a motif implicitly associated
products and services with symbols of productivity or
modernity that were quite irrelevant to the products
being promoted. Buildings that were not industrial
plants often showed smoke emanating from their
chimneys anyway. Stores, for example, do not have to
use power to warehouse and sell their goods. Yet the
ubiquitous symbol of industry and progress presided
over many stores such as the Bennett's Teas building on
their very finely engraved tin canister <Figure 12>. In a
similar vein, insurance companies do not produce goods
through steam power. Yet rather than miss an
opportunity to associate its company with modern
technology, the United Brotherhood Insurance Company,
a fraternal organization in Pennsylvania, portrayed a
steaming locomotive in front of its headquarters on a
large tin chromolithographed sign <Figure 13>.

While trains appear in Victorian advertisements
very frequently along with other symbols of
industrialization, they are also to be found alone.
Again to quote Leo Marx, "The image of the railroad in
the landscape was one of the more vivid embodiments
of the American ideal of material progress that emerged
in the nineteenth century...."[11] The extensive campaigns
of the Fast Mail Tobacco Company provided examples of
the many promotions that exploited the power of this
association. The Fast Mail was a very popular brand of
tobacco that was named for a heroic improvement in
speeding cross-country mail delivery. Its packaging and
advertisements always showed a racing, smoking
locomotive steaming its way across the prairie <Figure

14>. The image had nothing to say about the tobacco, but it did allow the purchaser to own an exciting portrayal of what Walt Whitman called the "emblem of motion and power--pulse of the continent...."

Factories that were featured in advertisements usually represented the place of production. On occasion, however, the abstract concept was adopted to advertise something manufactured elsewhere. The Milltown Stogies tin container from Pittsburgh, Pennsylvania, presented a truly astonishing profusion of smoke, filling the skies above a massive industrial complex <Figure 15>. In terms of design, the smoke provided a dramatic background for the name of the cigar. More significantly, the vastness of the smoke rising above myriad smokestacks is yet another indication that advertisers did not interpret the dangerous byproducts of industry negatively. At least one other cigar company, Pittsburgh Stogies, commissioned a similar package and other supporting advertisements. So it seems that even in Pittsburgh, where pollution from the steel mills presented a serious problem, the smokestack was considered by some to be a viable advertising motif.

The Decline of Industrial Imagery

By 1910, factories, smokestacks, and puffing engines had been all but erased from advertising strategies. There were many complex factors involved in this change, including changes in the communications technologies as well as social and cultural reactions against the Victorian values and lifestyles. There was even a strong reaction against the complexity of Victorian styles of visual beauty that affected the dominant styles of advertising images. In addition, the sheer volume of advertisements began to inundate the public by this time.[12]   As people became increasingly saturated with visual, and later aural, stimulation, individual advertisements had to become simpler with more immediate emotional impact. Advertisers could no longer expect their audiences to take the time to examine the details of a complex factory scene or multiple vignettes, such as those of the Gaar, Scott agricultural equipment poster.

Importantly, the factory itself also changed by this time. Insurance companies, concerned with reducing the losses by fire that occurred in the old, complex Victorian factories, suggested and enforced architectural changes to simplify industrial structures.

Figure 1. The Diamond Wine Co. Champagne; paper sign, 1896.

Figure 2. American Cutlery Co.; cardboard box for knives and forks, circa 1880.

Figure 3. August Wolf Milling Co.'s Works; paper sign, circa 1895.

Figure 4. Berry Bros. Varnish Manufacturers; advertisement in The Michigan Artisan, 1885

Figure 5. Dixon's Pencils; paper sign, circa 1882.

Figure 6. Fairbanks Scales; paper sign, circa 1875.

Figure 7. Willimantic Spool Cotton; tradecard, circa 1890.

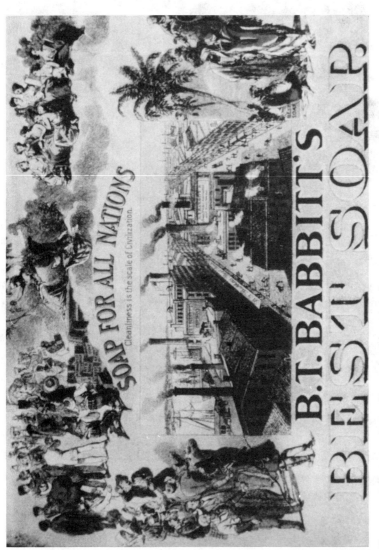

Figure 8. B.T. Babbitt's Best Soap; tradecard, circa 1885.

Figure 9. State Line Steamship Company; paper sign, circa 1890.

Figure 10. C. Aultman & Co.; paper flier, circa 1880.

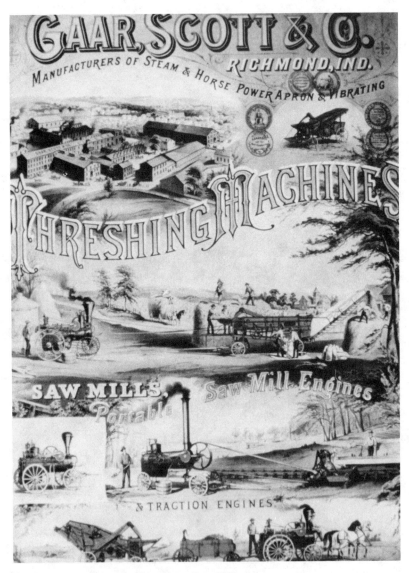

Figure 11. Gaar, Scott & Co.; paper sign, 1892.

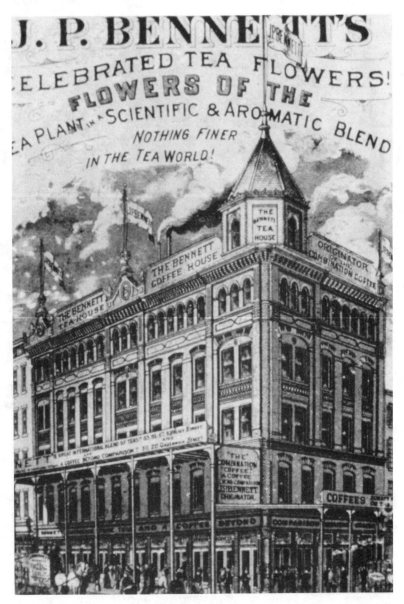

Figure 12. J.P. Bennett's Tea and Coffee Company; lithographed tin container, circa 1890.

Figure 13. United Brotherhood Mutual Aid Society of Pennsylvania; chromolithographed tin sign, circa 1880.

Figure 14. J.J. Bagley & Co. Chewing Tobacco; chromolithographed tin container, circa 1885.

Figure 15. Milltown Stogies; chromolithographed tin container, circa 1895.

Engineering and safety variables came to the fore in design, marking the end of the elaborate manufactory that had made such an appealing portrait.[13]   Another engineering variable that changed the image of the factory was the gradual shift to electrical power that eliminated the heavily puffing smokestack from most production sites.

The puffing engines of locomotives had never had much charm for passengers; their soot was much more appealing in an advertising image than on one's clothing.   Thus, at the end of the 1890s, Mark Twain complimented the Lackawanna Line's new passenger service for changing its fuel to anthracite coal that left his famous white suit clean.   On his advice, the company began to publicize that it ran on "The Road to Anthracite" and asked Elmo Calkins, one of the earliest advertising agents to become famous for his creative copy, for help with the campaign.   Calkins responded by inventing the lovely and very popular Phoebe Snow whose white dress and gentle nature survived decades of riding the rails unsullied by soot.[14]   Shortly after these and other changes began in factories and locomotives, coal and wood-powered steam equipment on the farm and elsewhere was also gradually replaced by electric motors and gasoline engines.   The advertisements for all these new technologies featured their relative cleanliness and efficiency, discrediting the symbolism as well as the reality of the steam engine.

The advertising field itself also underwent extensive changes that altered the style of American advertisements.   By the 1920s, the number of agencies had vastly expanded and the field had become almost entirely professionalized.   As a result, the agencies faced increasing competition between themselves and often responded to the competition by developing their abilities to provide emotionally charged messages that could elicit highly personal reactions.   Advertisers increasingly tried to sell by appealing to the personal needs and emotions of their markets, creating and then promising relief for anxieties, particularly identity and self-esteem anxieties.[15]   All these developments made it less appropriate for manufacturers to use their advertisements to boost their own prestige with portraits of their factories.

Another reason for the decline of industrial themes in advertising was the expansion of the market definitions to include those people who worked in the factories.   For them, the factory represented a distressful livelihood more than an inspirational symbol of progress.   Expressing this growing awareness of the workers' perspective, Carl Sandburg was one of many who increasingly rejected the Victorian idealization of smoke and labor.   In his classic poem of 1920, "Smoke and Steel," he begrudgingly recognized that grinding labor was necessary for the gains of industrial progress. But he voiced a bitter cry of protest with the line, "Smoke and blood is the mix of steel."   Furthermore, the public at large was becoming less inspired by the sacrifices of the work ethic and was more inclined to pursue consumerism and the various internal stages of mind that popular culture began to offer as temptations.[16]

Discussion: Competition For Cultural Authority
Competition in the commercial marketplace was only one of the colorful facets of the nineteenth-century American culture that intrigues historians.   In this period of dramatic changes, there was also a determined competition for cultural authority: whose ideas, whose values, whose truths would determine the course of this new era?   Writers and speakers of innumerable persuasions were intense and prolific in their proselytizing.   The Romantics, the Evangelicals, the myriad social and political reformers, the Social Darwinists who protested reform, the prophets of self-improvement, the Populists, and the Progressives, were among the most vocal of those who competed to influence the nation through persuasion.

The American industrialists were a new class in that century.   As important actors in the dominant changes which some people praised, some questioned, and yet others decried, the entrepreneurial industrialists were generally more self-conscious than most other Victorians about their status and identity relative to the ambient values.[17]   Although the industrialists saw themselves as the entrepreneurial engines of progress, there was very real cultural and political opposition to their actions and values that in turn exacerbated their self-consciousness.

While politicians, journalists, and philosophers all had their traditional means of propagating their attitudes, the businessmen had no ready access to public opinion in the early 1800s.[18]   Yet all of this class of aggressive entrepreneurs had investments of time, financial resources, family security and status, and personal reputation to enhance as well as to protect from criticism.   As the technologies of communication developed through the century, businessmen learned to exploit them to market goods and services.   In this context, some members of the new class of industrialists also used advertisements to express their own views of progress and their places in it.

In the early eighteenth century, long before the era of Victorian advertisements, Joseph Addison satirized the eagerness with which businessmen purchased their publicity. He believed that they very deliberately paid to place their names in newspapers along side of the great politicians and heroes of the day. Indeed, merchants who bought space in his journal, *The Tatler*, and other advertising media of that era took great liberties with their copy, oftentimes appearing to take advantage of their opportunity for self-aggrandizement more than to sell their wares.

The avenues of advocacy available to nineteenth-century businessmen were much broader and more attractive. They included, among other evolving communication technologies, the capacities for printing and distributing the beautiful chromolithographed images illustrated above. With whatever means they could command, like their eighteenth-century predecessors, Victorian entrepreneurs promoted their personal reputations and their claims to importance with the same iconography and messages by which they promoted their businesses.

The motif of smoke, be it from factory or equipment smokestacks, was unique to nineteenth-century advertisements. As such, it is intuitively appealing to historians searching for significant clues to Victorian attitudes. In addition to making connections between this unique symbol of progress and what we already know of the Victorian era, we can find additional support in communications theory and anthropology where scholars have long sought the meanings of cultural symbols. For instance, we can turn for guidance in interpreting the smoke motif to the important communications theorist James Carey. According to Carey, one purpose of art is that it makes the world strange. That is, it takes the familiar phenomena of life "out of the backdrop of existence and forces them into the foreground of consideration."[19] The passing of time can also make the ordinary strange. Because the everyday phenomena of the past were so commonplace as to be unworthy of recorded description or explanation by their contemporaries, their passing transforms them into mysteries. The lure of history derives in part from the challenge of deciphering the mystery of the past's ordinary phenomena. Billowing smokestacks were once such commonplaces in advertisements; now they appear strange--veritable mysteries to us in the late twentieth century. As such, they lure us into their past.

The artifacts of the past are too often our only clues to these mysteries and we must learn to interpret them. Every historian dreams of a Rosetta Stone to reveal the secrets of the particular symbol systems that come to him from whatever Sphinx lures him into its past. In his highly acclaimed book, *The Great Cat Massacre*, Robert Darnton recently suggested one way for historians to find the clues that they need. Taking his cues from anthropology, he defends the value of qualitatively interpreting historical resources that can be as varied as legends and household artifacts: "For one can read a ritual or a city just as one can read a folktale or a philosophical text. The mode of exegesis may vary, but in each case, one reads for meaning--the meaning inscribed by contemporaries in whatever survives of their vision of the world."[20] This is the sense in which I have tried "to read the texts" of the Victorian advertising images.

Darnton's analysis also justifies focusing on smoke as a significant symbol in nineteenth-century advertisements: "Anthropologists may have overworked the concept of culture-as-language, but it provides a tonic to historians. For if culture is idiomatic, it is retrievable.... We can stop straining to see how the documents 'reflect' their social surroundings, because they were imbedded in a symbolic world that was social and cultural at the same time." And, "My own suggestion about a way of making contact is to search for opacity in texts.... When we run into something that seems unthinkable to us, we may have hit upon a valid point of entry into an alien mentality."[21] When a post-1960s observer first looks at a Victorian advertisement with polluting clouds of smoke billowing over a factory scene or a piece of equipment, it seems indeed "unthinkable" that a businessman would expend his resources in publishing such an image. An advertiser would be loath to allow such an association for his business and his products today. This is truly the riddle of the Sphinx. Yet the very incongruence of this smoke to a late twentieth-century viewer is the first measure of its historiographical significance as well as a clue to the larger puzzle of Victorian values and attitudes. So at the same time as the smoke presented its riddle, it was also a Rosetta Stone of sorts, a "point of entry" into the mentality of the people for whom this image was a commonplace.

Still, Darnton admits that we must be cautious: how can we distinguish idiom from idiosyncrasy? Perhaps the "unthinkable" signal was in fact just a quirk. There is no guarantee that a historian can read the symbol systems of any past well enough to answer this question with complete confidence. Yet, when a symbol occurs as frequently as does the smoke motif in Victorian advertisements, it sends a powerful and consistent signal alerting alien historians to its significance. Furthermore, the explication of this particular symbol fits so readily into what we already know of the cultural context of the Industrial Revolution, that one seems to corroborate the other. By reading these images through their symbols and placing them within what we know of their context, perhaps we can follow Carey's aspiration to "grasp the imaginative universes in which the acts of our actors are signs."[22]

Thus, the prevalence of the smoke motif still conveys the enthusiasm with which advertisers accepted the dominant Victorian values of progress and enterprise. They accepted industry as the optimal avenue of pursuing a progress that would, according to Horace Greeley, secure "to each individual the largest liberty for his personal endeavors, and for society at large the greatest amount of material for its collective comfort and well-being."[23] The smokestacks and the engines that dominated the physical settings of steam-powered industry were essential factors in the growth of nineteenth-century productivity. This productivity generated abundant rewards for many entrepreneurs and their peers. Looking back a century, we can understand that those who enjoyed success within this system would have been strongly motivated to accept smoke and the other costs of industrialization as necessary evils. Yet their advertisements embodied more than an acceptance of the costs of industry. They enthusiastically glorified the most visible of those costs by representing smoke as a symbol of success. By promoting this symbol and the mentality it represented through their advertisements, the industrialists helped to shape myths of progress that have long outlived their time.

Notes

1   William Cullen Bryant, ed., *Picturesque America I* (New York, 1872), 527.

2   The following titles contain a wealth of evidence regarding the reactions to industrialization and urbanization. Asa Briggs, *The Power of Steam: An Illustrated History of the World's Steam Age* (Chicago, 1982); Samuel P. Hays, *The Response to Industrialism: 1885-1914* (Chicago, 1957); Humphrey Jennings, *Pandaemonium, 1660-1886: The Coming of the Machine as Seen by Contemporary Observers* (1985); John F. Kasson, *Civilizing the Machine: Technology and Republican Values in America, 1776-1900* (New York, 1976); Leo Marx, *The Machine in the Garden: Technology and the Pastoral Ideal in America* (New York, 1964); Norman Pollack, *The Populist Response to Industrial America* (New York, 1962); John R. Stilgoe, *Common Landscape of America, 1580-1845* (New Haven, 1982); and, "Moulding the Industrial Zone Aesthetic: 1880-1919," *American Studies* 16, 1, pp. 5-24; Herbert L. Sussman, *Victorians and Machines: The Literary Response to Technology* (Cambridge, Mass., 1968).

3   William Cullen Bryant, *Picturesque America I*, 527, 529.

4   Horace Greeley, *et al.*, *The Great Industries of the United States* (Hartford, 1872).

5   Daniel Pope, *The Making of Modern Advertising* (New York, 1983), Chapter 4.

6   For a broad discussion of many of the attributes of the valued Victorian, see Daniel Walker Howe, "American Victorianism as a Culture," *American Quarterly*, 26, 5 (December, 1975), 507-532. See also, John F. Kasson, "Civility and Rudeness: Urban Etiquette and the Bourgeois Social Order in Nineteenth-Century America," *Prospects*, 9 (1985), 143-167.

7   A great many nineteenth-century advertisements display strategies other than those to be discussed here. The strategies not included are those that simply associated the product with some visual symbol of nostalgia or of a Victorian ideal such as beauty, purity, or filial love. This genre of advertisement made no claims for the products' modernity or efficacy in the visual message.   The ads were pretty, but they were not particularly aggressive representatives of competitive marketing.   Most of these were relatively inexpensive stock images over-printed with the advertisers' names. They were designed to please their audiences rather than to promote the distinctive features of any product.   The rationales behind this genre of advertising and its images are very interesting and important to understanding the Victorian era, but they are not the topic at hand, particularly because their subjects were rarely innovations of the new technologies.

8   Interestingly, today's advertisements for these same groups of products still have little to say about their products and therefore continue to exploit strong emotional appeals for their primary impact.

9   For a survey of all of the ways in which electricity was used as a theme in Victorian advertising, see Pamela W. Lurito, "The Message was Electric," *I.E.E.E. Spectrum* 21 (September, 1984), 84-95.

10   Leo Marx, "Closely Watched Trains," *The New York Review of Books* 31, 4 (March 15, 1984), 28-30.

11   Leo Marx, "Closely Watched Trains".

12   Pope, *The Making of Modern Advertising*, 21-30.

13   Stilgoe, "Moulding the Industrial Zone Aesthetic."

14   One place where this oft repeated story can be found is Steven Fox, *The Mirror Makers: A History of American Advertising and its Creators* (New York, 1984), 44-48.

15   In the last few years, several studies have competently recorded these changes in the advertising profession. Both Fox in *The Mirror Makers*, and Pope in *The Making of Modern Advertising*, survey the critical years. For the most exhaustive study to date, however, see Roland Marchand, *Advertising the American Dream: Making Way for Modernity, 1920-1940* (Berkeley, 1985).

16   For broad discussions of this trend in American culture, see: T.J. Jackson Lears, "From Salvation to Self-Realization: Advertising and the Therapeutic Roots of the Consumer Culture, 1880-1930," in Richard Wightman Fox and T.J. Jackson Lears, ed., *The Culture of Consumption* (New York, 1983); William E. Leuchtenburg, *The Perils of Prosperity: 1914-1932* (Chicago, 1958); and David M. Potter, *People of Plenty: Economic Abundance and the American Character* (Chicago, 1954).

17   The self-conscious image-making of the Boston patricians who founded and profited from Lowell's industrialization has been documented by Richard A. McDermott in *The Claim to Power: The Foundations of Authority in American Industry, Lowell, 1820-1850*, (unpublished doctoral dissertation, Brandeis University, 1985). See also, Howe, "American Victorianism as a Culture."

18   One must be careful in this perspective not to portray the business class as overly plagued by ideological attacks. Practical folks, they of course all too often succeeded in achieving their immediate ends without concern for public opinion. Political favor and influence, however they were obtained, allowed many businessmen to bypass public sources of opposition.

19   James W. Carey, "A Cultural Approach to Communication," *Communication* 2 (1975), 11.

20   Robert Darnton, *The Great Cat Massacre and Other Episodes in French Cultural History* (New York, 1984), 5.

21   Darnton, *The Great Cat Massacre*, 260, 262.

22   James W. Carey, "Communication and Culture," *Communication Research* (April, 1975), 187.

23   Greeley, *The Great Industries of the United States*.

COMMENT: MANUFACTURING A PUBLIC IMAGE FOR BUSINESS AND INDUSTRY

Richard S. Tedlow

- I -

First, let me say that I welcome these papers as evidence of a growing interest on the part of the profession in the methods by which the corporation has presented itself to the public. The corporation lies at the center of one of the key paradoxes in American society. Americans are brought up to believe in political equality and equality before the law as such phrases as "All men are created equal"; "One person, one vote"; and "Equal justice under law" attest. Yet many have come to live their working lives in hierarchical organizations in which equality is an alien concept and where unequal power and economic reward are the rule. The management of image has been an important method by which the corporation has tried to dull the edge of this paradox by locating itself securely within the context of American values.[1]

These three papers all have in common a concern for image-oriented advertising. Such advertising can provide an indication of the self-conception of the people who created and financed it. The images about which she writes, Helena E. Wright tells us, were designed to "[sell] a new system, about which there was some controversy," as well as to vend particular products. Lowell's promoters wanted to put the best possible face on the massive changes they were bringing about. In 1825, this presentation meant the "factory-in-the-forest." A decade and a half later, views of the city were featuring "a solid wall of brick mills following the river bank." By 1876, Lowell was no longer a story of a machine in a garden. It was now a case of the machine in a "mature, developed city."

213

Apparently, smoke was not a particularly prominent part of the views of Lowell; but it was a recurring motif of late-nineteenth-century advertising, featured even for products or in circumstances where it was not particularly appropriate or, arguably, actually inappropriate.   In Pamela J. Lurito's paper, we see companies not only accepting but accentuating smoke as a symbol of industrial activity.

By the mid-1930s, Patrick J. Furlong shows us Studebaker spending precious dollars to establish an image as a craft-oriented firm. The company's campaign was a self-conscious rejection of contemporary industrial reality, but that very fact tells us much about how the company wanted to think of itself and position itself in the public mind.

- II -

It might be helpful in advancing the discussion of such issues to introduce some concepts from the world of modern marketing academics. I think these concepts might help us to a closer concentration and a more complete knowledge concerning what precisely is going on with these advertisements. One way to begin is by asking what advertising is. Where does it fit in the marketing strategy of a business? What is it supposed to do?

Marketing is commonly broken down into the four elements of the so-called marketing mix: product policy; price; distribution; communication.[2] It is under communication that advertising falls. Marketing communication itself is divided into two basic categories: interpersonal (measuring the management of, for example, the direct selling effort of the sales force), and mass. Advertising is mass communication. Thus, it is only one part, though often an important and expensive part, of the total marketing program.

Now that we have located advertising in its marketing context, we can proceed to ask specific questions designed to systematize and deepen our analysis. Marketers ask, either explicitly or implicitly, six questions about advertising. These are: motives or objectives, markets, messages, media, money, and measurement.[3]

1. *Motives or objectives*. What is it that the advertising is supposed to do? Is it designed to introduce a product, service, or idea to a market? Is it aimed to make this market more interested in what it already knows about? Is it supposed to increase the market's desire for that in which it may already be

interested?   Is it supposed to stimulate action?   Is it designed to reassure the customer after the purchase has been made?[4]

2. *Markets.*   At whom is the advertising aimed? Is it directed to an undifferentiated mass market?   Or can specific segments be identified and targeted?   If so, how can those segments be described in terms of demographics (age, income, education), psychographies (life-style), or other variables?

3. *Messages.*   What does the advertiser want to say to the target audience to achieve the stated objectives?

4. *Media.*   Through what channels does the advertiser elect to reach the target market?   Ms. Wright's paper provides an especially interesting discussion of the changing media of the time her paper covers and of the complications involved in using them.

5. *Money.* How much does the advertiser budget to achieve his or her goals?

6. *Measurement.*   How does the advertiser determine the extent to which his or her advertising has achieved the goals in question?

I think that any discussion of advertising must answer the kinds of questions posed above.   Too often, commentators give their opinions concerning whether advertising was successful or not without regard to what the advertising's goals were.   Without knowing that (and finding out sometimes requires archival work), such judgments are mere conjecture.

I would like to illustrate how the questions above can enhance our understanding by focusing, for the sake of brevity, on one of the three papers under discussion. If Professor Furlong, for example, wanted to make use of the model above in elaborations of an already very interesting essay, in what directions might it lead?

Beset by turmoil in the middle of the Great Depression, Studebaker launched its "medieval guild" campaign.   This theme, Professor Furlong informs us, was "unheard of" among the competition.   Why did Studebaker "choose to advertise itself in this fashion in 1935?   Why not Packard or Chrysler?"   Here we have question one above: Objective.   It is possible that Studebaker made this choice precisely because Packard, Chrysler, and the others did not.

Closely linked to the question of objective in this case is that of markets.   At whom was this advertising aimed?   There are a variety of possibilities, including consumers, dealers, the labor force, politicians, the local community, etc.   Professor Furlong asserts that the company wanted to sell to a "broad range of customers in a highly competitive market." One wonders how certain one can be of this assertion. Did not Studebaker attempt to segment the market? One would have thought that such a small competitor should have been looking for a closely defined, defensible niche in which to compete.

On the issue of money, it would be very interesting to know whether the complete budget was expended on this particular campaign. One would also like to know what Studebaker's advertising budget was in these years, what its advertising to sales ratio was, and how both compared to the competition in order to get an idea of the constraints under which the company operated.

Finally, there is the question of measurement. Professor Furlong writes that Studebaker "did sell cars with this type of advertising." But what role did the advertising itself specifically play as opposed to the many other factors which could have influenced sales, such as changes in the product itself, distribution policy, pricing, economic trends in general, or other factors? It is possible that Studebaker sold cars in spite of its advertising? It would not have been the first company of which that could be said.

I want to make it clear that the above comments are in no sense meant as criticisms of Professor Furlong's paper. To the contrary, I think he has found an important incident in the history of automobile marketing and handled it well, especially given the constraints of a brief presentation and the fact that his paper covers a lot more territory than this one advertising campaign. I was much informed by his work and will make use of it in the future. I also realize that the resources necessary to answer some of the questions posed above may not exist. My only aim in the preceding remarks has been to suggest specifically some future steps for the kind of work represented by all these papers.

Notes

1   Richard S. Tedlow, Introduction to the Japanese edition of *Keeping the Corporate Image: Public Relations and Business, 1900-1950* (Tokyo, forthcoming).

2   This well-known typology is from E. Jerome McCarthy, *Basic Marketing* (Homewood, Ill., 1960).

3   Paul W. Farris and John A. Quelch, *Advertising and Promotion Management* (Radnor, Penn., 1983), 1.

4   Philip Kotler, *Marketing Management* (Englewood Cliffs, NJ, 1984), 611-613.

REAL LIFE?
MOVIES AND AUDIENCES
IN EARLY 20TH CENTURY
AMERICA

Francis G. Couvares

Daniel Czitrom

Within a decade of their first exhibition in the late 1890s, movies became the amusement of choice among urban, immigrant, working-class Americans. Within another decade, movies secured an even vaster audience, becoming the first truly modern mass cultural phenomenon in America. Why did those audiences flock to the movie theaters and what effect did the films have on their patrons? How can we best understand the social significance of the movies in the first two decades of the twentieth century? What are the best strategies for the fullest comprehension of the cultural history of the movies: that is, the elusive and complicated historical relationship between the viewer and the viewed?

Among some younger American film historians, a new answer to these questions has begun to emerge. Simply stated, the current consensus holds that what appeared on the screen was less important than what happened in and around the movie house. Film content mattered little to audiences, and probably had little lasting impact on them; it was, according to Russell Merritt, "rather the act of going to the movies that mattered most."[1] Similarly, Roy Rosenzweig argues that "the moviegoing experience, rather than movie content" explains the "nickel madness" of the early twentieth century.[2] Even film historians such as Robert Sklar and Garth Jowett, who credit movies with the power to attract and influence audiences by virtue of what happened on the screen, nonetheless note the importance of factors extraneous to movie content in building audiences. These factors included the cheap price of

219

admission, the lack of affordable recreational
alternatives, the sociability of the movie house, the
physical attractiveness of new movie "palaces," and
condemnation of movies by blue-noses, which made
moviegoing almost an act of political defiance for
immigrants and other poor Americans.[3] We will return
to the important insights of these recent historians, but
we want first to explore the still plausible notion that
movie content both attracted and influenced audiences.

At least since the 1930s, when Benjamin Hampton
and Lewis Jacobs wrote the first comprehensive histories
of the movie industry, some sort of content analysis has
been central to explaining the "rise of American film."[4]
Writing in the midst of the Great Depression and
reflecting the spirit of New Deal cultural populism,
Jacobs especially celebrated the early movies for their
social realism and sympathy for ordinary people. The
characters found in early comedies, he argued, were
illustrative of "the common man or woman" and were
selected "because the audiences and film makers were
alike themselves of this class..." Referring to
melodramas of urban life, he made a similar point:
"Sympathy for the poor was matched" in such movies,
he claimed, "by distrust of rich bankers and
politicians."[5]

A corollary of this argument holds that by
around 1920 the movies lost contact with their original
audience. Studio consolidation, industry self-censorship,
and the movie producers' ambition to attract an
expanded, more respectable middle class audience,
combined to turn the medium toward society comedies,
costume melodramas, historical spectacles--all presented
as multi-reel "feature" shows. As Jacobs puts it:

> While living on the bounty of the
> poor, the 'first art child of democracy' (as
> movies had been called) had dealt with the
> working man's life and struggles. As the
> poor became less important as the
> mainstay of the movies, ... the ideals and
> tribulations of the masses lost some of
> their importance as subject matter for the
> motion picture. Patrons of the better-class
> theatres had more critical standards, more
> security in life, and different interests ...
> Pictures mow began to be devoted almost
> exclusively to pleasing and mirroring the
> life of the more leisured and well-to-do
> citizenry.[6]

We began this project with the aim of putting first Jacobs' and then the younger historians' theories to some empirical tests. An obvious first question presented itself: How many movies before 1920 portrayed working class or immigrant life in a manner that might be called socially realistic? The answer seems to be that, though the percentage was larger before 1920 than after, the number was always small in relation to total output. A study of movie reviews, producers' catalogues and bulletins, as well as a sample of the movies of the period (preserved in the Library of Congress Paper Print collection), convinces us that, at least in the form set forth by Jacobs, the notion that the first two decades of movie history were a golden age of socially conscious and sympathetic working-class entertainment cannot be sustained.[7] Pre-1920 movies that treated working-class life in a quasi-realistic way were simply too few in number to sustain such an argument (though we will never know the exact number or proportion of the total). On the other hand, there were probably more such films in this era than after 1920, and there seemed to have been enough of them to cause anxiety for the political and cultural establishment. Frederic C. Howe, first U.S. Commissioner of Immigration and later Chairman of the industry-supported National Board of Censorship, wondered out loud in 1914, "What shall we do about the motion picture show?" The question, he suggested, "will be raised again when the movie begins to portray labor struggles, conditions in mine and factory; when it becomes the daily press of industrial groups or classes, of Socialism, syndicalism, and radical opinion."[8]

One finds other tantalizing, yet frustratingly cryptic, shards of evidence on this issue. Suggestive accounts of audience response sometimes appeared in trade journals. For example, *Moving Picture World* in May of 1908 quoted a recent editorial from the Lowell *Sun*, recounting an editor's visit to a local movie house. What he saw shocked him: the story of a bankrupt recouping his losses by means of gambling; a live cock fight; a live bull fight. "BUT WORSE EVEN THAN THESE"--and this passage was printed entirely in capital letters--"WAS A PICTURE OF A LABOR STRIKE IN WHICH ONE OF THE STRIKERS KILLED THE BOSS AND WON GREAT APPLAUSE." We have been unable to identify this film, but, whatever its ultimate resolution or moral, the scene in question clearly evoked a response that had dangerous implications in a town with a long history of labor strife. In the same vein, the Worcester police censor anticipated an undesirable response to movie violence in 1910. In his first two weeks on the job, he cut not only "the duel and hell scenes from *Faust*," and the murder of Julius Caesar from the Shakespeare play," but also "a scene from a labor film in which strikers murdered a scab."[9]

The implications of movies about labor strife may have been especially disturbing insofar as movie houses served not only as working-class social centers,[10] but sometimes as centers of class mobilization. There is evidence, for example , that movie theaters occasionally held benefit performances for striking workers. Similarly, in 1904 in the small town of Winona, Minnesota, the manager of a storefront movie house, who was also an organizer for the State Federation of Labor, "gave a speech on unionism from the Bijou stage." Within days, the Bijou closed its doors and the manager was "politically coerced" to leave town. Possibly to avoid just this sort of retaliation, the Boot and Shoe Workers Union of Ardmore, Oklahoma, bought its own movie house in 1909, intending to admit all union members free, and to show films depicting "the conditions of the trades in all countries."[11] Depending on the circumstances surrounding their showing, therefore, movies about working-class struggles could have evoked a more or less class-conscious response from audiences. Unlike the saloon, with which the movie house was often compared, the new "clubhouse and academy of the workingman"[12] provided not only an opportunity to congregate and talk but a text to talk about.

After screening about forty early films dealing with labor and lower-class urban life, and after surveying movie reviews and producers' bulletins, we noted several recurrent themes or motifs that could have elicited the sort of audience identification feared by the censors. Eviction and unemployment are two of these. The 1904 Biograph one-reeler, *The Eviction*, can be summarized briefly:

> A landlord armed with a stick approaches an old couple standing in front of a rundown row house; after a few words are exchanged, the old man picks up a shovel and begins fighting with the landlord; his wife and neighbor join in, and the landlord is driven off; he returns with three policemen, but the door is locked and they are showered with water thrown from the second story; they break in the door and

enter; the old couple escape out the back, meet their adversaries in the street and, joined by neighbors, engage in a big melee; the police run off but the landlord is beaten unconscious, dumped in a wheelbarrow, and led off.

Two points should be made about this film. First, it is primitive even by the standards of 1904: it is shot by a stationary camera from a vantage point of about thirty feet from the action; there are no close-ups and no effort to develop characters or to explain the context of the action. Second, it is unrelievedly violent: from almost the first to the last moment, the frame is filled with bodies hitting, lunging at, and chasing one another. For the immigrant and working-class audience that saw this film, perhaps no explanation was necessary. Like job insecurity, residential insecurity was a fact of their lives, and they probably needed no prompting to identify with the beleaguered   tenants' defense of their home.

The theme of unemployment is treated in a second film from 1904, a series of eight episodes produced by Edison under the title, *The Ex-Convict*. It is more sophisticated than *The Eviction*, employing several camera angles and distances, multiple sets and locations, fuller characterizations, and a more complex narrative structure.

In the first episode, a man dressed in a suit and tie says goodbye to wife and daughter at the front steps and walks off. In the next, he is dressed in a work apron and is painting or otherwise working on a large box in front of a store; a policeman approaches, speaks to the man and then to his employer, who has left the store to listen; the employer suddenly fires the man--he has apparently learned from the cop that his employee is the ex-convict of the movie title. In subsequent scenes, the man returns home and anguishes with his wife over their bedridden daughter, whose medicine bottle is empty; later, after begging in the snow and being ignored by a well-dressed passerby, he starts to climb into the window of a house--in desperation he had returned to crime. In the sixth episode we see the man walking in a fine residential neighborhood--perhaps casing out new targets--when a little girl runs into the street; the man chases after her and saves her from an oncoming automobile ; the girl and her governess thank the man, but he slips off before the girl's father arrives on the scene and inquires after the rescuer. In the penultimate scene, the ex-convict breaks into a home, is caught by the householder, and weeps in despair; but at that moment, as the householder is calling the police a little girl comes into the room, recognizes the burglar as her rescuer and embraces him; the father shakes his hand, and, when the police arrive, sends them off. In the final episode, the ex-convict and his family are in their home when the wealthy man, his wife, and daughter arrive bearing food, medicine, and loads of gifts.

The film ends in reconciliation and with a plea for charity, as do many of these social-theme movies; but it is possible that audiences interpreted it much in the same way they might have *The Eviction*--as the story of familiar people in circumstances so desperate that even crime is justifiable and forgivable. Even films that explicitly condemned labor agitation and the criminal poor may have provided, in depicting the conflicts between poor and rich, a fleeting sense of empowerment or a moment of cathartic anger for their audiences. In this sense, these early films may foreshadow the nearly universal technique in later Hollywood of tacking on "morally correct" endings to films in which the world has been turned upside down.[13] Gangsters presented as heroic businessmen, the gender reversals of screwball comedies, suburban teenagers as juvenile delinquents-- these are only a few of the ways in which Hollywood refined the formula that allowed people to vicariously enjoy the forbidden as long as things returned to "normal" after ninety minutes.

Some anti-labor films left little room for interpretation. For example, Edison's *One Kind Of Wireless* of 1917 narrates the story of a strike among railroad workers in a heavy-handed and cartoon-like manner. Tony, a discharged Italian laborer, is simply bad; his former comrades on the work gang are simply ignorant and easily duped into supporting Tony's vengeful plot against those who fired him; and the managers are simply good guys who ultimately foil the plot through heroic action. Lest any viewer doubt the point of the action, the film is saddled with dozens of titles that remove all doubt, for example: "With a sense of having been unjustly injured, Tony revenges himself by sowing seeds of discord among the other laborers."

We saw few films as wooden or as resistant to multiple interpretations as this one, however. Most were sympathetic toward the suffering of poor workers, if not toward their struggles to overcome their circumstances. D. W. Griffith's films often portrayed hardworking but poor people who were abused by mean or frivolous or self-righteous bosses (for example, *The Song of the Shirt*, 1908; *The Child of the Ghetto*, 1910; *Simple Charity*, 1910; and the modern sequence from *Intolerance*, 1916). Often, he portrayed worker and employer locked in combat as a result of the moral failing of one or the other. Ultimately, for example, in such films as *The Iconoclast* (1910) and *The Two Sides* (1910), harmony is achieved when the offending party recognizes the humanity of the other, usually after catching a glimpse of the adversary in a domestic setting.

Indeed, many, if not most films about the working class were domestic melodramas. Perhaps what registered most strongly among working-class as well as middle-class audiences was the pathos of the family in crisis. Women, who were actively courted by movie exhibitors and producers and who were fully integrated into audiences by the second decade of the century, may have especially appreciated such themes. Mothers and daughters, often sick and near death, struggle in these movies to make a living in the city; they are often abused by husbands, bosses, landlords, or other men; sometimes they suffer because men cannot resolve their differences at the workplace, and occasionally it is women who step in to mediate and moralize the conflicts. Whatever the theme, domestic melodramas drew viewers into a realm in which class struggle was of subsidiary importance. Struggles between generations, between husbands and wives, and between families and an unpredictable and demanding world played themselves out in movies set in every social milieu. Viewers of a domestic melodrama with an explicit social theme may have paid less attention to that social theme than to familiar motifs of domestic crisis.

The sort of analysis sketched above can only suggest how some early social theme movies were interpreted at a given moment by a diverse audience. Moreover, social theme movies were only one kind of film melodrama, and not the most common; melodrama itself was only one among several popular genres, including "actualities," documentaries, travelogues, farces and comedies, romances and costume dramas. And the early audiences paid their nickels and dimes to see all of them. By considering another early genre, slapstick comedy, a form that was hugely popular and more ubiquitous, we may be able to refine our understanding of the relationship between early movie content and audiences.

Mack Sennett is a good source to begin with, both because his Keystone comedies were big at the box office and because he liked to talk about his art. The formula for his movies, he said, was simple: they "reduced convention, dogma, stuffed shirts and Authority to nonsense and then blossomed into pandemonium."[14] He consolidated every convention of earlier stage and movie burlesque into a perfectly predictable and repeatable, but utterly chaotic, style. In the world of Keystone, everything was up for grabs. Like the tradition of charivari, Sennett's comedies reminded its devotees (and the critics who were beginning to take notice) that every law--of the state, of decorum, even of gravity--was subject to repeal by this new cultural medium. Lewis Jacobs believed that Sennett's "Rabelaisian gusto" was suited to his working class audience, and that the newer, middle-class movie patrons preferred "polite comedy" and "sophisticated humor."[15] Robert Sklar echoes and elaborates this idea: "Reel after reel, week after week, year after year, Sennett's audiences were privileged to observe a society in total disorder." And, he makes clear those audiences were largely working class fans, who harbored "feelings of hostility and resentment against those who brought misery into their lives," and who therefore thrilled at seeing every enemy undone. His final judgment, however, both reinforces and subverts these comments, opening the way for a less class-specific interpretation of the appeal and influence of slapstick: "It is not too much to say that Sennett's comedies...gave audiences their first glimpses of a social perspective that was to become one of the most emotionally powerful of Hollywood formulas--the anarchic individual pitted against disordered violent authority--which re-emerged in later periods of upheaval in the early 1930s and the late 1960s."[16]

Sklar is undoubtedly right that the motif of the individual--whether "anarchic" or not--pitted against authority--whether "disordered" or "violent" or not--became a staple of Hollywood. This was true of both comedies and dramas, as it had been true of much nineteenth-century stage drama and popular literature in general. Indeed, as John Fell has persuasively argued, what the movies did was to appropriate the conventions of late nineteenth-century narrative (and also those of still photography), shaping these effectively for a new medium capable of reaching a hitherto undreamed of audience.[17] By the time of *Birth of a Nation* and Charlie Chaplin, i.e., about 1914, this transformation had matured--but it is evident in even the earliest attempts at narrative films, as in the *Ex-Convict.*

Like the domestic melodrama, the slapstick comedy was a highly conventionalized form. When the greatest artist of that form, Charlie Chaplin, played the role of a tramp or a hired hand, there is little evidence that he evoked a special response in working-class, as opposed to middle-class viewers. Nor is there any evidence that such roles succeeded better than those in which he played a cop or a department store floorwalker or a sodden dandy. It was probably easier for most viewers to recognize Everyman in a character of modest or ambiguous social status, but Chaplin's genius rested in his extraordinary physical prowess and in his uncanny ability to accentuate and harness the tensions within conventional slapstick. The impulsive anarchist balanced by the sweet and innocent underdog; the loser who is never defeated, and the winner who never quite takes the prize: in whatever guise and in whatever setting, Chaplin offered his viewers an opportunity to explore a world in which the lines of conflict between good and bad, wisdom and folly, beauty and ugliness, strength and weakness, love and hatred--and ultimately between freedom and authority-- were drawn not so much between individuals as within them.

If this is the case, then the attention paid to film content (i.e., defined as story line or subject matter) by older historians such as Jacobs, and even younger ones such as Lary May,[18] is, though perhaps necessary, not nearly sufficient for a full comprehension of the cultural history of film. If form is content--i.e., if genre and narrative convention are seen as the formal content of movies, which organizes stories and shapes the interpretation of them--then the correspondence of movie themes to social reality recedes in importance for the film scholar.

At this point in our discussion it might be useful to step back from the specific issue of the relationship between early film and its audience of mass culture for the values and behavior of twentieth-century Americans. This is not as radical a turn as it might seem. Indeed several historians, Lary May being the most forceful and persuasive, see the early film industry as the "birth of mass culture" in America. The mass culture debate is best understood as a spectrum. At one end are those who view mass culture as a powerful agency of social control, a significant shaper of consciousness. From Frankfurt critical theorists and some Marxists on the

Left, to conservative "mass culture critics" and evangelical censors on the Right, these observers insist that mass-produced goods and images have reduced consumers into increasingly passive and homogenous objects of sophisticated manipulation. The department store and the shopping mall, the movie and the TV, the ball park and the amusement park, have conspired to create and gratify superficial wants, and to make people unfit for sustained engagement with the real world.[19]

To one degree or another, all theorists of this sort lament--or at least note with regret the erosion by mass culture of older institutions that once played a larger role in shaping values and behavior, for example, church, family, ethnic neighborhood, school, workplace, etc. Thus, the decline of religious piety or of class consciousness, of community or of the work ethic, have all been attributed to the pernicious influence of mass culture.   At the other extreme are those who deny significant or at least primary influence to mass culture. Usually liberal pluralists, these theorists insist that mass culture exerts at most a secondary influence on people. They see consumers already constituted into what Herbert Gans has called "taste cultures"[20] before they make their choices in the marketplace of goods and entertainments.   Those choices reflect values that originate in families, neighborhoods, and other primary social contexts.   At most, the movie or the shopping mall can reinforce or give new expression to an already sturdy set of predispositions and preferences.   When significant social changes--class mobility, education, suburbanization, or the like--alter primary conditioning, tastes follow suit. As I. C. Jarvie, a sociologist who has studied the movies extensively puts it, "people are by and large seeing what they want."[21]   Only in a totalitarian state, where brute force limits the options available in the cultural marketplace, can "captains of consciousness" perform the oppressive and repressive functions ascribed to them by critics of mass culture.

The polar views sketched above are rather too bald and conceal great variety within each. Moreover, they do not indicate the extent to which the two views can be partly reconciled. Recent historians of popular culture in England and America have located in the early development of movies and other forms of mass culture evidence suggesting the furthering of class or ethnic consciousness. Following E. P. Thompson and Raymond Williams, these historians find what Antonio Gramsci called residual and emergent cultural formations coexisting in a state of tension with hegemonic forms--thus allowing, at certain moments, oppositional values and behavior to spring forth under the eyes of the ruling class. Like liberal pluralists, these historians emphasize the continuing power of family, ethnic neighborhood, workplace, and local solidarities, among others, to shape consciousness. They also call attention to the potential for innovation and unpredictable variation in the cultural realm. Unlike pluralists, however, those who employ the Gramscian perspective insist that the machinery of cultural incorporation relentlessly tries to neutralize oppositional initiatives by turning them into "wants" that can be gratified through consumption, or by marginalizing them as eccentric exceptions.[22]

We of course can't hope to "settle" the mass culture debate--one that has, after all, been raging at least since Matthew Arnold's *Culture and Anarchy*. But to return to the early movies, we can at least suggest that new historical thinking and research, guided partly by the insights of Gramsci and Williams, may help us produce a truer, fuller, and more subtle cultural history of film.

We need to begin, perhaps, with far more critical attention to a stilted vocabulary that frequently constricts our thinking about popular culture, especially as it appears in the past. Words like "effects," "mass," "impact," and "response" are deeply rooted in a tradition of communications and social science research that obscures as much as it explains. Certainly the "hypodermic needle" model that takes for granted a simple stimulus and a universal response is of little use to the cultural historian (or to the behavioral psychologist). Conversely, the "supermarket model" is equally inadequate. It hypothesizes sturdy consumers choosing what they want, but it never admits the possibility that the act of choosing and getting may disrupt or transform or reconstitute those very wants.

The Gramscian perspective may help us to balance these competing insights and, in particular, to reintegrate the interpretation of the moving image and the sociology of moviegoing. It may also help us to develop a more sophisticated psychology of spectatorship. That psychology must begin by recognizing a variety of possible relations between the movie and the viewer. There are at least three possibilities. Watching a movie may involve a simple "third person" experience, what a writer in *Nickelodeon* in 1910 referred to as the "life from the top of the omnibus" experience.[23] This helps explain the original and continuing fascination with travelogues and documentaries, as well as with those panoramas and cityscapes that play an important part in the "look" and "feel" of all kinds of movies, which include depictions of sheer motion, speed, and the most enduring movie cliche of all, the chase.

Viewing may also involve a "first person" experience, which occurs when a viewer identifies with a character and vicariously shares that character's screen adventures and struggles. The viewer thereby experiments with personal impulses, desires, and aspirations, free from an intractable and complicated world. The viewer relates to the moving image more actively in the first person, more passively in the third person. But there is also a "second person" experience, perhaps the most interactive and transformative of all. The quality of this experience--in which the viewer enters into a dialogue with the movie, and with the self, and with the "expanded text" within which both movie and self exist--is suggested by a remarkable short story written by Delmore Schwartz in 1937. Entitled "In Dreams Begin Responsibilities," it is the story of a teenage boy's coming to terms with his deepest anxieties about his parents and himself, all while inside a moviehouse.[24]

"I think it is the year 1909," the story begins. "I feel as if I were in a motion picture theater, the long arm of light crossing the darkness and spinning, my eyes fixed on the screen." The protagonist dreams himself watching a movie starring his mother and father, who meet, court, marry and forge the small but tragic evasions and cruelties that link them uncomfortably to one another and to their son. At first, the boy describes his experience as passive, almost sounding like a critic of mass culture: "I am anonymous, and I have forgotten myself. It is always so when one goes to the movies, it is, as they say, a drug."

If it is a drug, however, this movie is one that intensifies consciousness, that activates its viewer. As the movie unfolds, the boy cannot restrain himself from weeping and crying out to the characters--to stop what they are doing, to say something else, to start all over. "The old lady next to me pats me on the shoulder and says There, there, all of this is only a movie, young man, only a movie,' but I look up once more at the terrifying sun and the terrifying ocean, and being unable to control my tears, I get up and go to the men's room, stumbling over the feet of the other people seated in my row." He returns again, cries out again, and is finally put out by an officious usher who scolds: "Don't you know that you can't do whatever you want to do? ...you

can't carry on like this, it is not right, you will find
that out soon enough, everything you do matters too
much...."

Better than anything else we know, Schwartz's
story suggests one explanation of the power of motion
pictures, perhaps especially for the first generation of
moviegoers. Neither the boy, nor the old lady, nor the
usher can contain the movie's power to engage the
imagination. Though separate from the "real" world of
responsibility beyond the theater, the dream world
within can only with difficulty be neutered or ignored,
especially by those viewers whose struggles with
themselves, their families, and their society are most
pressing. Himself the child of immigrants, Schwartz
may have revealed one significant relationship between
the early audiences and those domestic melodramas and
slapstick comedies that filled the screen with conflict.
Movies both "blocked out" the real world and evoked it,
all in the context of a set of narrative conventions that
isolated the individual in tension with family, society,
authority, and self. For the immigrants, and also
perhaps for new migrants from the countryside, socially
mobile middle-classes, and others, the opportunity to
explore those conflicts silently, but by no means
passively, must have been compelling.

This long theoretical excursus has appropriately
led us back to a consideration of the social history of
early movies and audiences. The Gramscian perspective
allows historians to recognize that the moving image is
neither omnipotent nor impotent; that the audience is
neither entirely passive nor active in the face of the
moving image. In fact, some recent historians of film
have profited from that perspective. They have paid
serious attention to what happened on the screen, while
still recognizing that different people interpreted movies
in different ways. Elizabeth Ewen, for example, has
shown that, for the daughters of Italian immigrants in
New York, the movies were "manuals of desire, wishes,
and dreams." These young women learned from the
movies how to dress and how to act, but more
importantly, they found in movies an opportunity to
explore those powerful conflicts between personal
impulse and parental constraint that were a defining
condition of their lives. Their personal struggles had
even wider implications because they were part of a
rebellion against so-called "traditional" culture that cut
across lines of class, ethnicity, and gender.[25]

Middle class America was undergoing a family
struggle no less intense in the early twentieth-century.

As Lary May has shown, the party of "modernity" enlisted the exuberant Douglas Fairbanks, the spunky Mary Pickford, and the wildly impulsive yet ineffably graceful Charlie Chaplin on its side. In contrast to these, "tradition" seemed only so much Victorian sanctimony, pretense, and repression.

In retrospect, the star system seems an almost inevitable result of the developing "first person," and, especially, "second person" relationship between movies and audiences. The technical and narrative innovations pioneered by Griffith laid the foundation for a new kind of intimacy. "Looming over the audience, magnified, far larger than life," as Richard Schickel has suggested, "the movie players, these strangers, were seen with erotic narrowness and nearness. We do not see our closest friends so intimately, or the people who share our homes, or our lives, except perhaps in the act of making love."

The making of what Schickel calls "intimate strangers" by the movies inexorably led to a kind or emblematic celebrity, churned out with assembly line efficiency by the studio machines. Individual films came to be seen "not as ends in themselves, discrete creations, but as incidents in a larger and more compelling drama--the drama of the star's life and career, the shaping and reshaping of the image of him or her that we carry in our minds." And of course, this new form of celebrity, though perfected by the movie industry, quickly became appropriated by all forms of twentieth century public life, including politics.[26]

The movie stars were followed not merely on the screen but in the press and movie magazines. Most importantly, the star system indicates the extent to which watching a movie was only a portion of an "expanded text" that included learning about sex, fashion, and courtship, and the obsession with gossip about actors' "real" private lives. It included all or part of the movies one had seen before, as well as the act of movie-going, often unchaperoned with peers or dates. It even included a quasi-political opposition to all restraints upon individual freedom, from those that began in the family to those proposed by the snobs and censors who were trying to put the genie back in the bottle.

In the future, historians of film will need to continue in this line. For the early years, in particular, we might locate those specific moments when immigrants and middle classes attacked or defended the movies in the context of censorship battles on the local and national level. Similarly, memoirs, diaries, and letters, as well as local, especially ethnic, newspapers might reveal how ordinary people thought about specific movies or about movies in general.   Further study of movie magazines, studio public relations, and fan mail may reveal not only more about the manufacturing of the star system but also more about how fans incorporated stars into their lives.

In these and in other endeavors, however, film historians must attend equally to social analysis of audiences and textual analysis of films.   And we must resist the tendency both to exaggerate and to underestimate the power of the movies--or of mass culture generally--in shaping values and behavior in the twentieth-century.   Finally, toward this end, we might profitably reacquaint ourselves with Siegfried Kracauer's *Theory of Film* (1960).[27]   He insisted that the movie's ability to transform what it captures and to render convincing the stories and messages it carries, derives from its essential capacity as a recorder of "small moments of material life."   This means that the moviegoer is always free, no matter how engaging the story or persuasive the message, to subvert or, as it were, to deconstruct the movie.   When he does this to one or more "fragmentary moments" of a movie, each moment "disengages itself from the conflict, the belief, the adventure, toward which the whole of the story converges."   Thus disengaged, each moment may become part of a new construction composed of other moments drawn from that movie, from other movies, or from memory, experience, and dream.

As much as anyone, Kracauer recognized the enormous power of movies as propaganda, precisely because their moments of reality lend conviction to any story they inhabit.   But, because film (along with photography, but more so) is the "only art which exhibits its raw material," the viewer is, at least potentially, always free to reappropriate individual moments of reality and with them, the pulsing, material world that surrounds him, and "that is his home."

Notes

1   Russell Merritt, "Nickelodeon Theaters, 1905-Building an Audience for the Movies," in Tino Balio, ed., *The American Film Industry*, revised edition (Madison, 1985), 89; see also, Robert C. Allen, "The Movies in Vaudeville: Historical   Context of the Movies as Popular Entertainment," *Ibid.*, 57-82; Alan Hovig, "The Commercial Amusement Audience in Early 20th-Century American Cities," *Journal of American Culture* (Spring, 1982), 1-19.

2   Roy Rosenzweig, *Eight Hours for What We Will: Workers and Leisure in an Industrial City, 1870-1920* (New York, 1983), 199.

3   Robert Sklar, *Movie-Made America: A Cultural History of American Movies* (New York, 1975), especially Parts 1 and 2; Garth Jowett, *Film: The Democratic Art* (Boston, 1976).

4   Benjamin B. Hampton, *A History of the Movies* (New York, 1931); Lewis Jacobs, *The Rise of American Film: A Critical History* (New York, 1939).

5   Jacobs, *The Rise of American Film*, 17, 92.

6   *Ibid*, 271.

7   Kemp R. Niver, ed., *Biograph Bulletins, 1896-1908* (Los Angeles, 1971); Eileen Bowser, ed., *Biograph Bulletins, 1908-1912* (New York, 1973); *Motion Picture Catalogs by American Producers and Distributors, 1894-1908: A Microfilm Edition*, 6 reels with printed guide (Frederick, Md., University Publication of America); the films were viewed in August 1985 at the Motion Picture Section, Library of Congress, Washington, D.C. A guide to the Library's holdings of early films is Kemp R. Niver, *Motion Pictures from the Library of Congress Paper Print Collection, 1894-1912* (Washington, D.C.); holdings not listed in Niver can be found in the Library's card catalog. We would like to take this opportunity to thank Kathy Loughney, Reference Librarian at the Motion Picture Section, and Donald Brown, research assistant at Amherst College, for their help with this research.

8   Frederic C. Howe, "What To Do With the Motion-Picture Show: Shall It Be Censored?" *Outlook* 107 (June 20, 1914), 412; see also Daniel Czitrom, "The Redemption of Leisure: The National Board of Censorship and the Rise of Motion Pictures in New York City, 1900-1920," *Studies in Visual Communication* 10 (Fall, 1984), 2-6.

9   Rosenzweig, *Eight Hours for What We Will*, 205;   *Moving Picture World* (May 23, 1908), 456.

10   *Ibid.*, 191-221.

11   David O, Thomas, "From Page to Screen in Smalltown America: Early Motion Picture Exhibition in Winona, Minnesota," *Journal of the University Film Association* 33 (Summer, 1981), 9-10; *Nickelodeon* (March, 1909), 80, and (February 1, 1910), 77-78. Other kinds of mobilization might also occur in the movie house: In *Moving Picture News* (January 7, 1911), 10, a correspondent reported that "a great number of Chicago moving picture theaters" had run a slide in support of a political campaign against the local gas utility.

12   *Nickelodeon* (January, 1909), 7-8.

13   See Kathleen Karr, "The Long Square-Up: Exploitation Trends in the Silent Film," *Journal of Popular Film* 3 (Spring, 1974), 107-128.

14   Qouted in Stuart and Elizabeth Ewen, *Channels of Desire: Mass Images and the Shaping of American Consciousness* (New York, 1982), 92. See also, Theodore Drieser, "The Best Motion Picture Interview Ever Written," *Photoplay* (August 1928), 32-35, 124-129.

15   Jacobs, *Rise of American Film*, 212.

16   Sklar, *Movie-Made America*, 104-105, 107, 212-13.

17   John L. Fell, *Film and the Narrative Tradition* (Norman, Oklahoma, 1974); see also, Fell, ed., *Film Before Griffith* (Berkeley, 1983).

18   Lary May, *Screening Out the Past: The Birth of Mass Culture and the Motion Picture Industry* (New York, 1980).

19   For examples of the "Left" critique of mass culture see Ewen, *Channels of Desire*; Stuart Ewen, *Captains of Consciousness: Advertising and the Social Roots of the Consumer Culture* (New York, 1976); Christopher Lasch, *The Culture of Narcissism: American Life in an Age of Diminishing Expectations* (New York,1979); for the "Right" critique, along with a variety of views, see Bernard Rosenberg and David Manning White, eds., *Mass Culture: The Popular Arts in America* (Glencoe, IL, 1957). See also, Daniel J. Czitrom, *Media and the American Mind from Morse to McLuhan* (Chapel Hill, 1982).

20   Herbert J. Gans, *Popular Culture and High Culture: An Analysis and Evaluation of Taste* (New York, 1974).

21   I. C. Jarvie, *Movies and Society* (New York, 1970), 217.

22   See especially Raymond Williams, *Problems in Materialism and Culture* (London, 1980), and *Marxism and Literature* (London, 1977).

23   *Nickelodeon* (May 15, 1910), 264.

24   Delmore Schwartz, "In Dreams Begin Responsibilities" in *In Dreams Begin Responsibilities and Other Stories* (New York, 1948).

25   In S. & E. Ewen, *Channels of Desire*, 81-108.

26   Richard Schickel, *Intimate Strangers: The Culture of Celebrity* (Garden City, 1985), 35, 36. On the star system, see also May, *Screening Out the Past*, 96-146, and Alexander Walker, *Stardom: The Hollywood Phenomenon* (New York, 1970).

27   Siegfried Kracauer, *The Theory of Film: The Redemption of Physical Reality* (New York, 1960); quotes that follow are from 302-303.

HOLLYWOOD'S LABOR FILMS: 1934-1954

Francis R. Walsh

This paper deals with the treatment of organized labor in films between 1935 and 1954. It is part of a larger study of Hollywood's role in shaping the public's image of the labor movement dating back to the beginnings of the motion picture industry. It is hard to underestimate the influence of Hollywood during this period. Noting that history reaches the public in a variety of ways, one of the conference panelists pointed out that a museum exhibit may reach a much larger audience than an academic monograph. Popular films, for better or worse, also play a role in shaping our understanding of the past. Consider for a moment the drawing power of Hollywood films during those years when average weekly movie attendance grew from 60 million in the early thirties to 90 million at the end of the 1940s.

I have decided to focus on this particular historical period, 1935-1954, because it offers a greater variety of labor films than any other twenty-year period in Hollywood's history. This is not to imply that Hollywood produced a surfeit of labor films during this or any later period. One of the first tasks for anyone interested in this particular topic is to try to figure out why there have been relatively so few labor films when compared to other Hollywood genres such as the western, the musical, or the gangster film. It is certainly not due to a lack of exciting personalities or dramatic incidents. One might at least expect Hollywood to have taken a careful look at this subject in the thirties when union membership increased by 300 percent and the country was rocked by a number of major strikes.

The popular explanation for the relatively small number of labor films in the thirties is that depression audiences were only interested in escapist films, a situation best summed up in the old Hollywood rubric, "If you've got a message, send it Western Union." There was, of course, considerable support for escapist films during those years.   The head of President Hoover's Organization on Unemployment Relief, for example, advocated giving free tickets to the poor and New York's Jimmy Walker urged film makers to "show pictures that will reinstate courage and hope in the hearts of the people."[1]

Nevertheless, Hollywood did produce a number of message films during this period ranging from *I am a Fugitive from a Chain Gang* earlier in the depression to *The Grapes of Wrath* at its end.   But we are half-way through the depression before we come across our first serious labor film, *Black Fury*, which was released early in 1935.

Part of the reason for the small number of labor films in the thirties lies in the fact that Hollywood writers along with John Steinbeck, Dorothy Lange, Woody Guthrie, James Agee, and others chose to focus on the farmer as the symbol of depression dislocation. Robert McElvaine has argued that industrial workers have never fit the self-image that Americans have developed.[2] It is the farmer who symbolized American independence and not the industrial laborer who is dependent on his employer for wages and who must resort to collective action to gain a modicum of power.

Another possible reason for the relative neglect of labor stories lies in the fact that the motion picture business is just that--a business run by business people with their own anti-labor bias.   Even in its early years when the industry did produce a number of working-class films, its portrayal of organized labor was hardly flattering.   One can get a flavor of these early films from their titles: *Lazy Bill and the Strikers*, *The Loafer*, and *The Good Boss*. As Philip Foner has noted, most of these films portrayed labor leaders as bomb-throwing foreigners and strikes as futile efforts which only left the workers worse off than before.   Anti-labor films had become so numerous by 1910 that the American Federation of Labor convention that year urged its members to protest the showing of such films at their local theatres.[3]

What appears to have been a traditional prejudice on the part of Hollywood against unions was compounded by changes within the industry in the late twenties.   Forced to equip their studios and theatres with expensive equipment for talking pictures, MGM, Warner Brothers, and other studios were compelled to borrow large amounts of investment capital from New York.   This meant that controversial story lines now were forced not only to gain the approval of the

Hollywood moguls, but also to clear another hurdle in the financial offices in New York.

Hollywood's own labor difficulties in the thirties also made the industry less receptive to scripts championing the cause of labor. The studio owners engaged in a bitter but futile effort to block actors, directors, screen writers, stage hands and technicians from forming their own unions. One actress recalls that in the early years of union organizing efforts, opposition to the union was so great that meetings of the Screen Actors Guild had to be held in secret in Boris Karloff's garage.[4]

Management-labor antagonism meant that any labor script could lead to disputes between writers and producers as to how unions would be depicted on film. Since traditional Hollywood films required a conflict between good and evil as personified by the hero and villain, any labor script would have to determine which side played which part. My investigation of those films which did deal with organized labor indicates that there was a considerable amount of rewriting of labor scenes which meant increased costs in time and money. It is possible that Hollywood resolved this conflict by simply not producing such films in large quantity.

Pressure also came from forces outside of the studios. Hollywood had been able to stave off censorship through self-regulation in the form of the Hays Office until 1934 when a national campaign to clean up the film industry forced a change. The result was the establishment of the Production Code Administration headed by a Hays office employee, Joseph I. Breen, who had the power to approve, censor, or reject all American-made films. The code that Breen enforced focused on crime, obscenity, and vulgarity and most of the research on the Breen office has dealt with sex and gangster films. But Breen was also sensitive to how social problems including labor issues were presented on film.

The paucity of labor films can also be explained in part by the political pressures to which Hollywood was subjected. The industry may have been able to shrug off the original 1938 House Un-American Activities Committee (HUAC) that charged forty-two Hollywood personalities including eight-year old Shirley Temple with being red stooges, but the hearings which began in 1947 and led to the imprisonment of the Hollywood Ten had a chilling effect on the selection of film topics. We need to know much more about this period. Did HUAC, as the traditional interpretation goes, use Hollywood personalities to gain additional publicity, or, as Edward Dmytrick, one of the Hollywood Ten, has argued, did some of the losing participants in the industry's labor wars of the thirties use HUAC to even old scores? Clearly some welcomed the hearings. Ayn Rand, for example in her critique of the industry, "Screen Guide for Americans", recommended: "Don't glorify failure, don't deify the common man, don't smear industrialists." Others worried about the effect of the hearings. Eric Johnston, president of the Motion Picture Association of America, was heard to say of the hearings in private: "We'll have no more *Grapes of Wrath*...no more pictures that deal with labor strikes."[5]

In order to illustrate the various forces that both limited and shaped Hollywood's image of organized labor in this period, I have selected five different films: *Black Fury*, 1935; *Riffraff*, 1935; *How Green Was My Valley*, 1941; *An American Romance*, 1944; and *Salt of the Earth*, 1954.

The first film in the thirties to focus on labor unrest was *Black Fury* which was released in 1935. The film was based on a story by Pennsylvania judge M. A. Musmano who had played a key role in investigating the exploitation of coal miners in his state. The idea for the story stemmed from an incident in 1929 in which a miner had been beaten to death by the state's notorious iron and coal police.[6]

Musmano's first script was a hard-hitting indictment of the coal industry.[7] The script begins with a cataloguing of a series of mining disasters followed by a list of pitched battles between management and the miners dating back to the turn of the century which were to be flashed on the screen after the title and film credits.

The script goes on to describe a plot by the mine operators to break their contract with the workers in order to take advantage of the depressed wage levels. They hire a detective agency which sends in an agent to infiltrate the union and create a strike. This enables the owners to charge the union with breaking the contract and allows them to import scabs protected by the iron and coal police. The cruelty of the police who are nothing more than uniformed thugs leads to a confrontation with the strikers in which thirty-five people are killed including a ten-year old boy.

The hero of the first script is Jan Volkanik whose courageous leadership of the strikers wins the sympathy of the public. In order to get a better understanding of what is happening in the coal fields, President Roosevelt

invites Jan to the White House and arranges for him to
speak to the head of the Labor Department.   A
committee hearing is arranged and Jan traces the root of
the current dispute to cut-throat practices among the
operators who have resorted to wage cuts to gain a
competitive edge in the industry.   His solution is an
agreement among the owners to give the workers a
shorter workday and workweek in order to create more
jobs.   The owners would also agree to a minimum wage
and the right of the workers to form their own unions.
In case anyone in the audience missed the point of all
of this, the script called for the insertion of a newspaper
headline immediately after Jan's testimony which
announces: "NRA drafts code to settle troubles in the
coal field."
     The Musmano script was completed on the eve of
the motion picture industry's decision to establish the
Breen office.   After reading the script, Robert Lord, a
Warner Brothers executive, informed Hal Wallis, head of
production at the studio, that although the Musmano
story was an excellent one, it was bound to run into
trouble from the censors.   "You know," he wrote, "the
capital-labor subject is an extremely touchy one with
them."[8] Lord was soon proven correct.   On August 29,
1934, the executive secretary of the National Coal
Association wrote Breen that he had heard that Warner
Brothers was making a film critical of the coal industry.
Reminding Breen of the importance of coal to the
nation's economic recovery, he went on to assert that
management-labor conflict in the coal industry was a
thing of the past.[9]
     Breen immediately forwarded a copy of the
complaint to Jack Warner along with his own
recommendation that the script should be changed to
show that "working conditions while not ideal...are
getting better all the time. The point here," he added,
"is to establish the fact that the miners have little to
complain about."[10]   Ten days later, Breen dashed off
several other recommended script alterations including
making it "clear that if the miners go out on strike, the
company will be *justified* in employing other workers to
do the work." He also expressed the hope that the film
would make it "clear that the owners are opposed to
violence on the part of the police." Breen concluded by
pointing out that his office was especially interested in
reducing the amount of violence in the film.   This
meant playing down the "vicious brutality of the coal
and iron police" and eliminating any scenes showing
miners doing any great damage to property.   "This is

especially important at this time," he reminded Warner, "with so much individual unrest prevalent throughout the country."[11]

As it turned out, Breen had little to worry about. On receipt of Breen's first letter, production head Hal Wallis ordered a rewriting of the Musmano script, noting that, if necessary, "we should bend over backwards to eliminate anything unfavorable to the coal mining industry."[12]

The new script, which with a few minor changes became the final film, was completed five weeks later.[13] Closely following the suggestions made by the Breen office, it represents a major transformation of the Musmano story. The company's labor relations are generally favorable. More important, the owners are no longer interested in breaking the contract. Instead, we are presented with an industrial detective agency that foments strikes in order to hire out guards and scabs to management.

For a time the agency's agent who infiltrates the union is thwarted by a labor leader who reminds his members that "things ain't as bad as they used to be, and they're gettin' better all the time." He attributes this progress to the common-sense philosophy of the union: "Half a loaf is better than none! That's the idea we've been working on and it's gettin' us somewhere."

Meanwhile, the hero of the story, renamed Joe Radek, is a popular but apolitical miner uninterested in union activities. On the night of the crucial debate between the secret agent and the union leader, Joe learns that his girlfriend has run away with a member of the coal and iron police. After a night of drinking, he stumbles into the union hall just in time to hear the men arguing about whether or not to fight the company. Joe, still preoccupied with his own problem, shouts, "Sure--fight! Betchem my life fight." This swings the tide; the union is split with the dissidents going out on strike with Joe as their new union president.

To the well-intentioned owners, the strike appears to be a doublecross by the workers. The frustrated company president exclaims, "We tried to play ball...by granting them everything we reasonably could." A court agrees, clearing the way for the company to hire new workers and guards from the scheming detective agency. But even at this point, the company stands for fair play as the president warns the agency to avoid abuse or mistreatment of the strikers.

As the strike drags on with little hope for success, the miners blame Joe for their problems. At that point, the only violent scene takes place. Making it clear that it is personally motivated and not reflective of the typical behavior of the coal and iron police, an officer beats and kills Joe's friend.   Learning that the strikers are about to return to work on unfavorable terms and realizing that he has been used, Joe wires the mine with dynamite and threatens to blow it and himself up unless the original contract is restored. After spending five days in the mine, a feat which captures national attention, the federal government intervenes.   A subsequent investigation reveals that the strike was engineered by the detective agency, the contract is restored, the men go back to work, and Joe gets his girl back.

Reaction to *Black Fury* was mixed.   In typical Hollywood fashion, the film was ballyhooed as a daring depiction of life in the raw.   "See it..." advised the ads, "See it...while you can!...The screen may never take such a chance again!" Despite Warner Brothers' efforts to revamp the script to meet Breen's objections, the film was banned in Maryland and in Chicago for being "inflammatory and conducive to social unrest." The New York board of censors threatened to cut its "inflammatory scenes" but eventually allowed the film to be shown in its entirety.[14] New York senator Robert Wagner praised the film as a "vivid portrayal of a coal mine strike." John L. Lewis, apparently taking the position that half a loaf was better than none in film reviewing, characterized the Warner Brothers' effort as "a great contribution to the comprehension of the deep seated problem involving industrial relationships."[15]

On the other hand, the bulk of the film reviews make it clear that the Breen office had accomplished its goal. *Variety* commended the film for steering "clear of the general embarrassment that usually attends any labor versus capital theme."   If anything, the reviewer added, "intelligent management is given a subtle boost." *The New York Times* critic saw it as a rousing defense of the conservative point of view in labor management, while his counterpart on the *New York American* observed that the mine owners "are hallmarked with benevolence."   Not surprisingly, the *New Masses* interpreted the   film as "a calculated attack upon the rank and file movement."[16]

It is a much more difficult task to determine how the depression audiences reacted to *Black Fury*.   In typical Hollywood fashion, a great deal of time and money was spent on scenery design.   A mine and coal town were built on a 135 by 280 foot section of the Warners' lot.   The script directions called for "long rows

244   Francis R. Walsh

of ...grimy frame houses...covered with dilapidated
roofs...The houses are squalid and grubby and have no
indoor plumbing." On the other hand, at the beginning
of the film Joe is pictured living comfortably in a house
well-stocked with food. Even more misleading are the
scenes of work in the mines. As reviewer Albert Maltz
pointed out, the miners in the film work cheerfully "in
well-lighted rooms' ten feet high instead of lying on
their bellies or crouching down, their feet in water, the
roof but two inches over their heads."[17]

It is easier to compare what audiences saw with
what they would have seen had the Musmano script
formed the basis of the film. Neither the original nor
the final script offer any real understanding of how
unions function. Strikes occur without any preparation,
committees, picket lines, or thought of relief. However,
the first script presents union members in a much more
positive manner. There, it is Washington that responds
to the hero's recommendations, whereas in the film it is
the governmental agency that intervenes to save Joe and
resolve the strike. The film presents the workers as
sheep easily manipulated by the agent and mistakenly
swayed by an obviously intoxicated miner to go on
strike. The owners benefit the most from the script
changes: transformed from a group of devious strike-
breakers into honest captains of industry who are as
much the victims of the agency as are the strikers. It is
left to the spokesman for the government investigation
at the end to deliver the film's message: "There was
never a real issue in this controversy."

Real issues, of course, abounded in the 1930s.
The task of Hollywood's labor films during those years
appears to have been one of trivializing the forces that
turned issues into strikes. A case in point is MGM's
Riffraff released in 1935.

Interestingly, the original script for *Riffraff*
ignored the labor issue.[18] But while the writers were
working on the story, the maritime strike which had
tied up west-coast shipping for months erupted into a
bloody confrontation in San Francisco. West-coast
publishers sought to create a red scare in order to gain
governmental support to break the strike. Meanwhile in
Hollywood, rewrites were ordered, and by August a
new script had been produced which centered on a
strike in the fishing industry.[19]

Once again, the naive hero, in this case Dutch
Miller, is manipulated by an outside agitator. Only this
time, the red menace replaces *Black Fury*'s detective
agency as the instigator of the strike. "Red" Belcher,
reflecting Hollywood's view of a radical organizer,

urges: "Rise up men! Take your necks from under the
iron heel! The workers shall be free! Strike the fetters
from your starved bodies!" Red is able to use Dutch to
get the men to strike. And once again, strikes are shown
to hurt labor more than management as newspaper
headlines announce: "Fishermen on strike ten weeks face
starvation--Red Cross to aid hungry workers." Like Joe
Radek, Dutch is blamed for the result and is ostracized
by his fellow workers. Fortunately, Dutch too is able to
redeem himself by thwarting Belcher's attempt to blow
up the waterfront.

While a number of labor films followed *Riffraff*,
the only one to attempt to deal seriously with
unionization before World War II is *How Green Was My
Valley*, released in 1941. The film is based on the best-
selling novel by Richard Llewellyn which told the story
of the gradual disintegration of a Welch family and the
disappearance of their way of life against the
background of a troubled coal industry.[20] Darryl Zanuck,
the head of Fox studio, paid an unprecedented $300,000
for the rights to the story in the hope that it would be
another *Gone With the Wind*.

The first script, completed on May 18, 1940,
traced the development of a miner's union and a
turbulent strike through the experiences of the Morgan
family. The plot pits the patriarchal head of the family
who views the union as doing the devil's work against
his elder sons who are active in the labor movement.[21]

As wages are cut at the local colliery, support for
the union grows. Even the new minister, Mr. Gruffyd,
endorses it, telling an audience in the Morgan home that
"only a union can make a bad owner act with fairness--
and a sensible owner will not object." Warming to his
subject and sounding more like an organizer than a
cleric, he tells them: "Your weapon is the strike.
Without the right to strike you have no union." To Mr.
Gruffyd, the fight at the mine is no parochial issue, but
"a struggle for justice and decent living waged by the
whole working class."

The firing of two of the Morgan brothers
combined with continuing wage cuts leads to a walkout.
As the strike lengthens, workers are evicted from their
homes and according to the script directions, there is
"an atmosphere of misery and hunger about the street,
houses and the working men and women." Violence
erupts, spurred on by a speaker who urges his "brothers
and comrades" to "flood the mines, burn down the
collieries and if we must,...take ownership into our own
hands." Soldiers are called out, and despite something

approaching a local war, the miners eventually win out with the help of Mr. Gruffyd.

This first script received uniformly negative reviews from the studio readers.[22] But the major attack came from Zanuck who felt that the script had turned into "a labor story and a sociological problem story instead of a great human, warm story about real living people." He found the negative portrayal of the mine owners especially disturbing. They "are nothing but villains with mustaches," he wrote. "That might have been alright a little while ago, but I'll be damned if I want to go around making the employer class out-and-out villains in this day and age." Zanuck charged the script writer with trying to produce an English *Grapes of Wrath*. This might be acceptable if the story was happening today, he noted, but "this is years ago and who gives a damn?" Finally, picking up on the criticism made by some of the studio reviewers, he argued that the film could be interpreted as an attack on the English capitalist class. "Producing this picture," he concluded, "is about the best Nazi propaganda you can find."[23]

A new screen writer, Philip Dunne, who was more receptive to Zanuck's view of the film, was brought in to rewrite the script. Responding to a steady flow of suggestions from Zanuck, Dunne produced five scripts between June 25, 1940 and January 23, 1941. These changes worked to drastically cut the amount of footage devoted to the labor scenes, reduce the radicalism of the workers, and soften the image of the owners. For example, by the completion of the third script on November 11, all of the violent clashes between the strikers and the army had been eliminated. Three weeks later, the strike itself all but disappears from the screen. On January 23, 1941, Zanuck wrote that "there is no need to go into the union business which is now a closed issue."[24] What remained were two brief scenes amounting to a few minutes of screen time.

Needless to say, the speech urging the strikers to seize control of the mines was also excised from the final film. Gone also at Zanuck's suggestion was Mr. Gruffyd's stirring defense of the right to strike. Fortunately, Dunne balked at Zanuck's recommendation that they be replaced with a "paraphrase of some of President Roosevelt's recent remarks on unions."[25]

Criticism of the owners also disappeared on the way to the final version. For example, the script had originally suggested that the two Morgan brothers had been fired because of their union activities. The final version reflects several line changes by Zanuck which explains their firing in terms of a surplus of labor in the coal fields, a condition which was beyond the control of the owners.[26]

Scenes depicting the squalor and poverty of the mining town also disappeared."I believe that the illusion should be given of all of these things," Zanuck wrote, "but ...it should not be shown."[27] Unfortunately, it was impossible to present the illusion without the reality. As a result, audiences saw a "typical" turn-of-the-century Welch home with lace curtained windows and fresh hams hanging from the rafters; where the women wore well-starched aprons and the men changed their clothes for supper.

It is, of course, hard to argue with success. *How Green Was My Valley* won five academy awards including best picture of the year. But anyone seeking a better understanding of the problems that had plagued England's coal fields since the turn of the century would have to look elsewhere. We know nothing about the issues that triggered the strike, how the strike is conducted, or for that matter, how the strike is resolved. We can only assume that the final settlement was not a favorable one, for two of the Morgan brothers active in the union leave for America after the strike is over.

The next major film to take a look at organized labor was *An American Romance* which was released in 1944. Although it was one of the costliest films of its day, it was neither an artistic nor a box-office success. Nevertheless, anyone interested in Hollywood's view of American industry during World War II will find it a valuable resource.

The original story was conceived of by King Vidor, one of Hollywood's leading producer-directors. The first script, entitled *Man of Tomorrow*, was completed in July, 1941 and tells the story of a Minnesota farmboy from his early interest in tinkering with model T's to his work in the California aircraft industry.[28] With the outbreak of the war, Vidor decided to turn the story into a tribute to the industrialists "who made this country what it is and will save it." According to Vidor it was to be a film about "American strength, American know-how, and a way of doing things."[29]

The hero of the new story is Steve Dangos who emigrates to America at the turn of the century. In a Cook's tour of American industry, Steve starts out as a laborer in the Mesabi iron range, but his drive and curiosity take him to a steel mill in Ohio and eventually to where he heads his own automobile company. Finally, with the outbreak of World War II, Steve applies his talents to the aircraft industry which is experiencing the same kind of production problems that he had overcome in the automobile industry.

Every effort was made to present an accurate picture of the production process in each of the industries in which Steve works. At times, the film takes on an almost documentary character, a condition which came in for heavy criticism from the film reviewers. For example, a camera crew visited the Carnegie Illinois steel plant in Chicago in order to use an abandoned section of the factory to film an outdated method of steel production. Many of the scenes were filmed on location in war plants which required a great deal of paper work. Film crews also had to cope with the unexpected in local factories. For example. they arrived at an Indianapolis auto plant to find that it had just been converted into an aircraft engine plant. Working at night, the crew had to take the airplane engines off the line and bring in some military cars which they partially disassembled in order to show the assembly process. The cars also had to be painted in civilian colors and then repainted Army drab before they were returned to the military.[30]

I mention this careful attention to detail in the industrial segments of the film because it presents such a stark contrast to the haphazard and unrealistic manner in which union and strike scenes are handled. Organized labor had not been a part of the original pre-war script, but was added in Vidor's words to represent "America's growing pains." A strike was written into the script to show "that we have lived through that era and now we enjoy better relationships between nanagement and labor than we have ever enjoyed in our history."[31]

The new script called for a clash between Steve and his workers who have lost their easy relationship with him as the company grows in size. Frustrated, they engage in a sit-down strike which forces Steve to bring in an industrial protective service. Eventually the militia has to be called out to maintain order.[32]

The Breen office had no problem with the portrayal of the strike scenes in the new script. The major trouble came from the Bureau of Motion Pictures which reviewed films for the Office of War Information. The Bureau was especially disturbed by the inclusion of the sit-down strike in the film. It felt that the film's presentation of unions as radical violent conspiracies to be "a fascist tactic pure and simple." The Bureau was also troubled that the remainder of the sit-down strikes of the thirties ran counter to the War Labor Board's

efforts   to   foster   harmony   between   labor   and
management.[33]

With the sit-down strike and the ensuing violence
eliminated from the script, Ludwig had to develop
another approach to the topic. The result is one of the
strangest strikes in films since the advent of sound. In
the film, Steve arrives at his plant to find it empty--
there are no workers, no strike notices, and no picket
lines.

The next scene shows a delegation of workers
filing into the boardroom to meet with Steve and his
directors. The workers are so obviously unprepared for
the strike that they have chosen Steve's son Teddy who
has been learning the business to represent them.

In an earlier version which led to the sit-down
strike, the workers had enumerated their own labor
grievances such as speed-ups and seniority rights. In
their place we have a speech by Teddy to his father
which mirrors the Bureau of Motion Picture's "Manual
for the Motion Picture Industry" which called for
presenting the war as not merely a struggle for survival,
but a fight for a new people's democracy based on the
four freedoms. Teddy informs the board that the
workers have no intention of telling management how to
run its business. "In fact," he says, "most of us are
willing to admit that we are not good enough to be
where you are." All the workers want is to be just part
of the team and unions are one way of doing it. "Men
get together," Teddy points out, "because they need each
other's strength. We learned that lesson from the
colonies." And when Steve asks the men to have faith
in him, Teddy responds, "How about having faith in
us?--or better still gentlemen, why don't we have faith
in each other?"[34]

An American Romance has been viewed as a
symbol of the country's more tolerant attitude toward
organized labor.[35] There is no longer any question, for
example, of the workers' right to organize. On the
other hand, that tolerance had clearly defined limits
which ruled out any interference by labor in
management decisions. Moreover, little has changed in
Hollywood's portrayal of the rank and file workers.
Once again we are presented with a picture of workers
incompetent to manage their own affairs and who must
be saved by a government agency in *Black Fury*, a
minister in *How Green Was My Valley*, or the owner's
son in this case. And although Teddy talks about a
partnership between management and labor, the film
makes it clear that the strength of American industry

lies in the ingenuity and hard work of its captains of industry.

Ironically, *Salt of the Earth*, the only film to champion organized labor during this period, can trace its origins back to the House Un-American Activities Committee investigation of Hollywood. As Dorothy Jones has demonstrated, the hearings frightened the industry and led to a sharp drop in the number of social problem films from 20.9% in 1947 to 9% in 1950 and 1951.[36] A number of members of the film industry, including the famous "Hollywood Ten", were blacklisted.

Unable to find work in Hollywood, several of the outcasts decided to produce their own films. Searching about for a suitable topic they seized upon a recent fifteen-month strike that had taken place in a New Mexico copper mine in 1950-1951. As Paul Jarrico, the producer of *Salt of the Earth* later recalled, the film was "a crime to fit the punishment." The strikers, mostly Mexican Americans, belonged to local 890 of the Mine, Mill and Steel Smelters union which had been expelled from the CIO for alleged Communist influences in 1949. "We were kicked out of Hollywood for the same reason," said Jarrico.[37]

The film was a cooperative effort between Jarrico, Herbert Biberman, and Michael Wilson, who had been blacklisted by Hollywood, and the local miners and their wives who had taken part in the strike. The workers and their families played most of the parts in the film including the male lead. Rosaura Revultas, a major Mexican actress, was brought in to play the leading female role.

The film tells the story of how the miners are subjected to dangerous working conditions and how their company housing is inferior to that supplied to Anglo workers in the neighboring mines. The strike is almost defeated when the company secures a Taft-Hartley injunction prohibiting the strikers from picketing the mines. Pointing out that the injunction only prevents the striking workers from picketing, the women of the community overcome the reluctance of their husbands and take their place on the picket line while the men are forced to take care of the children. The courage of the women on the picket line combined with the solidarity of the miners eventually forces the company to negotiate with the workers.

The story of how *Salt of the Earth* was made is as dramatic as the film itself.[38] All elements of the motion picture industry sought to stop the film from being made, and when that failed, they moved to block its distribution. Members of the International Alliance of

Theatrical Stage Employees were not allowed to participate in any facet of the film's production or distribution. Bending to pressure, Pathe Laboratories reneged on its agreement to process the film. Musical scoring for the film had to be done secretly.

Public pressure was also brought to bear. Congressman Donald Jackson of California denounced the film as "a new weapon for Russia," while Hearst columnist Victor Riesel warned that Communists were making a film close to the atomic testing grounds at Los Alamos. Meanwhile, local vigilante groups attacked the film crew on location.[39] Before the film was completed, its star Rosaura Revultas was deported to Mexico and the film had to be completed with a stand-in who was shot at a distance. With union projectionists refusing to show the film and the studios pressing theatre owners not to book it, Salt of the Earth had only a brief showing in a handful of cities.

Reviewers who had a chance to see the film varied in their reaction. Bosley Crowther of the New York Times was surprised in light of the controversy surrounding the film to find it "in substance, simply a strong pro-labor film." Pauline Kael, on the other hand, branded it "ridiculously and patently false" and "as clear a piece of Communist propaganda as we have had in many years."[40]

One can criticize the film for offering a romantic image of the strikers while presenting a one-dimensional picture of the mining company and police "bad guys." But the film makers had no models on which to build. Salt of the Earth is the first feature film to focus on and present a strike by a militant union from the workers' point of view. Unlike the other films that I have discussed, Salt of the Earth shows a strike from beginning to end replete with a strike committee, union meetings, picket lines, and emergency plans. The film also must be credited with presenting a women's perspective on union activity beginning with their initial resentment of the men's use of the local as an excuse to get out of the house. And perhaps the most refreshing part of all, it shows union members making decisions and playing an active role in determining their own destiny without the help of government agents, ministers, or the boss's son.

Notes

1   Ralph A. Brauer, "When the Lights Went Out--Hollywood, the Depression, and the Thirties," *Journal of Popular Film and TV*, 8 (Winter,1981),19; Robert S. McElvaine, *The Great Depression* (New York, 1984), 208.

2   Robert S. McElvaine, "Workers in Fiction; Locked Out," *New York Times Book Review*, Section 7 (September 1, 1985), 1.

3   Philip S. Foner, "A Martyr to His Cause: The Scenario of the First Labor Film in the United States," *Labor History*,24 (Winter, 1983), 103-104.

4   Thomas J. Knock, "Hollywood and the Historian: The Oral History Project at SMU," *OAH Newsletter*, (August, 1985), 4.

5   *Ibid*, 4; Rand quoted in Keith Reader, *Cultures in Celluloid*, (London, 1981), 74; Peter Roffman and Jim Purdy, *The Hollywood Social Problem Film*, (Bloomington, Ind., 1981), 296.

6   *New York Times*, April 21, 1935.

7   Undated Script, *Black Hell*, University of Southern California, Special Collections (USCSC).

8   Robert Lord to Hal Wallis, May 2, 1934, USCSC.

9   J.D. Battle to Joseph I. Breen, August 29, 1934, USCSC.

10   Joseph I. Breen to Jack L. Warner, September 2, 1934, USCSC.

11   Joseph I. Breen to Jack L. Warner, September 12, 1934, USCSC.

12   Hal Wallis, "inter-office memo," September 13, 1934, USCSC.

13   *Black Hell* (later, *Black Fury*) script, October 8, 1934, USCSC.

14   *New York Times*, April 6, 1935.

15   *Motion Picture Herald*, April 13, 1935, 18.

16   *Variety*, April 17, 1935; *New York Times*, April 11, 1935; *New York American*, undated, in *Hollywood Reporter Clipping Service*, University of California, Los Angeles, Theater Arts Collection, (UCLATA); Peter Ellis, "The Movies", *The New Masses*, April 23, 1935, 28-29.

17   Albert Maltz, "Coal Diggers of 1935," *New Theatre*, April, 1935.

18   *Riffraff* scripts: July 23, 27, 1934, USCSC.

19   Irving Bernstein, *Turbulent Years*, (Boston, 1971),285; *Riffraff* scripts: August 27, September 17, 1934, USCSC.

20   Richard Llewellyn, *How Green Was My Valley* (New York, 1940).

21   *How Green Was My Valley script*, May 18, 1940, UCLATA.

22   Script comments: Aidan Roark, May 20, 1940; Henry Duffy, May 20, 1940; Henry Lehrman, May 21, USCSC.

23   Darryl Zanuck, script comments, May 22, 1940, UCLATA.

24   Philip Dunne recorded interview, undated, USCSC; *How Green Was My Valley* scripts: June 25, 1940, UCLATA; August 23, 1940, USCSC; November 11, 1940, UCLATA; November 30, 1940, January 23, 1941, USCSC; Darryl Zanuck to Philip Dunne, January 23, 1941, USCSC.

25   Darryl Zanuck to Philip Dunne, April 11, 1941, USCSC.

26   Darryl Zanuck to Philip Dunne, December 16, 1940, USCSC.

27   Darryl Zanuck to Philip Dunne, November 15, 1940, USCSC.

28   *Man of Tomorrow* script, July 19, 1941, King Vidor Collection, University of California, Los Angeles Special Collections (UCLASC).

29   King Vidor to J. J. Cohn, June 2, 1944, USCSC; Nancy Dowd interview of King Vidor, Directors Guild of America Oral History Project, USCSC, 248.

30   Nancy Dowd, King Vidor Interview, 253-54.

31   King Vidor to M.E. Gilfond, February 2, 1943, USCSC.

32   *An American Miracle* (later *An American Romance*) script, August 13, 1942, UCLASC.

33   Clayton R. Koppes and G. D. Black, "What to Show the World, The O.W.I. and Hollywood , 1942-45,", *Journal of American History*, 64 (1977), 99-100; Richard R. Lingeman, *Don't You Know There's A War Going On?* (New York, 1970), 187.

34   *An American Miracle* script, April 2, 1943, Vidor Collection, UCLASC.

35   Roffman and Purdy, 262.

36   Dorothy B. Jones, "Communism and the Movies: A Study of Film Content," in John Cogley, *Report on Blacklisting* I, *Movies* (Fund for the Republic. Inc.) 231.

37   Paul Jarrico in the documentary film, "A Crime to Fit the Punishment" Mack-Moss, Inc., 1982.

38   See Herbert Biberman, *Salt of the Earth* (Boston, 1965) and Michael Wilson and Deborah Silverton Rosenfelt, *Salt of the Earth* (Old Westbury, N.Y., 1978).

39   Nora Sayre, *Running Time* (New York, 1982), 174.

40   *New York Times*, March 15, 1954; Pauline Kael, *I Lost It at the Movies* (New York, 1966), 298-311.

AUTHORS

MARY H. BLEWETT is Professor of History at the University of Lowell. Her publications include *Men, Women, and Work: A Study of Class, Gender, and Protest in the New England Shoe Industry, 1780-1910.*

FRANCIS G. COUVARES is Associate Professor of History at Amherst College. His publications include *The Remaking of Pittsburgh: Class and Culture in an Industrializing City, 1877-1919.*

DANIEL CZITROM is Associate Professor of History at Mt. Holyoke College. He is author of the forthcoming *New York Naked: City Culture and the Uses of the Underworld.*

MICHAEL BREWSTER FOLSOM is the former Director of the Charles River Museum of Industry in Waltham, Massachusetts. His publications include *The Philosophy of Manufactures: Early Debates Over Industrialization in the United States,* co-edited with Steven D. Lubar.

PATRICK J. FURLONG is Professor of History at Indiana University at South Bend. He has published articles in various scholarly journals on subjects ranging from political and military aspects of Revolutionary America to topics in Indiana history.

BRENT D. GLASS is the former Executive Director of the North Carolina Humanities Committee. He is presently Director of the Pennsylvania Historical and Museum Commission.

JACQUELINE A. HINSLEY is Research Associate at the Hagley Museum. She is the co-author of *Sophie duPont, a Young Lady in America: Sketches, Diaries, and Letters, 1823-1833.*

GARY KULIK is Assistant Director for Academic Programs at the National Museum of American History, Smithsonian Institution. He is also Editor of *American Quarterly.*

THOMAS E. LEARY is a principal member of Industrial Research Associates, a consulting group specializing in public history and social policy. He is the former Director of Research and Interpretation at the Buffalo and Erie County Historical Society. His publications include *From Fire to Rust: Business, Technology, and Work at the Lackawanna Steel Plant, 1899-1983.*

PAMELA WALKER LURITO has taught courses in business, social sciences, and history at Chamberlayne Junior College, Emerson College, and Tufts University and has made numerous presentations at professional meetings around the country.

MARSHA A. MULLIN is the former Curator at Discovery Hall Museum in South Bend. She is presently Curator of Collections at the Ladies Hermitage Association in Hermitage, Tennessee.

FRANCES ROBB is a doctoral candidate in the History of Science and Technology at West Virginia University. She has researched the industrial history of the antebellum Potomac Valley and served as a predoctoral fellow at the Smithsonian Institution.

LORETTA A. RYAN teaches history at the Calhoun School in New York City. Her article in this book is based on her doctoral dissertation, "Lowell in Transition: The Uses of History in Urban Change."

RICHARD S. TEDLOW is Associate Professor of Business History at the Harvard University Graduate School of Business Administration. He is also the Editor of *Business History Review.*

MIKE WALLACE teaches history at John Jay College of the City University of New York. His past essays on public history include "Visiting the Past: History Museums in the United States" and "Reflections on the History of Historic Preservation."

FRANCIS R. WALSH is Professor of History at the University of Lowell. He has published a number of articles on ethnic history, urban studies, women's history, and film history.

ROBERT WEIBLE is the Historian at Lowell National Historical Park. He served as Chairman of the Lowell Conference on Industrial History from 1980 to 1987.

NICHOLAS WESTBROOK is Curator of Exhibits at the Minnesota Historical Society, where he supervises all aspects of state museum exhibit development. His research on British museums was done as part of his work as a Winston Churchill Travelling Fellow.

MICHAEL WORKMAN is a Park Ranger for historical interpretation at Friendship Hill National Historic Site. He is presently completing his doctoral degree in the History of Science and Technology at West Virginia University.

HELENA E. WRIGHT is Curator of the Division of Graphic Arts at the National Museum of American History, Smithsonian Institution. She has published numerous studies of labor and textile history.